Connecting the Internet of Things

IoT Connectivity Standards and Solutions

Anil Kumar
Jafer Hussain
Anthony Chun

Apress®

Connecting the Internet of Things: IoT Connectivity Standards and Solutions

Anil Kumar
Chandler, AZ, USA

Jafer Hussain
San Ramon, CA, USA

Anthony Chun
Los Altos, CA, USA

ISBN-13 (pbk): 978-1-4842-8896-2
https://doi.org/10.1007/978-1-4842-8897-9

ISBN-13 (electronic): 978-1-4842-8897-9

Managing Director, Apress Media LLC: Welmoed Spahr
Acquisitions Editor: Susan McDermott
Development Editor: James Markham
Coordinating Editor: Jessica Vakili

Distributed to the book trade worldwide by Springer Science+Business Media New York, 1 NY Plaza, New York, NY 10004. Phone 1-800-SPRINGER, fax (201) 348-4505, e-mail orders-ny@ springer-sbm.com, or visit www.springeronline.com. Apress Media, LLC is a California LLC and the sole member (owner) is Springer Science + Business Media Finance Inc (SSBM Finance Inc). SSBM Finance Inc is a **Delaware** corporation.

For information on translations, please e-mail booktranslations@springernature.com; for reprint, paperback, or audio rights, please e-mail bookpermissions@springernature.com.

Apress titles may be purchased in bulk for academic, corporate, or promotional use. eBook versions and licenses are also available for most titles. For more information, reference our Print and eBook Bulk Sales web page at http://www.apress.com/bulk-sales.

Any source code or other supplementary material referenced by the author in this book is available to readers on the Github repository: https://github.com/Apress/Connecting-the-Internet-of-Things. For more detailed information, please visit http://www.apress.com/source-code.

Printed on acid-free paper

Table of Contents

xiii

About the Authors

Anil Kumar is a Principal Engineer in the High Speed Silicon and Platform Engineering Division of IOTG at Intel Corporation and is responsible for the Connectivity Platform Architecture across IOTG. In this role, he led the effort with the planning team to create IOTG's first ever roadmap for connectivity solutions. He is currently driving platform and chip level integration of several key connectivity and communication technologies which are critical for Cyber Physical Systems. Anil joined Intel in 2007 as a design engineer in Digital Home Group. He served as Platform Architect for several Intel Architecture based Media Processors for TV and Set Top Box applications. As the chief architect in Intel Media Group, Anil led several designs that resulted in award-winning consumer electronic device designs at CES. The world's first Google TV devices were based on reference design efforts led by Anil as well. Prior to joining Intel, Anil held design engineering positions at multinational companies such as Fujitsu and Alcatel. He was instrumental in taking several designs from concept to production throughout his career. Anil is a co-author of *Demystifying Internet of Things Security* (Apress 2019).

Jafer Hussain is a Platform Architect in the Internet of Things Group at Intel Corporation. Jafer joined Intel in 2014 in Wireless Communications Group where he led the development and integration of wireless connectivity solutions in Intel Architecture platforms. In his current role, he supports wireless connectivity strategy, enablement, and customer engagements for a variety of IoT segments. Jafer is an accomplished inventor who has co-authored 10 patents in the area of embedded systems, wireless technologies, and system-on-chip. He received a B.S. in Electrical Engineering from the University of Engineering and Technology, Taxila, Pakistan, and an M.S. in Management of Technology from the National University of Singapore.

Dr. Anthony (Tony) Chun is an architect and wireless planner in the Internet of Things Group at Intel Corporation. Anthony Chun joined Intel in 2000 and was a research scientist in Intel Labs where he developed architectures for reconfigurable software defined radios and accelerators. In his current role, he is responsible for the definition of wireless connectivity roadmaps for the IOTG business units. He has co-authored 20 patents in the area of wireless architectures and accelerators. He has co-authored several papers in engineering journals and received best paper awards at Intel Design Technology and Test Conference 2011 and at the IEEE Computer Society Annual Symposium on VLSI, 2009. He has B.S., M.S., and Ph.D. degrees in Electrical Engineering from Stanford University, Stanford, California.

Introduction

The Internet of Things (IoT) is essential for increasing the productivity of many industries and quality of life of all humankind. Key goals include making the world smart and autonomous. IoT is here now, and IoT is transforming the way we live and work. From saving lives by connecting people and technology in the medical space, to lowering costs across industries through automation and actionable business insights, IoT offers massive potential for society and business to build a more connected, secure, and engaging world.

We find that the role of IoT in improving the quality of life for all humankind is particularly important as we are writing this book in the spring of 2020 during the Covid-19 pandemic that has engulfed the world. Applications of IoT include assisting first responders in the diagnosis and treatment of patients, in ensuring that people are maintaining social distancing, assisting in the development of treatments, and in supporting contact tracing.

The Internet of Things (IoT) is a term that was coined by Kevin Ashton in 1992[1] and defines an ecosystem consisting of (1) the "Internet" that is used to connect (2) "Things."

The first part of the definition incorporates connectivity: "the *Internet.*" As we will discuss later in the book, the Internet is used to connect nearly every computer, smartphone, tablet, server, etc., in the world and is key to scaling connectivity to billions or even trillions of "Things" to enable data to be processed in the "Edge" or "Cloud."

---

[1] Ashton, K. (22 June 2009). "That 'Internet of Things' Thing"

The second part of the definition is the term *"Things,"* which includes any device that bridges the physical world to the digital world: computational platforms, machines, appliances, cars, trains, and sensors such as cameras to name a few. Thus, IoT literally defines connecting physical devices via the Internet.

Implicitly, IoT also includes the following key attributes:

- Scalability: Trillions of Things readily deployed across multitudes of use cases and connected via the Internet. It enables each Thing to be identified uniquely and addressed so that data can be received or sent from or to the Thing from anywhere on the Internet.

- Communications: The digital data and measurements from the Things are sent reliably, securely, and punctually to be analyzed in the "Edge" or the "Cloud"; conversely, commands from the Edge or Cloud are received reliably, securely, and in a timely manner by Things so that time critical operations can be executed.

- Analytics: Data from trillions of Things are analyzed to derive understanding and insights that produce actions that benefit entities – humans, corporations, and the world community.

Besides the way IoT is transforming the way we live and work, the business growth opportunity is tremendous. The number of devices connected to Internet Protocol (IP) networks will be more than three times the global population by 2023.[2] Both wired and wireless connectivity

---

[2] Cisco Annual Internet Report (2018–2023) White Paper www.cisco.com/c/en/us/solutions/collateral/executive-perspectives/annual-internet-report/white-paper-c11-741490.html

technologies are essential ingredients in an IoT product. However, navigating the fragmented IoT connectivity ecosystem of standards, protocols, architectures, hardware, software, business models, etc., is challenging, and a well-thought-out approach is needed for scaling a solution to a viable product.

This book will guide the reader through this fractured landscape with real-world examples that they can leverage for an IoT product. We will discuss state-of-the-art connectivity solutions that are used in IoT applications. We provide enough foundational material to provide the reader with the background necessary to make informed decisions on the connectivity technology that will lead to a viable IoT product. We leverage our cumulative industry experience at Intel Corp. and elsewhere to discuss the complete process of selecting, designing, developing, and deploying connectivity solutions for IoT products. While there are many books discussing aspects of IoT, there is not a text that guides a reader through the entire process of developing and deploying connectivity for IoT products. Our book attempts to fill this gap.

This book is intended for researchers, managers, strategists, technologists, makers, and students in the embedded and Internet of Things (IoT) space trying to understand and implement connectivity in their devices and platforms. Our goal is to help you to develop an understanding of the essentials of connectivity including standards, protocols, hardware, software, and security. As the industry is constantly advancing, we hope this book equips you with the foundation needed to explore and adopt the emerging connectivity technologies for your solutions in the future.

CHAPTER 1

IoT Connectivity Considerations

IoT at a Glance

Internet of Things (IoT) is a set of technologies and capabilities that are enabling new use cases and delivering services across a wide variety of markets and applications. In simple terms, IoT is about connecting the unconnected, making them smart and autonomous, and providing the ability to remotely monitor, control, and manage devices on a massive scale. When people think of IoT, they often think of home or personal IoT. IoT is much more than a smart door lock, smart garage door opener, smart lighting, or a wireless video doorbell. IoT will play a role in many commercial applications such as smart manufacturing, smart cities, autonomous cars, building automation, and healthcare.

Implicitly, IoT also includes the following key attributes:

- Scalability: Trillions of Things readily deployed across multitudes of use cases and connected via IP. IP enables each Thing to be identified uniquely and addressed so that data can be received or sent from or to the Thing from anywhere on the Internet.

- Communications: The digital data and measurements from the Things are sent reliably, securely, and punctually to be analyzed at the "Edge" or the "Cloud"; conversely, commands from the Edge or Cloud are received reliably, securely, and in a timely manner by Things so that time critical operations can be executed.

- Analytics: Data from trillions of Things are analyzed to derive understanding and insights that produce actions that benefit entities – humans, corporations, and the world community.

One of the core aspects of IoT is about M2M (machine-to-machine) communication where billions of smart and autonomous things and devices will connect to the Internet and leverage AI, cloud technologies, and big data analytics to make our lives much smarter, healthier, and better. A typical end-to-end IoT system concept is shown in Figure 1-1.

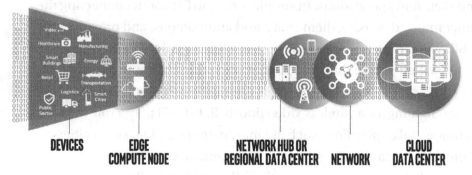

| DEVICES | EDGE COMPUTE NODE | NETWORK HUB OR REGIONAL DATA CENTER | NETWORK | CLOUD DATA CENTER |

Figure 1-1. End-to-end IoT system concept

How will an IoT-enabled device communicate what it knows to the Internet? Suitable connectivity solutions range from a multitude of wired connectivity technologies such as Ethernet to wireless technologies like Wi-Fi and even 5G cellular.

Many solutions need a combination of multiple communication technologies. For example, a smart car system playing video or using GPS navigation might need 4G LTE in order to communicate with the outside world and Wi-Fi and Bluetooth to communicate with devices like phones and rear seat entertainment (RSE) used by the passengers. In this book, we will look at a select set of connectivity technologies that enable these applications.

Wired or Wireless?

Wired connectivity solutions such as Ethernet-based on twisted pair copper or fiber optics are used today and will continue to be used in many IoT applications as they have many benefits in terms of high speed, excellent reliability, support for long cable runs, inherent security, and relatively low latency.

However, wired connectivity solutions alone are not enough for enabling the IoT ecosystem. Consider the following: using wireless to connect battery-powered IoT sensors simplifies deployment and reduces installation costs and enables economical scaling of IoT solutions. For example, imagine the cost and construction time required for running miles of cabling for a Smart Agriculture or Smart City use case or rewiring an existing Smart Building to reroute cables to environmental sensors. The cost of installing the wired connectivity infrastructure could overwhelm the potential savings due to the high-cost deployment of IoT solutions. Thus, wireless connectivity could enable the scaling of a financially viable solution. For devices that are in motion such as robots, mobile terminals and cars, or devices that need to be placed in different locations on a temporary basis such as mining and agricultural equipment, wireless connectivity is needed to meet the needs of applications that require mobility and seamless connectivity. Thus, we can see that wireless technologies are essential to building the IoT ecosystem. However, we

3

acknowledge the inherent limitations of wireless technologies, and we will devote several chapters of this book on the strategies for reducing and mitigating these limitations and optimizing the potential of wireless solutions for IoT applications.

Note that in both wired and wireless connectivity, the data are transmitted as an electromagnetic wave.

Wired connectivity: Electrical or optical signals are sent over a physical wire or cable between IoT devices; the electrical or optical signals are constrained within the physical cable. The electromagnetic carrier wave is transmitted over a cable that consists of a conductive material that acts as a transmission line. The types of cable that are used depend upon the wired standard and can include twisted pair or shielded twisted pair such as telephone cables, coaxial cables, fiber optic cables, and even powerlines such as household electrical wiring. The physical properties of the cable determine the data rate and reliability of the transmitted data.

Because the messages are restricted to the physical cable or wire, they are secure from being intercepted unless the cable is physically accessed. Cables are subject to crosstalk interference from adjacent cables. Shielding used in coaxial cables provides immunity from such noise and interference.

The electromagnetic energy that is sent over a cable attenuates with distance due to the impedance of the cable and impedance mismatches from different components connected to the cable. For example, the maximum length of Ethernet cables is typically 100 meters.[1]

Wireless connectivity: Radio Frequency (RF) or optical signals are broadcast across the environment between IoT devices. For wireless connectivity, the carrier waveform is launched as an electromagnetic wave into "free space" from the transmitting device to the receiving device. The

---

[1] https://infinity-cable-products.com/blogs/performance/attenuation-in-cable#:~:text=Some%20of%20the%20major%20causes,as%20they%20increase%20in%20length

electromagnetic waveform could be sent over an antenna that radiates the energy in a specific direction; at the receiver, another antenna is used to convert the electromagnetic wave into a voltage and current that is processed to recover the transmitted data.

In theory, "free space" is considered to be a vacuum. In reality, "free space" includes physical obstacles such as the ground, buildings, walls, people, trees, moisture and rain, etc. which affect the fidelity of the wave that arrives at the receiver antenna. Practical communication solutions need to overcome these impairments and several different techniques are adopted by various connectivity standards.

In addition, it is certainly possible that the transmitted wave is an optical signal sent via a laser or infrared pulse. It is also possible to use non-radio techniques such as ultrasonic signals to send data between IoT devices. Such techniques are not yet widely deployed for IoT applications today and could become popular once the solutions mature.

Which Wireless Technology?

The IoT will require several wireless technologies if it's to meet its potential. No such thing as "one size fits all" wireless technology exists for IoT, and many times combination of multiple wireless technologies is needed. For example, Bluetooth Low Energy and IEEE 802.15.4 are good choices for battery-powered sensors, but for devices that are constantly moving, or are not near a LAN (Local Area Network), or Wi-Fi Access Point (AP), such relatively short-range wireless technologies are not suitable for connecting to the Internet.

Even if a Wi-Fi network is present, manufacturers might prefer longer-range wireless technology for its convenience and autonomy. For example, a white goods manufacturer could select cellular technology over Wi-Fi because it enables a refrigerator or washing machine to connect to the Cloud automatically, eliminating the need for a consumer to enter a password to add the appliance to the home's Wi-Fi network. In these situations, low-power wide area networks (LPWAN) or Narrowband IoT technologies could come to the rescue.

Considerations for Choosing Wireless Technologies for IoT

There are many wireless networking technologies that are deployed in IoT today, each with a different set of capabilities. Here are some of the key considerations when choosing these different solutions.

Spectrum

Wireless spectrum can be characterized as either licensed or unlicensed. Access to licensed spectrum is typically purchased from a local government to provide an organization exclusive access to a particular channel in a particular location. Operation in that channel should be largely free of interference from competing radios. The drawback is that the spectrum of interest may be extremely scarce or expensive to access. In some other cases, radio connectivity bands allowed in one country may not be available in other geographical area for same usage. For instance, mobile networks in India use the 900 MHz and 1800 MHz frequency bands, while GSM (Global System for Mobile communications) carriers in the United States operate in 850 MHz and 1900 MHz frequency bands. To deploy an IoT device globally, then it may have to support multiple radio bands making the device costly as well as time-consuming to develop. Even when more easily accessible, it can take months to gain the approval to operate, so licensed bands are not well suited to rapid deployments.

Unlicensed spectrum is generally open and available to anybody to use with no exclusive rights granted to any particular organization or individual. The downside is that competing systems may occupy the same channel at different power levels leading to interference. Manufacturers of radio systems operating in unlicensed bands include capabilities in these radios to adapt their operation for this potential interference. These techniques include adaptive modulation, automatic transmit power control and out-of-band filtering, and so on.

Range and Capacity

Several factors impact the amount of data capacity that can be delivered at a particular distance. Those factors include spectrum, channel bandwidth, transmitter power, terrain, noise immunity, and antenna size. In general, the longer the distance to be covered, the lower the data capacity. The longest propagation distance can be achieved by using a low-frequency narrowband channel with a high-gain antenna, while higher capacities could be achieved by selecting wider channels, with limited range. For optimal performance for each application, we need to choose the best combination of channel size, antenna, radio power, and modulation schemes to achieve the desired capacity.

A radio link can be described as being line of sight when there is a direct optical path between the two radios making up the link. A link is called non-line of sight when there is some obstruction between the two radios. Near line of sight is simply a partial obstruction rather than a complete obstruction. In general, lower-frequency solutions have better propagation characteristics than higher frequencies. Higher-frequency solutions that operate in multi-gigahertz range are typically line-of-sight or near line-of-sight systems. From 1 GHz to 6 GHz range, the propagation characteristics capabilities will vary depending on other factors, and typically below 1 GHz the propagation becomes much better, making those frequencies suitable for longer range. Figure 1-2 shows a landscape of data rates and ranges of common wireless technologies.

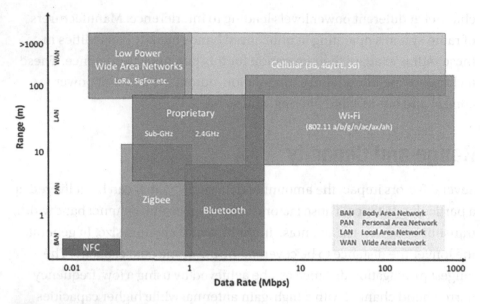

Figure 1-2. *Range and data rate comparison of wireless connectivity technologies*

Network Topology

Network topology is the arrangement of the elements in a network, including its nodes and connections between them. Common network topologies used for wireless connectivity are depicted in Figure 1-3.

Point-to-point topologies are best suited for delivering lots of capacity over long distances. Point-to-point connections cover longer distances that are less susceptible to interference as the antenna patterns are narrower so the energy can be focused in the direction of the desired transmission. Point-to-point links are also used for short-range connections to the wireline backbone. Resiliency in a point-to-point link can be provided by deploying in 1+1 or other redundant configurations with parallel sets of radios.

Ring topologies are excellent for resilient operations of high-capacity links covering a large area. This configuration is typically used in the backhaul network.

Mesh networks can be built using multiple point-to-point links or with specialized meshing protocols to enable multiple paths from point A to point B. Mesh networks are more resilient since the failure of one device does not cause a break in the network or transmission of data.

Adding additional devices does not disrupt data transmission between other devices, so it is easy to increase the coverage area or add additional nodes without re-configuring the entire network. Mesh networks have the downside of each packet traversing multiple hops and so can lead to lower capacity and increased latency for a given infrastructure.

Point-to-multipoint (or **star**) networks provide scale and capacity over a geographic area. Point-to-multipoint networks are typically deployed to cover sectors or cells. The key differentiating capability to look for in point-to-point networks is their ability to scale in the number of nodes per cell but also the ability to place cells next to each other without interference.

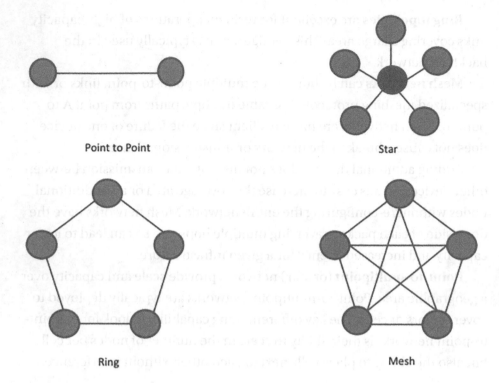

Figure 1-3. *Common network topologies*

Quality of Service

System builders and operators need to make the most efficient use of available spectrum and other networking infrastructure by deploying multiple services on the same network and making sure that mission-critical information is transmitted with highest priority. Quality of Service (QoS) is a set of technologies that work on a network to guarantee its ability to dependably run high-priority applications and traffic under limited network capacity. QoS technologies accomplish this by providing differentiated handling and capacity allocation to specific flows in network traffic. They enable the network administrator to assign the order in which packets are handled, and the amount of bandwidth afforded to that application or traffic flow. A network should support multiple Quality of Service (QoS) levels and the ability to sort traffic based on standard traffic classifiers. In this way, the transmitter of the data packet can mark the class of service or priority, and the end-to-end network will ensure that the packet is delivered with the desired level of low latency and availability.

Network Management

The capability to manage a network has a direct impact on the total cost of ownership of the IoT system. Networking systems that allow centralized management of configuration, fault detection, performance tuning and continuous monitoring, and security validation minimize the cost and effort. They also reduce unplanned outages and increase system availability and reliability.

Security

The security of wireless communications is growing in importance. Primary techniques to look for here are the ability to encrypt the over-the-air link, using a network, mesh, or link key. Besides this we need to secure management interfaces with HTTPS and SNMP. Systems should also provide the ability to create multiple user accounts with password complexity rules. Previously, many traditional automation and control solutions have not been exposed to security issues faced by the IT systems, but recently have become hacking targets as their solutions get connected to the Internet. Major security breaches could slow down the adoption of IoT.

As can be seen from Figure 1-4, several local area network (LAN) and wide area network (WAN) technologies with different levels of security and network management requirements need to work seamlessly to realize an end-to-end IoT system.

11

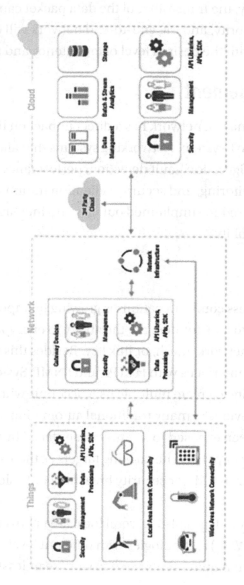

Figure 1-4. End-to-end IoT systems need various connectivity technologies

Connectivity Standards

In the IoT domain, networking standards are the most important ones. Standards define rules and formats for setting up and managing IoT networks, along with how data are transmitted across these networks. Communications standards are essential to making sure that the data gets to the destination, error-free and on time. The protocols make sure that both the transmitter and the receiver can understand the meaning of the data, or they speak the same language to ensure interoperability.

Standards establish a transparent, consistent, and universal understanding of a technology. They enhance compatibility and interoperability among products from different vendors and accelerate the development, global adoption, and large-scale deployment of IoT technologies. Overall system costs are significantly reduced when we adopt standards-based technology. Consumer choice and competition will result in lower device prices. Research, development, and maintenance costs are all driven down when solution providers and customers can focus on one standard technology rather than several different proprietary protocols and solutions.

According to the European Telecommunications Standards Institute (ETSI), a standard is a "document, established by consensus and approved by a recognized body, that provides, for common and repeated use, rules, guidelines or characteristics for activities or their results, aimed at achievement of the optimum degree of order in a given context."[2]

There are several standardized communications technologies that were widely deployed on a global scale. The most successful examples include wired and wireless technologies such as Wi-Fi (based on IEEE 802.1, 802.3, and 802.11 specifications), ZigBee (based on IEEE 802.15.4 specifications), and Wireless Cellular Communications such as 2G/3G/4G/ LTE (based on standards developed by ITU and 3GPP).

---

[2]www.etsi.org/standards/why-standards Derived from ISO/IEC Guide 2:1996, definition 3.2

However, these previously existing standards are not optimized for a majority of large-scale IoT deployments that require interconnection of large number of battery-operated devices. Limited range and coverage, low penetration capability, power-hungry transmissions, and high costs are factors that hamper their applicability in many IoT use cases.

We should consider the following when we choose connectivity standards for an IoT application:

Environment/location: Operating location of IoT devices and whether it is fixed or mobile. Environmental factors such as operating temperature range, humidity, vibration, presence of explosive gases, etc. need to be considered. A primary input into the design/section process which determines power, communication range, and serviceability constraints is described later.

Size: Device enclosure size. May introduce constraints on antenna size, power supply, or cooling solutions used. If you have a small device, it will affect the size of the battery that can be used and the amount of time the device can operate before the battery needs re-charging.

Cost: Each sub-system in the IoT system should have a cost target and determines the overall viability of the IoT system. A primary input that will introduce constraints everywhere. Variable costs such as any monthly subscription fees or usage-based fees for connectivity shall be considered.

Data: The amount and frequency of data to be captured and sent (e.g., 8 Bytes every 125 millisecond) as well as the lifespan of that data (how long will it persist in each storage location). A primary input that could often be constrained by environment, size, or cost. Establishes bandwidth and spectrum requirements as well as storage and processing requirements onboard a device locally and, in the Edge, or Cloud remotely. If your device transmits large amounts of data frequently, then you will need a high bandwidth solution.

Serviceability/availability: Each system will have a finite life or a service requirement. System availability is the probability that the system is operating at a specified time. Typically constrained by environment

14

and cost, may introduce constraints on power. Also, drives standard or proprietary technology preferences to ensure future upgrades.

Power: Power becomes a significant design consideration with dependencies on size, environment, cost, amount of data, serviceability, and available computing power. For example, battery-powered sensors used for environmental monitoring need to avoid frequent battery replacement.

Onboard processing: Requirements for onboard vs. remote processing power and storage capabilities determine the bandwidth and frequency of data transfer. Constrained by size, cost, and power.

Transmission mode: The connectivity standards chosen depend on mode of operation. In simplex mode, the communication is unidirectional. The half-duplex mode is used in cases where there is no need for communication in both direction at the same time. In full-duplex mode, both stations can transmit and receive simultaneously.

Security: Since IoT devices are connected into the Internet, the effective surface of attack is increased, and the communication links can become a backdoor for hacking and unauthorized access. Privacy may be considered as the authorized, fair, and legitimate processing of personal information. When selecting an IoT solution, the security and privacy requirements and applicable regulations shall be considered.

For successful implementation of an IoT solution, tradeoffs are necessary. If our device must transmit data over a long distance wirelessly, the radio solution will need to operate at a lower data rate, use a lower frequency, implement a larger antenna, or increase the transmitted power. If our battery-powered device is at location that cannot be easily reached and it must operate for days without a re-charge or battery replacement, we will need to reduce the amount of data transmitted and reduce the frequency (how often) at which data is transmitted or limit the range of operation. Alternatively, one could invest in a more expensive battery technology or use a bigger battery.

In reality, many IoT endpoints and gateways will employ multiple communication technologies based on cost, improved flexibility, and interoperability. A primary example is connected thermostat which incorporates both Wi-Fi and ZigBee. Many smart meters support cellular, ZigBee, RF mesh, and Wi-Fi capabilities. A key advantage of Wi-Fi and Bluetooth is that they are already embedded in essentially all smartphones.

This type of coexistence of multiple technologies in a single system is illustrated in the smart home IoT system example shown in Figure 1-5.

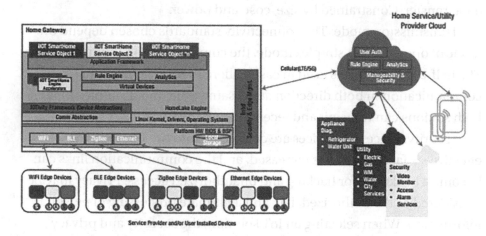

Figure 1-5. *Smart home system using multiple connectivity*

The gateway supports Wi-Fi and Ethernet for LAN connections that need higher bandwidth such as audio and video applications. PAN and mesh networks based on Bluetooth Low Energy and ZigBee are used for energy-efficient sensors and controllers for lighting, security, and so on. The gateway provides WAN connectivity to Cloud using cellular technologies like LTE and 5G and local analytics. Cloud service providers enable cloud-based applications to deliver various services such as utilities and security.

Summary

Today, many of the underlying systems for IoT applications are based on proprietary standards and could present integration and interoperability challenges. A lack of a broader network ecosystem perspective in terms of business systems, platforms, and standards as well as interoperability could present a significant challenge for the adoption of IoT into modern workflows. Consortia, industry, and government bodies as well as standards associations are working to establish standards, associated profiles, and tests. It is incumbent upon everyone involved in the ecosystem to work with partners to stay current on evolving standards, make them interoperable, and coexist to maximize the value delivered by IoT. By using a standards-based foundation, system designers and engineers would be able to architect a network that will stay current with evolving use cases. The rest of this book will discuss the evolution of existing standards and the emergence of new standards to address the IoT use cases.

Problem Set

1. I have designed a perfect wireless system that provides maximum range, maximum throughput, and minimal battery usage for my transmitter and receiver. I therefore would like to keep my implementation proprietary without any standardization and ensure that my company is the only source for hardware and software for this ecosystem. What are potential pitfalls in this approach?

2. The existing machinery and connectivity
    solution in my factory are 20 years old. In order
    to increase the productivity of my factory to be
    better than my competitors, I will need to replace
    my manufacturing equipment and my means of
    connecting my control devices to the equipment.
    The equipment will need to be in place for the next
    20 years in order to amortize my costs and yet be
    more flexible and agile as my product mix changes
    over time. What are some considerations on the
    connectivity technology that I should implement?

3. Much has been made of the rise of autonomous
    devices (i.e., cars, robots, factories) that rely on
    machine learning and artificial intelligence. For
    these autonomous devices, do you think there is a
    need for wireless connectivity? Why or why not?

4. Consider two potential paths to developing a
    wireless sensor node: (1) take an off-the-shelf CPU
    from manufacturer A and attach it to a wireless
    module from manufacturer B onto a circuit board
    that I develop and manufacture or (2) develop a
    custom chip that combines a CPU with a wireless
    radio IP. What are some tradeoffs between options
    (1) and (2) in terms of developing a viable business
    case for my product?

5. Consider (a) a battery-powered moisture sensor in
    an agricultural field, (b) a Point-of-Sale terminal,
    and (c) an automatic robot in a factory. All are
    connected to the cloud. How would you choose the
    connectivity technologies to be optimal for each
    use case?

CHAPTER 2

Back to Wireless Basics

Chapter Overview

In this chapter, we go back to wireless basics and discuss the challenges and limitations that are inherent in wireless communications as compared to wired communications and the techniques that have been developed to solve these issues. We will classify the different wireless standards that are applicable to IoT solutions that we will discuss in subsequent chapters. We also describe the criteria that you can use to select the right wireless technology for your solution.

Introduction

We will begin our discussion on wireless connectivity basics by revisiting the fundamental goals of Internet of Things solutions (please refer to Figure 2-1):

1. Collect measurement data from "things": sensors or devices in the physical world.

2. Send the data reliably, securely, and in a timely manner from the things to the Edge or Cloud via the Internet.

© Anil Kumar, Jafer Hussain, Anthony Chun 2023
A. Kumar et al., *Connecting the Internet of Things*,
https://doi.org/10.1007/978-1-4842-8897-9_2

3. Analyze data in the Edge or Cloud to derive insights into the physical world.

4. Perform actions back in the physical world based on the insights from this analysis in order to accomplish a goal.

Some examples of this process include

- Using temperature sensors to measure room temperature and human presence in an office building, sending the data via the *ZigBee* wireless protocol to a building management server, and sending commands back to the building's HVAC system to adjust the temperature of an unoccupied room by turning off the HVAC in order to save energy.

- Using solar-powered or battery-powered sensors to detect soil moisture in a field, transmitting the measurements to a gateway via the long range *Bluetooth Low Energy* (BLE) wireless protocol signals, analyzing the moisture data along with weather patterns in an Edge *server*, and sending commands via Bluetooth Low Energy to the drip irrigation valve to turn on crop watering in order to optimize water usage.

- Detecting preferred customers' (who opt in to get discounts) Bluetooth addresses from their smartphones via Bluetooth beacons to detect their presence in the shoe department of a store, transmitting this information to a gateway, looking up the customer's order history, and sending new content to a digital sign near the customer with the latest shoe sale in order to increase sales.

- Smart city: Sensors monitor air quality and vehicle traffic patterns and street imagery and relay the data back to the analytics functions to determine optimum strategies for reducing city traffic. The resulting action includes aligning traffic light and mass transit schedules to mitigate traffic congestion.

- Retail Point of Sale: Restaurant orders are relayed by a mobile Point of Sale terminal to the data analytics software running on the cloud; based upon the customer orders on a particular night, the inventory of those items that are in demand can be increased, and specials to promote specific menu items can be offered

- Inventory management: Bluetooth sensors attached to a pallet of merchandise relay the location of the pallet in the warehouse to a management system which schedules a robot to pick it up for shipping.

- Covid-19 mitigation: Measuring the body temperatures of passengers in an airport terminal via wireless thermal sensors and relaying this data to a gateway to alert medical staff.

- Covid-19 mitigation: Measuring the location of customers in a shopping mall via their Bluetooth received signal strength or their angle with respect to Bluetooth beacons in order to determine if people are following social distance guidelines.

- Covid-19 mitigation: Using wireless presence detection in an office building to determine if Shelter-in-Place rules are being followed.

In this book, we are focused on optimizing step 2 (sending the data from the sensors to the edge or cloud) and step 3 (sending messages back to actuators to perform actions).

We will assume that the IoT devices present measurement data accurately, reliably, in a timely manner and securely to the communications system. We will assume that the IoT analytics in the Edge and Cloud have been designed to perform an appropriate action using the received IoT data. There are numerous references on IoT sensors and IoT analytics; for example, please see this paper that compares three IoT Cloud platforms.[1]

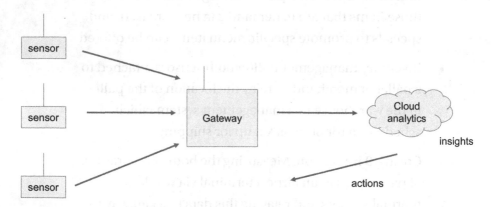

Figure 2-1. *Depiction of IoT showing data being sent from sensors to a Gateway and then to the Cloud for analysis*

In order to accomplish these goals, the sensor data must be sent accurately (without errors), securely (so that it is only received by the owners of the data or cannot be fabricated by an adversary), and on time (without delay), especially if the necessary actions are time critical.

---

[1] P. Pierleoni, R. Concetti, A. Belli, and L. Palma, "Amazon, Google and Microsoft Solutions for IoT: Architectures and a Performance Comparison," in IEEE Access, vol. 8, pp. 5455-5470, 2020, doi: 10.1109/ACCESS.2019.2961511.

In addition to the physical data that are sent from the sensors to the cloud, control messages are sent from the cloud to the sensors and actuators to commission, configure, command, and manage the IoT devices and physical actuators. The control messages include setting up the schedule for when data are to be sent from the sensors, setting sleep states, sending software updates and patches, checking the status of the device, etc. These control and management messages need to be sent securely and received reliably and at the appropriate time as well.

Finally, data privacy and security need to be strictly maintained by preventing unauthorized adversaries from accessing the devices and intruding into the overall network.

The Ideal Wireless World vs. Reality

Let's visualize an *ideal* wireless IoT world. In an ideal IoT world, key attributes of the wireless technology are

- Accuracy: Data that are transmitted and received are accurate and without distortion or error.

- High throughput: Transmissions from the devices are at data rates that are fast enough to meet the customer's target Quality of Service.

- Low latency: Data from each device are sent and received within the delay that meets the customer's target Quality of Service.

- Energy efficient: The wireless components consume low power leading to long battery life of the device (ideally years without replacing the battery of an inaccessible device such as a remote sensor).

- Secure: The transmitted messages both to and from the device are secure from eavesdroppers.

- Hacker-proof: Adversaries are not able to "spoof" legitimate traffic and send fake messages nor access the underlying infrastructure to obtain user data or disable or corrupt the system.

- Reliable: Messages are successfully received reliably so that customer's target Quality of Service (as defined by the number of 9s; i.e., 99.999% is called "five 9s" and is the probability of a packet being received both correctly and on-time) is met.

- Uniform coverage: Connectivity is maintained across the coverage area (i.e., factory floor or retail space) without blind spots that cause loss of connectivity or poor throughput.

- Mobile: Devices can be moving on the ground or in the air and still reliably transmit and receive messages; in some wireless systems, this may require seamless handoff between base stations or access points.

- Rugged: Wireless technology can be used in rugged environmental conditions over a wide temperature, moisture, pressure, humidity, and shock range including exposed to weather outdoors or in high temperatures a manufacturing environment.

- Easy-to-commission: It is easy for the authorized end customer or system integrator to deploy and commission their numerous devices without requiring expensive support from the original equipment manufacturer (OEM) or original design manufacturer (ODM). (Conversely, it should be impossible for an unauthorized person to commission the network.)

- Easy-to-update: Software updates and patches can be sent wirelessly to the multitude of deployed devices so that physically updating the software by an authorized technician can be minimized.

- Manageable: The devices can be easily managed from a central location either onsite or at a corporate headquarters so that support personnel do not need to physically tend to the devices if issues arise ("truck rolls") and thus reduce operating expenses (OpEx) and Total Cost of Ownership.

- Scalable: The devices with their wireless components can be easily and economically manufactured (mass produced) and installed.

- Certifiable: Radio equipment must adhere to the regulations of the country where they are deployed and be officially certified that they are transmitting in their approved frequency spectrum and their transmissions are not interfering with other radio devices by keeping the wireless transmission power within the limits defined by the country. The units will be easily certified in all the countries where the end customer deploys their products.

- Design: The physical design of the product and the placement of RF components such as the antenna can be easily done within the constraints of the development team's expertise in antenna or Radio Frequency (RF) knowledge.

- Safety: The wireless equipment must ensure that human safety guidelines for radio transmission are met.

The preceding list is by no means exhaustive, and the reader can come up with additional criteria relevant to their use cases.

In 2022, how far are we from achieving the ideal wireless world with our current wireless connectivity technologies?

Challenges of Wireless Connectivity

In 2022, we are far from this ideal wireless world:

- Wireless transmissions that are in the *unlicensed* bands such as the Instrumentation, Scientific and Medical (ISM) band at 2.4GHz or other bands in the sub-1GHz spectrum are subject to interference from other devices that are transmitting in the same frequency band; wireless transmissions in *licensed* bands that are used by cellular devices are managed to prevent interference but are subject to monthly fees.

- Wireless transmissions are attenuated by obstructions in the environment between the transmitter and receiver such as walls, people, rain, etc. that affect the distance between IoT devices and the Edge server.

- Wireless transmissions are affected by fading and multipath due to reflections of the radio signal by objects such as people, buildings, vehicles, and vegetation in the environment between the transmitter and receiver.

- Wireless transmissions are affected by interference from radio noise in the environment due to microwave ovens, machinery, and other electrical equipment.

- Wireless transmissions are limited in transmit power for regulatory and safety reasons leading to challenges in the distance between IoT devices and the Edge server and in correctly receiving the data.

- Robustness and reliability: Measured probability of packet error on Wi-Fi is 11 to 30% for a 200-byte packet;[2] for Bluetooth Low Energy, a packet error rate of 1×10^{-3} can be met at the 1Megabits/sec data rate with sufficient range for industrial channels.[3]

- Security: Wireless signals are broadcast over the air and adversaries with the appropriate radio equipment such as a scanner can intercept the wireless signals; also, adversaries can "spoof" legitimate signals in order to attack a network via a "man-in-the-middle attack" which involves intercepting the legitimate messages and replacing them with fake messages.

- Manageability: Connecting and maintaining wireless devices may require a complex provisioning procedure in order to provide new nodes with access to the network. This is especially challenging for "headless" IoT devices that do not include a display or graphical user interface. One common example is connecting a Smart Speaker (such as Amazon Echo™-trademark) that does not include a display to a Wi-Fi network by using the installer application on his/her smartphone to first connect the speaker via Bluetooth.

---

[2] David Murray, et al., "Measuring the Reliability of 802.11 WiFi Networks," *2015 Internet Technologies and Applications* (ITA), 8-11 Sept. 2015.

[3] Díez, et al., "Reliability Evaluation of Bluetooth Low Energy for Industry 4.0," *2019 24th IEEE International Conference on Emerging Technologies and Factory Automation* (ETFA), 10-13 Sept. 2019.

- Power consumption: Radio transmitters and receivers require a certain amount of power which limits the battery life of remote sensors.

- Throughput: The data rate that is available is dependent upon the wireless standard and other variables including the number of competing users on the network, distance between network nodes, the amount of noise and radio interference, and the channel conditions including obstacles between the transmitter and receiver.

- Multiple access techniques are implemented to control access between competing devices to the wireless resources; for very simple "best effort" access schemes, it is possible that a given device may have to make multiple attempts to gain access to the network in order to send data which causes a long delay.

- Latency may be high due to "best effort" decentralized protocols that deliver messages when bandwidth is available which can be limited if there are numerous competing devices on the network.

- Scaling and deploying thousands and millions of devices in an efficient and cost-effective manner is challenging because technicians may be required to install, set up, configure, and maintain the sensors.

As we have indicated, the capabilities of wireless technology today fall short of the attributes of an ideal connectivity solution. Given these limitations, why not use wired connectivity (such as Ethernet) instead?

The unique advantages of convenience, flexibility, and mobility may outweigh the challenges of using wireless connectivity instead of wired connectivity for many use cases. Furthermore, steady improvement in wireless technologies as well as rigorous and thorough site planning, engineering, and design can provide solutions that are "good enough" to provide sufficient Quality of Service for your customers' use cases.

Connectivity Basics

In subsequent chapters of this book, we will discuss both wireless and wired connectivity standards for IoT products. Before we start that discussion, let's review the basics of both wired and wireless connectivity:

Wired connectivity: Radio Frequency (RF) or optical signals are sent over a physical wire or cable between IoT devices; the electrical or optical signals are constrained within the physical cable.

Wireless connectivity: Radio Frequency (RF) or optical signals are broadcast across the environment between IoT devices.

Note that in both wired and wireless connectivity, the data are transmitted as an electromagnetic wave that is defined by Maxwell's equations.[4] The electromagnetic wave consists of time-varying electrical and magnetic fields and is characterized by

- Carrier frequency $f_{carrier}$ Hertz (cycles per second): can range from 0Hz (i.e., direct current or DC) to 2.4GHz (Bluetooth and Wi-Fi) to 10^{14} to 10^{15} Hz in optical fiber[5]

- Wavelength λ meters

- Speed c = speed of light = 3×10^8 meters per second in free space

---

[4] Ramo, et al. *Fields and Waves in Communication Electronics*. Wiley, 1994 ISBN 8126515252, 9788126515257.

[5] www.sciencedirect.com/topics/engineering/fibre-optic-cable#:~:text=The%20light%20sent%20down%20the,14%20to%201015%20Hz

- Phase θ in radians where there are 180 degrees in π radians

- Amplitude A in volts

- Power P in watts=joules/second

- Energy E joules = power accumulated over time

- Bandwidth B Hertz which is the amount of spectrum that is used for the information or data that modulates the wave

The expression for the Radio Frequency (RF) waveform without data modulation as a function of time t is given by

$$X(t) = A\sin\left(2\pi f_{carrier}t + \theta\right) \tag{1}$$

For example,

- If $f_{carrier}$=2.4GHz = 2.4x10^{9}Hz, then the wavelength is

$$\lambda = \frac{c}{f_{crrier}} = \frac{3\times10^8 \; meters / s}{2.4\times10^9 \; Hz} = 0.125 \; meters$$

- If $f_{carrier}$=5GHz = 5x10^{9}Hz, then the wavelength is

$$\lambda = \frac{c}{f_{carrier}} = \frac{3\times10^8 \; meters / s}{5\times10^9 \; Hz} = 0.06 \; meters$$

Please refer to Figure 2-2.

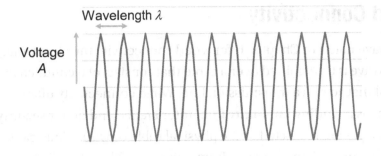

Figure 2-2. *Depiction of key parameters of a carrier wave*

The waveform that we have described is denoted as a *Carrier Wave* as it carries data. The set of frequencies that is used is called the *spectrum*.

For most of the applications in this book, we will focus on sending digital data that is mapped to binary sequences of 0s and 1s.

We send digital data over this carrier wave by *digital modulation* where the modulation is characterized by

- Modulation type: Translating the binary data to changes of the characteristics of the carrier wave – frequency, amplitude, or phase or combinations of these.

- Bandwidth *B* Hertz: The amount of spectrum that is used to send the modulated data; this defines the available throughput or data rate (the more bandwidth the higher the data rate).

- Energy per Bit E_b joules/bit = watts.

- Data Rate *R* bits per second.

Wired and wireless connectivity standards share the same concepts for ensuring that the data are sent reliably and securely over the transmission medium including *Information Theory* and *Communication Theory*; later in this chapter, we will discuss these techniques that are used to satisfy the requirements for an IoT solution.

Wired Connectivity

As we have noted in Chapter 1, for wired connectivity the electromagnetic carrier wave is transmitted over a cable that consists of a conductive material that acts as a transmission line. Wired connectivity offers advantages including immunity from interference and better security as the messages are restricted to the physical cable or wire. While cables are subject to crosstalk interference from adjacent cables, shielding in coaxial cables provides immunity from noise and interference.

Wireless Connectivity

As we also noted in Chapter 1, for wireless connectivity the carrier waveform is launched as an electromagnetic wave into "free space" from the transmitting device to the receiving device. In reality, "free space" includes physical obstacles such as air, the ground, buildings, walls, people, trees, moisture and rain, etc. that affect the fidelity of the wave that arrives at the receiver antenna. In addition, noise and interference in the radio environment can impact reception of the wave at the receiver. Because the wave is broadcast into free space, anyone between the transmitter and receiver can receive the waveform and with the right type of equipment collect it. We will go into detail on these issues later in this chapter.

What Is a Radio?

As we begin the discussion of wireless for IoT, we will begin with a brief introduction into what is a *radio*. While we associate a "radio" with wireless connectivity, there is an analogous component in the "PHY" (physical layer) that is used in wired connectivity.

A radio is the component of the IoT device or platform that

1. Receives digital data from the Central Processor Unit
    (CPU) or microcontroller (MCU) on the IoT device,
    prepares the data in accordance with a wireless
    standard or protocol, modulates and converts it to
    an analog radio frequency (RF) waveform within the
    frequency spectrum allocated to the standard, and
    transmits it from an antenna through the medium to
    the radio in the destination device that receives and
    processes the messages

2. *Receives* RF waveforms via an antenna that have
    been transmitted from other devices in its network,
    mitigates the effects of the transmission medium
    including noise and interference, converts the
    waveforms to data packets in accordance with
    a wireless protocol or standard, and passes the
    packets to the processor or controller on the IoT
    sensor device or platform

Some additional key points include

-   Another term for radio is *modem* which is a contraction
    of "modulator demodulator." The term modem is often
    used interchangeably with radio.

-   We are focused on a *digital* radio which is used to
    transport binary data as we mentioned, in contrast to
    analog radio formats such as AM and FM that were
    used to transmit analog audio and voice. Analog radio
    is not widely used for data transmission today.

-   The radio may have standard hardware interfaces to the
    host central processing unit (CPU) or microcontroller
    unit (MCU) on the SoC (system on chip), as seen in
    Figure 2-3. Having a standard host interface enables

radio manufacturers to mass produce radio products (comprised of silicon chips or radio modules) and reduce the manufacturing cost and selling price. Popular host interfaces include *USB, UART, SDIO*, and *PCI express*.

- Alternatively, the radio may be integrated into the SoC with the microcontroller, as an integrated chip with the CPU and radio in the same package.

- Software *drivers* between the host CPU or MCU and the radio may also be available for the operating system that is being used by the platform. The operating system can be Microsoft Windows,[6] Linux, Android,[7] Chrome OS, a Real-Time Operating System (RTOS) that executes operations in a deterministic manner such as Zephyr,[8] VxWorks,[9] Free RTOS,[10] etc., or bare metal (no operating system). Depending upon the operating system, the software drivers may be open source (via an open source project such as Linux) that is maintained by a community or proprietary from the radio manufacturer or the CPU manufacturer.

- Wireless standards and corresponding certification organizations ensure that multiple manufacturers in the ecosystem can develop equipment that can

---

[6] Windows is a trademark of Microsoft.

[7] Android is a trademark of Google LLC.

[8] https://zephyrproject.org/.

[9] https://experience.windriver.com/redefining-rtos/p/1?utm_source= google&utm_medium=sem&utm_campaign=vp-dg-amer-vhs-sem-vxworks-exact- brand-07012021&gclid=CjOKCQjw39uYBhCLARIsAD_SzMQHg7ec3eBdUz8mrJbg8aA 3rai4Crcult18k2fiXIrdercbEVUWG1saApQuEALw_wcB

[10] https://github.com/FreeRTOS/FreeRTOS

interoperate over the same standard and be certified
as adhering to the standard. Wireless standards ensure
that multiple suppliers provide a range of products
at different price points and that the industry can
continue in the event of a failure of one company.
Wireless standards are key to widespread adoption of a
technology and the build out of a complete ecosystem
of hardware manufacturers, software developers,
Original Design Manufacturers (ODMs), Original
Equipment Manufacturers (OEMs), and System
Integrators.

- The radio module may also include standard interfaces
  to attach an *antenna*. The selection of an appropriate
  antenna is a function of numerous factors including
  the desired antenna gain, antenna pattern (antenna
  gain as a function of direction), device form factor, size,
  cost, range to the receiver, and country certification
  requirements.

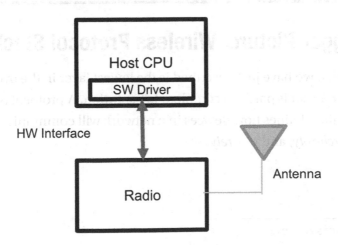

Figure 2-3. *Depiction of key radio interfaces*

| **ONE PAGER ON COMMON HOST INTERFACES** |

The use of common host interfaces enables wireless vendors to provide components that can be used on multiple devices. Some of the most common interfaces include

- PCIe: Peripheral Component Interconnect express is a standard developed by the PCI-SIG for defining the high-speed interfaces for connecting computer components.[11]

- SDIO: Secure Digital Input Output is a standard developed by the SD Association (SDA) that defines the interfaces between SD card peripherals.[12]

- USB: Universal Serial Bus is a standard developed by the USB Implementers Forum that defines the interface between computer components.[13]

- UART: Universal Asynchronous Receiver-Transmitter is a standard for interfacing a computer with peripheral devices.

The Bigger Picture: Wireless Protocol Stack

The radio that we have just described is the lowest layer in the overall *protocol stack* that is part of a complete IoT solution. A protocol is a procedure that defines how devices in a network will communicate *efficiently*, *reliably*, and *securely*.

---

[11] https://pcisig.com/

[12] www.sdcard.org/

[13] www.usb.org/about

This complete protocol stack is necessary to provide a successful solution to the customer that combines reliable, secure, and timely communications from Things to the Edge and Cloud with data analytics applications that derive actionable decisions from the data.

The wireless protocol defines the mechanisms for how devices access and send messages reliably across the network. The protocol stack defines the messages used by the components of the network (refer to OSI model). The protocol also allocates network resources such as bandwidth to devices that are sharing the network.

The protocol may use a scheduling mechanism to grant each device access to the network resources. The complexity of this scheduling mechanism depends on the Quality of Service requirements including latency and bandwidth.

Finally, the protocol stack's key role is to guarantee that data is reliably transported from end to end across the network. To do this successfully, the protocol layers are architected so that their combined efforts enable data to be transmitted and received correctly and in a timely manner so that Quality of Service requirements are met.

The resulting IoT solution is very complex with many hardware and software components from multiple vendors that have to be engineered, validated, integrated, and deployed. The solution will need to be deployed for a long period of time in order to recoup the development and installation costs and must be easily serviceable and maintainable.

The protocol is defined by technical contributions from stakeholders in the ecosystem and standardized by technical consortia, industry special interest groups, government agencies, and international standards bodies.

Standardization is essential to enable multiple manufacturers to develop compatible equipment and scale the technology across an ecosystem and drive down manufacturing costs.

Certainly, the ratification of a protocol stack as a standard requires technical compromise among the industry stakeholders, and it is possible that a proprietary protocol may offer technical advantages. However, we suggest that a standard protocol stack should be used if available in order to simplify the system engineering, design, validation, and maintenance of the IoT solution.

OSI Model: Basis for Defining a Protocol

The standard approach to defining a connectivity protocol begins with the Open Systems Interconnection (OSI) Model that was developed in 1984 and standardized by the International Standards Organization (ISO) and the International Telecommunications Union (ITU).[14]

Connectivity standards, whether wired or wireless, implement the different layers of the OSI model that are shown in Figure 2-4. The OSI model was developed to provide a common structure to the definition of network protocol stacks.

We will provide a brief description of the OSI model as it facilitates understanding of the software implementation of the connectivity stack. Details of the OSI model can be found in references on networking.[15]

---

[14] Andrew S. Tanenbaum, David J. Wetherall, *Computer Networks*, Prentice Hall Press, One Lake Street Upper Saddle River, NJ United States, ISBN:978-0-13-212695-3.

[15] Andrew S. Tanenbaum, David J. Wetherall, Computer Networks, Prentice Hall Press, One Lake Street Upper Saddle River, NJ United States, ISBN:978-0-13-212695-3.

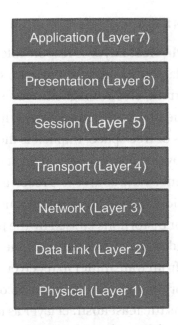

Figure 2-4. *The OSI model consists of seven layers*

The purpose of the OSI layered model is to enable systematic development of communications network standards by defining the functions that the standard must implement. The OSI model provides increasing abstraction as we move up the layers of the model. Each layer of the model does not see the inner details of the layer below it or above it.

Functionally, the communication between two devices (Device 1 and Device 2) is abstracted to be the communication between the corresponding layers of the model as shown in Figure 2-4. In reality, data from Device 1 are passed from Layer 7 to Layer 6, etc., down to Layer 1 via a set of well-defined interfaces between the layers and across to Layer 1 of Device 2 and then back up through the layers to Layer 7 as shown in Figure 2-4.

The OSI layers are as follows:

- Layer 1: The **Physical Layer** is responsible for transmitting data bits as electromagnetic signals (voltage or current, electromagnetic waves or optical pulses) over the physical medium which includes wires or cables or free space. Implicit is the capability to reliably recover the transmitted data at the receiver (if a "0" was sent by the source it is received as a "0" at the destination despite impairments such as noise, interference, or distortions caused by the physical medium.) In addition, the amount of time it takes to transmit a bit from transmitter to receiver determines the *data rate* or *throughput* in bits per second. The physical layer is the least abstract layer as it involves physical signals.

- Layer 2: The **Data Link Layer** ensures that a collection of bits called a *data frame* that is sent from the transmitter are received correctly by the Data Link Layer of the receiver. At the transmitter, the data frame is sent from Layer 2 to Layer 1, and at the receiver the data frame is sent from Layer 1 to Layer 2. The Data Link Layer at the destination device determines that the data frame was received correctly and sends an *acknowledgment* to the source device; if the source device does not receive an acknowledgment for a previous data frame, it resends the same data frame via Layer 1.

- Layer 3: The **Network Layer** groups data from the source device into *datagrams* or *packets* that are routed through the network to the destination device. The routing of packets may be through a series of nodes or routers in the network. The Network Layer also mitigates network congestion that can occur if multiple nodes in the network send packets at the same time. The combination of Layer 3 with Layer 4 enables the scalability of the IoT solution to the Internet.

- Layer 4: The **Transport Layer** takes data at the source device and sends it to the destination device such that it arrives in the proper sequence. It does this by creating connections between the source device and destination device through a series of *routers*. It is assumed that the data packets between the source and destination devices may be routed over different physical paths and that the data packets may arrive at the destination device *out-of-order* and may need to be reordered. Obviously, this is especially important if the payload consists of audio or video data. Different connection topologies are possible: point-to-point between the source and destination or broadcast from one source to multiple destination devices. Layer 4 is an end-to-end layer in that it runs on the source and destination devices; in contrast, Layers 1–3 run between intermediate nodes that combine to form the abstract connection.

- Layer 5: The **Session Layer** establishes the connection between the source and destination devices on the network. This connection is called a *session*. In order to do this, the source device needs to know the address of the destination device which is used to set up a connection in the transport layer.

- Layer 6: The **Presentation Layer** performs transformations of data that are being sent to the session layer, such as data compression and encryption and file conversions. An example would be applying compression of an image or video file. Encryption may be required depending upon the underlying security requirements.

- Layer 7: The **Application Layer** is the top layer of the model and provides the user or device-specific messages or data. For example, the application layer in a temperature sensor could be a software routine that reads the temperature value from the sensor at a specific time interval. On the Edge server that is connected to the temperature sensor over Bluetooth, the application is a software routine that displays the temperature value on a graphical user interface.

As we have indicated, Layers 4–7 abstract the intermediate node connections that are implemented in Layers 1–3. The implementation of the Layers 1–3 differs between the different wireless standards and are optimized to provide the best performance for each standard. Later in this book, we will focus on details of Layers 1 to 3 for the different wireless standards.

The actual implementation of the layers of the model in an IoT device will depend upon the application requirements such as speed, flexibility, power constraints, cost, etc. Layer 1 is usually implemented in hardware, and Layer 2 could be a combination of hardware, firmware, or software. Layers 3 and above are usually implemented in firmware or software. Note: Firmware is software that is embedded with the hardware vs. software that interacts with the user.

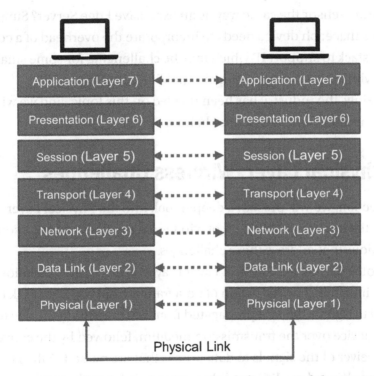

Figure 2-5. *OSI model standardizes the definition of the protocol stack used to connect devices. In the model, functional connections are between the corresponding layers. Each layer interacts with the adjacent layers on the device*

Why Is It Called the Internet of Things?

In Chapter 1, we reviewed the definition of IoT, and the word "Internet" is prominent in the definition. The word "Internet" implies that Internet Protocol is used. Using **Internet Protocol** (IP) to address each of the trillions of Things enables the ecosystem to scale in the number of uniquely addressable devices that can be accessed by the Cloud.

However, does it really make sense to treat a small, battery-powered temperature sensor the same way as an expensive Edge Server? Support of IP implies that each device needs to incorporate the overhead of a complex software stack to support IP which may be challenging for some small devices with limited computational capabilities and battery life.

Certainly, the industry has been divided on this topic, and we will address this question later in this chapter.

The Physical Layer: Wireless Challenges

In this section, we will present a deeper look into the Physical Layer and focus on the inherent challenges of wireless. We will also address some of the solutions that address these challenges.

As noted earlier, the Physical Layer (Layer 1) of a communication protocol includes the conversion of data frames from the Data Link Layer (Layer 2) to signals that are propagated from the transmitter device to the receiver device over the transmission medium, followed by the conversion in the receiver of the signals to data frames that are passed to the Data Link Layer. The physical medium could be a wire, cable, or fiber in the case of wired communication or through air as in the case of wireless.

The properties of the physical medium create inherent limitations that are mitigated in the design physical layer and the layers above it. For example, as we shall see shortly, the wireless medium includes obstacles, interferers, and noise that make it challenging to design a reliable, robust, and secure communications network.

After discussing some of these wireless challenges, we will present techniques for meeting these challenges and making the wireless PHY robust and reliable.

Frequency Band Considerations

In this section, we will discuss the frequency spectrum that is used for wireless connectivity. The choice of frequency spectrum affects the range of the wireless signal (distance between a transmitter and receiver), the data rate (throughput), and the number of users/devices that can be supported.

As we mentioned earlier in this chapter, wireless signals are broadcast as electromagnetic waves consisting of time-varying electrical and magnetic fields that propagate through free space.

The range of carrier frequencies $f_{carrier}$ that can be used for a specific wireless standard is allocated by international standards bodies such as the **Wireless Radio Congress** (WRC) and the **International Telecommunications Union** (ITU).

The standards bodies determine the constraints such as

- The frequencies that are allocated to a particular *frequency band*

- The division of the frequency band into smaller segments called *channels*

- The frequencies that are allocated to each channel

- The allowable signal power within each channel

- The allowable amount of signal power that is allowed to spill outside of the channel that is being used into neighboring channels (called Adjacent Channel Interference)

- The regulatory process for equipment makers and service providers to have products and services approved to use the frequency band

These constraints are set to prevent a device from interfering with other radio devices in that band or in adjacent bands. There could also be safety constraints as well; for example, transmission power is constrained for devices that are used in close proximity of a person's body such as handheld smartphones. Another example is prevention of interference with radar systems that are used by aircraft which has important safety implications.

The usage of the spectrum is regulated within each country by a local government agency. For example, in the United States the Federal Communications Commission (FCC) polices the RF spectrum and certifies all radio devices. In Europe, "Conformité Européenne" (French for "European Conformity") approval indicates that the product meets EU for radio devices.[16]

In order for the product to be certified for a given country, the product must be tested and approved by a regulatory agency that it meets these requirements.

The key frequency bands that are used for IoT applications are shown in Table 2-1 and Table 2-2.

For most standards, there has been an effort to *harmonize* the spectrum worldwide so that it can be used in most countries so that devices can be used worldwide with little or no modification of the radio.

---

[16] https://en.wikipedia.org/wiki/CE_marking

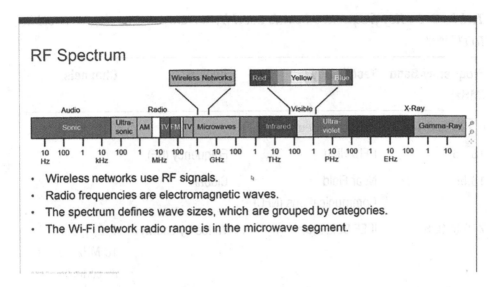

Figure 2-6. *Depiction of RF bands that are used for IoT devices (900, 2.4, 5GHz, UWB, GPS bands, cellular, 60GHz) (from Cisco)*

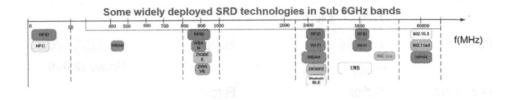

Source: ITU Workshop on Spectrum Management for Internet of Things Deployment, 22 November 2016, Geneva

Figure 2-7. *Depiction of key IoT RF bands*

Table 2-1. *Key frequency bands used by wireless technologies used in IoT*[17,18,19]

Frequency Band (MHz)	Technology	Region	Channels
0.125 to 0.134	RFID Low Frequency (LF)		
13.56	RFID High	Frequency (HF)	
13.56	Near Field Communications (NFC)	Global	
775 to 928	IEEE 802.11ah	Varies by county	1, 2, 4, 8, 16 MHz (varies by country)
433	RFID Ultra High Frequency (UHF)		
860 to 960	RFID Ultra High Frequency (UHF)		
867 to 869	LoraWAN	Europe	Up: 125/250kHz Down: 125kHz
868 to 869	SigFox	Europe	
868–868.6	ZigBee	Europe	

(continued)

---

[17] www.electronics-notes.com/articles/connectivity/ieee-802-15-4-wireless/basics-tutorial-primer.php

[18] https://en.wikipedia.org/wiki/List_of_WLAN_channels

[19] www.testandmeasurementtips.com/what-you-should-know-about-wi-fi-6-and-the-6-ghz-band/

Table 2-1. (*continued*)

Frequency Band (MHz)	Technology	Region	Channels
868.40, 868.42, 869.85	Z-Wave	Europe	
902 to 928	LoraWAN	North America	Up: 125/500kHz Down: 500kHz
902 to 928	SigFox	North America	
902–928	ZigBee	USA and Australia	
908.40, 908.42, 916	Z-Wave	USA and North America	
1227.6	GPS L2	Global	
1575.42	GPS L1	Global	
2400 to 2483.5	Bluetooth	Global	1MHz
2401–2495	Thread	Global	
2401–2495	Wi-Fi IEEE 802.11 b/g/n/ax	Global with differences between North America, Japan, and Indonesia and most of world	20MHz
2401–2495	ZigBee	Global	2MHz
5030 to 5990	Wi-Fi IEEE 802.11a/h/j/n/ac/ax	Differences between countries	10, 20, 40, 80, and 160MHz)

(*continued*)

Table 2-1. (*continued*)

Frequency Band (MHz)	Technology	Region	Channels
5925 to 7125	Wi-Fi IEEE 802.11ax (Wi-Fi 6E)	USA only (April 23, 2020)	10, 20, 40, 80, and 160MHz)
5925 to 6425	Wi-Fi IEEE 802.11ax	European Commission 2021	10, 20, 40, 80, and 160MHz)
57240–70200	IEEE 802.11ad/ay		2160MHz

Table 2-2. *Key LTE frequency bands.*[20] *These bands are applicable to Low Power WAN systems such as NB-IoT and LTE-M that will be described later*

Frequency Band (MHz)	Name	Cellular Band	Channels
2100	IMT	1	5, 10, 15, 20
1900	PCS[A 4]	2	1.4, 3, 5, 10, 15, 20
1800	DCS	3	1.4, 3, 5, 10, 15, 20
1700	AWS-1[A 4]	4	1.4, 3, 5, 10, 15, 20
850	Cellular	5	1.4, 3, 5, 10
2600	IMT-E	7	5, 10, 15, 20
900	Extended GSM	8	1.4, 3, 5, 10
1500	Lower PDC	11	5, 10

(*continued*)

---

[20] https://en.wikipedia.org/wiki/LTE_frequency_bands#cite_note-UL-3

Table 2-2. (*continued*)

Frequency Band (MHz)	Name	Cellular Band	Channels
700	Lower SMH[A 5]	12	1.4, 3, 5, 10
700	Upper SMH[A 6]	13	5, 10
700	Upper SMH[A 7]	14	5, 10
700	Lower SMH[A 8]	17	5, 10
850	Lower 800 (Japan)	18	5, 10, 15
850	Upper 800 (Japan)	19	5, 10, 15
800	Digital Dividend (EU)	20	5, 10, 15, 20
1500	Upper PDC	21	5, 10, 15
1600	Upper L-Band (US)	24	5, 10
1900	Extended PCS[A 9]	25	1.4, 3, 5, 10, 15, 20
850	Extended Cellular	26	1.4, 3, 5, 10, 15
700	APT	28	3, 5, 10, 15, 20
700	Lower SMH[A 10]	29	3, 5, 10
2300	WCS[A 11]	30	5, 10
450	NMT	31	1.4, 3, 5
1500	L-Band (EU)	32	5, 10, 15, 20
2000	IMT	34	5, 10, 15
1900	PCS[A 12]	37	5, 10, 15, 20
2600	IMT-E[A 12]	38	5, 10, 15, 20
1900	DCS–IMT Gap	39	5, 10, 15, 20

(*continued*)

Table 2-2. (*continued*)

Frequency Band (MHz)	Name	Cellular Band	Channels
2300	S-Band	40	5, 10, 15, 20
2500	BRS	41	5, 10, 15, 20
3500	CBRS (EU, Japan)	42	5, 10, 15, 20
3700	C-Band	43	5, 10, 15, 20
700	APT	44	3, 5, 10, 15, 20
5200	U-NII[A 13]	46	10, 20
5900	U-NII-4[A 14]	47	10, 20
3500	CBRS (US)	48	5, 10, 15, 20
3500	C-Band	49	10, 20
1500	L-Band (EU)	50	3, 5, 10, 15, 20
1500	L-Band Extension (EU)	51	3, 5
3300	C-Band	52	5, 10, 15, 20
2400	S-Band	53	1.4, 3, 5, 10
2100	Extended IMT	65	5, 10, 15, 20
1700	Extended AWS (AWS-1–3) [A 15]	66	1.4, 3, 5, 10, 15, 20
700	EU 700	67	5, 10, 15, 20
700	ME 700	68	5, 10, 15
2600	IMT-E[A 12]	69	5
1700	Supplementary AWS (AWS-2–4)[3]	70	5, 10, 15

(*continued*)

Table 2-2. (*continued*)

Frequency Band (MHz)	Name	Cellular Band	Channels
600	Digital Dividend (US)	71	5, 10, 15, 20
450	PMR (EU)	72	1.4, 3, 5
450	PMR (APT)	73	1.4, 3, 5
1500	Lower L-Band (US)	74	1.4, 3, 5, 10, 15, 20
1500	L-Band (EU)	75	5, 10, 15, 20
1500	L-Band Extension (EU)	76	5
700	Extended Lower SMH[A 5]	85	5, 10
410	PMR (APT)	87	1.4, 3, 5
410	PMR (EU)	88	1.4, 3, 5

2.4GHz ISM Band

Of special interest for IoT is the frequency band that is commonly used for IoT applications: the Instrumentation, Scientific and Medical (ISM) band at 2.4 GHz. In most countries this band is kept as unlicensed spectrum meaning that devices can operate without being subject to the arduous process of being granted a license in this band. As a result, the ISM band is used for Wi-Fi, Bluetooth, and the IEEE 802.15.4 radios such as ZigBee, Thread, etc. However, note that devices in this band may be subject to interference from other devices that use this band.

Nevertheless, each device must be certified by the local government wireless agency such as the FCC in the USA or CE in Europe before it can receive product approval in that country and legally operate. The certification process impacts the schedule and cost of developing an IoT product and is discussed later in this book.

Just Enough Information Theory

Information Theory is a specialty in electrical engineering that defines the amount of data required to represent a physical analog value (encoding) and the amount of data that can be transferred reliably over a communications medium. There are numerous references on Information Theory.[21] Please see our sidebar on Claude Shannon.

One of the key questions that Information Theory addresses is the representation of physical quantities: the number of bits that are required and how often a sensor signal output must be sampled in order to accurately represent a physical behavior.

Another important contribution of Information Theory is the maximum throughput (data rate) that information can be sent **reliably** over a given *communications channel*. The communications channel is a model of the physical environment that the transmitted signal propagates through including the type of noise, interference, obstacles, and other impairments. This maximum data rate is called *channel capacity* and will be discussed later in this chapter.

Sending data reliably over the channel is the key point of Information Theory: at channel capacity the Bit Error Rate (BER) can go to 0 and the data can be sent without errors! However, Information Theory does not prescribe how the arbitrarily small BER can be achieved. The methods and techniques for transmitting data reliably is the role of **Communications Theory**.

---

[21] Cover, T. M. & Thomas, J. A. (2006), Elements of Information Theory 2nd Edition (Wiley Series in Telecommunications and Signal Processing) , Wiley-Interscience.

Just Enough Communications Theory

The information theorist will indicate the conditions that are required to send data without error over the IoT wireless (or wired) link. However, her friend, the wireless (or wired) solution architect, has the practical challenge of designing, selecting, and deploying a wireless technology that will meet the requirements for the target use case.

The physical layer is optimized to account for the limitations of the physical medium and to meet the system requirements including data rate, latency, reliability, range, etc. In order to understand the design of the radio at high level, we will first study the basics of the physical layer which are incorporated into *Communications Theory*.

Communications Theory defines how data can be processed and reliably sent over a communications medium. Key questions that Communications Theory addresses include how to design a communications system that works robustly in the presence of noise, obstructions, interference, power limitations, bandwidth limitations, power limitations, multiple competing users, and other constraints. For additional details on communications theory, please consult these references.[22]

Signal-to-Noise Ratio (SNR)

The ratio of Signal Power to Noise Power or Signal-to-Noise ratio (SNR) as measured at the destination receiver is the single most important indicator of performance of the communications system. It is intuitive that the higher the noise power is with respect to the signal power, the less likely it is that a radio signal will be received correctly. This result is formalized in the channel capacity equation from Information Theory.

---

[22] Proakis, *Digital Communications*, 5th Edition, McGraw Hill, 2007.

To improve the overall performance of the wireless communications system, we should design the radio to

1. *Increase* the numerator (received signal power)

2. *Reduce* the denominator (received noise power)

Later in this section we will discuss wireless impairments that (1) reduce the signal power and (2) increase noise and interference. Once we understand these impairments, we can devise strategies on how to mitigate them.

Bit Error Rate and Packet Error Rate

For digital communications, the design goal is to achieve reliable communications within the constraints of transmission power, target throughput, channel characteristics, noise level, and interference levels as well as meeting implementation constraints such as battery power limitations and device size. The overall metrics of wireless performance are the measured **Bit Error Rate** (BER) and **Packet Error Rate** (PER).

The Bit Error Rate is the ratio of the number of received information bit errors to the number of received information bits.

The Packet Error Rate is the ratio of the number of received information packets that are in error to the number of received packets. Note that a Packet is in error if at least one bit in the packet is incorrect.

Let us specify that the packet consists of N_P bits. We can denote a packet as bits $b_0 \, b_1 \, b_2 \, ... b_{NP-1}$.

We can relate the packet error rate and bit error rate mathematically: each packet contains N_P bits and if any of the N_P bits from that packet are received in error, then the entire packet is received in error, so the probability of the packet being received in error is

$P_p = 1 - $ (*probability of all of the bits in the packet being correct*)

=1-((probability of bit b_0 being correct) × (probability of bit b_1 being correct) × (probability of bit b_2 being correct) × ... × (probability of bit b_{NP-1} being correct)

=1-(1- probability of bit b_0 being **incorrect**) × (1- probability of bit b_1 being **incorrect**) × (1- probability of bit b_2 being **incorrect**) × ...

× (1- probability of bit b_{NP-1} being **incorrect**)

$$p_p = 1 - (1 - p_b)^{N_p}$$

where

p_p is the packet error rate

N_p is the length of the packet in bits

p_b is the bit error rate

Example: Suppose our wireless thermostat uses 32-bit packets to send temperature measurements to a hub.

- Question: If the bit error rate $p_b = 1 \times 10^{-5}$, what is the packet error rate p_p?

- Answer: plugging in to the expression above:

  $p_p = 1 - (1 - 1 \times 10^{-5})^{32} = 3.20 \times 10^{-4}$.

- Question: How many 9s of reliability can we expect?

- Answer: 1- p_p =1- 3.20× 10^{-4}=0.99968005 or at least 999 out of 1000 packets will be received correctly or three 9s of reliability.

The BER and PER are functions of the type of digital modulation that is used to apply the information to the carrier waveform along with the SNR and channel conditions.

We can also equate packet error rate to the "number of 9s of reliability" which is 1- Packet Error Rate:

- Two 9s of reliability = 99% reliability = 99/100 packets received correctly.

- Three 9s of reliability 99.9% reliability = 999/1000 packets received correctly.

- Four 9s of reliability 99.99% reliability = 9999/10000 packets received correctly.

- Five 9s of reliability 99.999% reliability = 99999/100000 packets received correctly.

The number of 9s of reliability is an important metric for industrial and manufacturing solutions.

Radio Impairments

Communications Theory was developed for both wired and wireless communications to develop methods for mitigating *impairments* which include the effects of noise, signal attenuation, and signal distortion. Both wired and wireless communications incorporate comparable techniques to mitigate these limitations in order to provide reliable and robust communications.

First, let's consider impairments that reduce the received signal power (the numerator in the SNR). Later we will discuss the impairments that increase the amount of noise (the denominator in the SNR).

What Factors Determine How Far We Can Send Our Wireless Data?

One of the key limitations of wireless communications is range: the distance from an IoT device to an Access Point, Gateway, base station, or hub through which messages can be sent with acceptable reliability, quality, and latency. Most readers are probably aware from their personal experience with their smartphones and computers that the distance from an Access Point or cell tower to their device can affect their experience in downloading and uploading content. *Why can't I receive Wi-Fi on the second floor of my home if the Access Point is on the first floor? Why does my Bluetooth device only work if I am 20 feet away? Why do I only have one bar on my phone and why is my video downloading so slowly?*

This range limitation is the result of numerous factors including the frequency spectrum that is being used, the allowed signal power from their device, the presence of obstructions such as walls and buildings, interference from other devices, the type of antenna, and the noise power.

RF Environment Examples

Consider some of the RF environments of some typical IoT applications:

- Smart home: Interference from many people on their devices, competing access points from adjacent homes, microwave ovens, and baby monitors, and fading and blockage due to walls and furniture

- Smart building: Interference from many people on their devices, many competing access points and base stations and machinery, and fading and blockage due to walls, conference rooms, furniture, and people

- Smart factory: Interference from many people on their devices, many competing access points and base stations and machinery, and fading and blockage due to buildings, machinery, and people

- Smart agriculture: Interference from farm machinery and blockage due to buildings, crops, and animals

- Shopping mall: Interference from many people on
  their devices, many competing access points and
  base stations, and fading and blockage due to walls
  and people

- Smart city: Interference from many people on their
  devices, many competing access points and base
  stations and cars, busses, and trains, and fading and
  blockage due to buildings, vehicles, and people

Attenuation due to Free Space Loss

For wireless systems, radio signals are transmitted with a finite amount of
power due to energy constraints that are determined by regulatory, safety,
and design considerations.

Suppose we wish to transmit data from our IoT sensor to our hub
a distance of r meters. **Free Space Loss** is the amount of signal energy
being dissipated as the transmitted radio signal expands over a sphere of
radius r meters with surface area proportional to $A = 4\pi r^2$ meters squared,
as depicted in Figure 2-8. The received energy at the receiver antenna is
proportional to the wavelength squared. The radio energy dissipated can
be envisioned as an effective energy **loss** that is given by L_{free}

$$L_{free} = \left(\frac{4\pi r}{\lambda}\right)^2 = (4\pi f r/c)^2$$

where

λ is the wavelength of the transmitted signal in meters
f is the frequency of the transmitted signal in Hertz=1/seconds
c is the speed of light = 3×10^8 meters/second
r is the distance between the transmitter and receiver in meters

Note that $\lambda = \dfrac{c}{f} = \dfrac{3 \times 10^8 \text{ meters/second}}{f}$

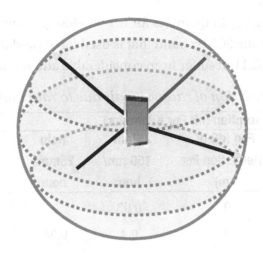

Figure 2-8. *Depiction of radio transmission from a device as energy dissipated over a sphere of radius r*

Note that in this idealized case, Free Space Loss assumes that the transmitting device is sitting in the middle of empty space. In reality, both source and destination are usually on a planar surface (i.e., the ground).

In addition to the dissipation of radio signal energy over distance, the objects in the environment absorb and block the radio signal.

Attenuation due to Absorption by the Atmosphere

Water vapor in the air absorbs and attenuates radio signals in certain frequency bands. Radio engineers have compiled data on the absorption of radio signals by rain and fog by radio frequency for different regions of the world based on typical rainfall.[23] Table 2-3 summarizes the attenuation of radio signals due to rainfall, fog, and atmospheric gases (water vapor

---

[23] Roger L. Freeman, Telecommunication Transmission Handbook, Wiley, 1975.

and oxygen) at the key frequencies for IoT wireless systems. For example, it is apparent that the 30GHz band that is used for 5G and the 60GHz band that is used for 802.11ad suffer from considerable attenuation due to rain.

Table 2-3. *Attenuation of radio signals due to rain and fog*[24]

Frequency (MHz)	Absorption (dB Per Kilometer)			
	Fog (dB of Attenuation Per km)	Rain 150mm/ hour	Rain 25mm/ hour	Atmospheric Gas
2400	0	0.03	0	0
5000	0	0.4	0.04	0
30000	0.06	28	5	0.08 (H_2O)
60000	0.2	40	9	15 (O_2)

Attenuation due to Obstacles

Depending upon the frequency band, signals may be partially blocked by objects including buildings, walls, doors, vegetation, and humans. For example, a wall consisting of 2x4 studs and drywall on each side causes 6dB of attenuation.[25]

---

[24] Roger L. Freeman, *Telecommunication Transmission Handbook*, Wiley, 1975.
[25] https://en.wikipedia.org/wiki/Link_budget

IMPACT OF ATTENUATION ON LINK BUDGET

Wireless signals are blocked or attenuated by objects in the radio environment that are between the transmitter and receiver, including buildings, walls, vegetation, people, vehicles, rainfall, etc. The degree of this attenuation depends upon the frequency that is being used.

Some example attenuation values are shown in Table 2-4.[26,27,28,29,30]

[26] Perry Lea, *Internet of Things for Architects*, Packt Publishing, 2018, ISBN: 9781788470599.

[27] https://blog.ibwave.com/a-closer-look-at-attenuation-across-materials-the-2-4ghz-5ghz-bands/

[28] www.ekahau.com/blog/2015/09/07/wi-fi-planning-walls-and-dbs-measuring-obstruction-losses-for-wlan-predictive-modelling/

[29] www.ofcom.org.uk/__data/assets/pdf_file/0016/84022/building_materials_and_propagation.pdf

[30] www.signalbooster.com/blogs/news/how-much-which-building-materials-block-cellular-wifi-signals

Table 2-4. *Radio attenuation of common materials*

Material	Attenuation (dB)	
	2.4GHz (dB)	5GHz (dB)
Heavy concrete	22.792	44.769
Lime brick	4.295	7.799
Dry wall	5.388	10.114
Chip board	0.463	0.838
Clear glass window[31]	0	0
Triple-glazed ultra-low e-glass[32]	35	20
Triple-glazed low-emission window[33]	30	20
Double-glazed energy saving window[34]	0	10
Aluminum[35]	5dB/micron of metal	7dB/micron of metal
Trees[36]	0.4 dB/meter of forest	1 dB/meter of forest
Wood	15dB/meter	32dB/meter

---

[31] Ängskog, et al., "Measurement of Radio Signal Propagation through Window Panes and Energy Saving Windows," *2015 IEEE International Symposium on Proceedings of Electromagnetic Compatibility* (EMC), pp. 74-79.

[32] Ängskog

[33] Ängskog

[34] Ängskog

[35] Rudd et al., *Building Materials and Propagation Final Report Ofcom at* www. ofcom.org.uk/__data/assets/pdf_file/0016/84022/building_materials_ and_propagation.pdf.

[36] *Attenuation in vegetation*, Recommendation ITU-R P.833-9, (09/2016).

ONE PAGER ON RSSI

Received Signal Strength Indicator (RSSI) is a measure of the power of the signal that has been sent from a transmitted device. The developer is familiar with the "number of bars" that is associated with the base station or access point when they connect their smart phone. RSSI indicates the relative signal strength of the AP as measured at the device and can be used by the user to position the device to improve the signal strength.

Note that having a "good" RSSI does not guarantee that the device will achieve maximum throughput. Interferers and multipath can also degrade performance.

How is RSSI measured?

RSSI is measured by computing the signal power over the received data. Typically, the preamble of the data frame is used.

Where is RSSI measured?

Signal strength is measured on the receiving device after the receive antenna but before the power amplifier boosts the signal. The value is reported by the device driver.

What are the units of RSSI?

RSSI is an arbitrary unitless quantity and has a relative value. In this definition, RSSI does not map to an actual received power level in milliwatts or dBm and may be indicated on a scale from 0 to 100 where 100 indicates maximum power. RSSI may also be depicted graphically as the number of bars.

Received channel power indicator (RCPI)

RCPI is a specific definition for 802.11 Wi-Fi. RCPI is measured over the received signal preamble and the received frame. RCPI is defined in IEEE 802.11k-2008.[37]

What are some tools for measuring RSSI?

Some devices incorporate RSSI measurements as an application. Some examples include *WiFi Analyzer* from Microsoft that is available for Microsoft Windows.

Figure 2-9. *Screenshot from "WiFi Analyzer" showing the measured Wi-Fi signal strength*

ONE PAGER ON AWGN

If you open any wireless communication textbook, you will see the term "AWGN" mentioned early and often. What is AWGN and what does it mean?

AWGN stands for Additive White Gaussian Noise and is an idealized but mathematical tractable representation for the noise that is encountered in a wireless communications system. Specifically, the noise is

---

[37] IEEE 802.11k-2008 "IEEE Standard for Information technology-- Local and metropolitan area networks-- Specific requirements-- Part 11: Wireless LAN Medium Access Control (MAC)and Physical Layer (PHY) Specifications Amendment 1: Radio Resource Measurement of Wireless LANs.", https:// standards.ieee.org/ieee/802.11k/3951/.

- Additive: The wireless noise is treated as a separate source that is added to the received wireless signal.

- White: The noise spectrum is evenly distributed or flat across the wireless bandwidth (each noise sample is uncorrelated from any other). The term "White" means that the noise is comprised of all frequencies.

- Gaussian: The noise samples are random and have a Gaussian or normal probability distribution function given by

$$f(x) = \frac{1}{\sigma\sqrt{2\pi}} e^{-\frac{1}{2}\left(\frac{x-\mu}{\sigma}\right)^2}$$

where

f(x) is the probability distribution

x is the Gaussian random variable

σ is mean of the Gaussian random variable

μ is of the Gaussian random variable

For the purposes of this book, the AWGN representation of wireless noise is sufficient. For more details, you can consider a digital communications reference.[38]

Noise

In the previous section, we discussed signal attenuation that affects the numerator of the SNR. We now address noise, which is the denominator of the SNR expression. Noise is random in nature and is characterized by probability. Noise can be attributed to both internal sources such as the radio components and the platform as well as external sources that are located in physical environment between the transmitter and receiver.

---

[38] Proakis, *Digital Communications*, 5th Edition, McGraw Hill, 2007.

Internal Noise Sources

Internal noise sources include the components in the radio receiver such as the antenna and *Low Noise Amplifier* (LNA) that increases the level of the received radio signals. In wireless radio systems, all of the noise sources in the radio are combined and characterized by an effective noise temperature T in degrees Kelvin. This receiver noise includes thermal noise that is physically due to movement of electrons in resistors, shot and flicker noise in transistors, and the noise seen by the antenna.[39]

Ideally, the LNA in the receiver will increase the level of the received signal without distorting the signal. In reality, there is likely to be a measurable amount of Intermodulation Distortion caused by nonlinearities in the receiver processing such as the amplification process.

Another key source of internal noise is the actual IoT computing device or platform. The computing device hardware, whether it is a small sensor or a Point-of-Sale terminal, will have clocks on the circuit board that are required for the CPU and digital logic; these clocks could produce harmonics (at multiples of the clock frequency) that might end up in the wireless spectrum and affect the radio performance. Platform noise can be mitigated by adjusting the clock rates so that any harmonics would be outside of the frequency band that is used by the radio, by shielding the radio components or by physically positioning the radio and antenna away from the digital components.

External Noise Sources

The environment produces radio noise that can impact the performance of the radio. These noise sources include

---

[39] Roger L. Freeman, *Telecommunication Transmission Handbook*, Wiley, 1975.

- Appliances such as microwave ovens

- Other communication devices such as portable phones and baby monitors

- Machinery in factories

- Lighting such as fluorescent lamps

- Space sources such as cosmic background noise

Characterizing Noise

Most noise is random in nature. The key parameters that define a noise signal include

- Probability distribution: We assume that most noise sources are AWGN an associated mean and variance (see sidebar on AWGN).[40] The spectrum of white noise is depicted in Figure 2-10.

- Power that is proportional to the variance of the noise distribution. Noise power in Watts is given by the following expression:

$$N = kTB \text{ Watts} \tag{2}$$

where
k is Boltzmann's constant$=1.38064852 \times 10^{-23}$ m^2 kg s^{-2} K^{-1} or Joules/Kelvin
T is the noise temperature of the wireless radio in Kelvin[41]
B is the receiver bandwidth in Hertz

---

[40] Proakis, *Digital Communications*, 5th Edition, McGraw Hill, 2007.
[41] https://en.wikipedia.org/wiki/Noise_temperature

In order to minimize noise, the bandwidth should be reduced to the minimum possible to accommodate the required throughput, and the receiver noise temperature T should be reduced through careful design of the radio.

In dBm, the noise power is given by

$$N_{dBm} = k_{dBm} + T\ dBK + B\ dBHz\ \text{dBm} \tag{3}$$

where

k is Boltzmann's constant in dBm

T is noise temperature in dB K

B is the bandwidth in dB Hz

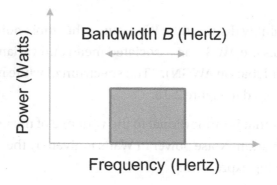

Figure 2-10. *Depiction of the spectrum of white noise with bandwidth B*

ONE PAGER ON DECIBELS (DB)[42]

Many wireless data sheets express KPIs in units of "dB" or "dBm." This section provides a quick introduction to these units.

---

[42] https://en.wikipedia.org/wiki/Decibel

The "bel" unit was created by Bell Telephone Laboratories in 1928 and was named after Alexander Graham Bell who invented the telephone. The bel is the base 10 logarithm of the ratio of two values and is a dimensionless value.

$$(\frac{P_2}{P_1})\ bel= \ log_{10}\left(\frac{P_2}{P_1}\right)$$

The decibel is one-tenth of a bel and is 10 times the base 10 logarithm of the ratio of two values:

$$(\frac{P_2}{P_1})\ decibel= \ 10\times log_{10}\left(\frac{P_2}{P_1}\right)$$

The decibel is abbreviated as "dB."

Why Use dB?

In many link calculations, there is a very large dynamic range of values meaning that the difference between the largest and smallest values is very large. The advantage of using decibels for link calculations is reducing this dynamic range to values that are easier to manage and that multiplications and divisions in linear units become addition and subtraction in dB units.

For example, the Signal-to-Noise ratio $\frac{S}{N}$ when expressed in dB becomes

$$(\frac{S}{N})\ decibel= \ =10\times log_{10}\left(\frac{S}{N}\right)=10\times log_{10}(S)-10\times log_{10}(N)\ =S_{dB}-N_{dB}$$

Some additional usages of dB include the following:

Power in watts is expressed in dB relative to 1 Watt:

$$P_{dBwatt}\ (dBW)= \ 10\times log_{10}\left(\frac{P}{1watt}\right)$$

Note that 0dBW = 1 Watt.

Power in milliwatts is expressed in dB relative to 1 milliwatt:

$$P_{dBmilliwatt} \text{ (dBm)} = 10 \times log_{10}\left(\frac{P}{1miliwatt}\right)$$

Note that 0dBm = 1 mW.

A factor of two increase (or decrease) in power corresponds to an increase or decrease of $10 \times log_{10}(2) = 3dB$.

To convert from dBm to milliwatts $P\,mW = 10^{\frac{P_{dBm}}{10}}$

Example: Wi-Fi modules are typically limited to a maximum output power of 15dBm which corresponds to $10^{\frac{P15dBm}{10}} = 31.6mW$

To convert from dBm to dBW subtract 30 from the dBm value (which is equivalent to dividing by 1000):

P dBW = P dBm – 30

For example, 1mW = 0 dBm = -30dBW.

To convert from dBW to dBm add 30 to the dB value (which is equivalent to multiply by 1000):

P dBm = P dBW + 30

For example, 1W = 0 dBW= 30dBm.

Example: Digital Communications System with Noise

In this section we will describe an example of the impact of noise on digital communications. The classical digital communications block diagram is shown in Figure 2-11. The figure shows a source that generates a data sequence $x(n)$ that is modulated and transmitted and received at the destination with additive white Gaussian noise.

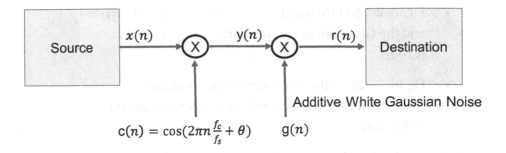

Figure 2-11. *Digital communications block diagram*

Figure 2-12(a) shows a binary data sequence in which we map "0" to "-1" and "1" to "+1." Each "bit" corresponds to 16 samples of simulated data.

- Figure 2-12(b) shows the carrier waveform given by the expression $c(n) = \cos\left(2\pi n \dfrac{f_c}{f_s} + \theta\right)$, n=0, 1, 2, ... and fc/fs=1/8. In other words, the carrier waveform is sampled at a rate of 8 samples per cycle.

- Figure 2-12(c) shows the carrier waveform modulated by the binary data; this modulated waveform is transmitted from the source device to the destination device.

- Figure 2-12(d) shows a Gaussian noise sequence, where the noise power is set to 20dB below the signal power so that the SNR is 20dB.

- Figure 2-12(e) shows the sum of the modulated carrier and the Gaussian noise waveform. This is the signal that is received at destination device.

- Figure 2-12(f) shows the sum of the modulated carrier and the Gaussian noise waveform where the SNR is 10dB.

- Figure 2-12(g) shows the sum of the modulated carrier and the Gaussian noise waveform where the SNR is 5dB.

At the destination device, the demodulator receives the noisy signal and must accurately recover the data sequence that was sent by the source. It is apparent that this task becomes more challenging as the SNR decreases. If the SNR becomes low enough, it is impossible to recover the original source data.

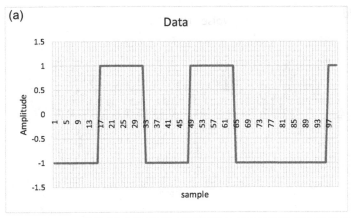

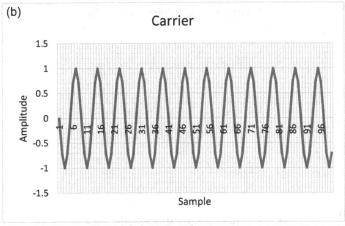

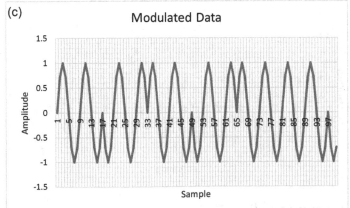

Figure 2-12. *Example illustrating digital communication and the effects of noise*

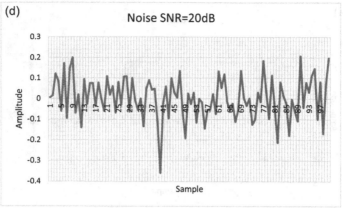

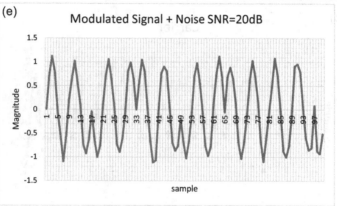

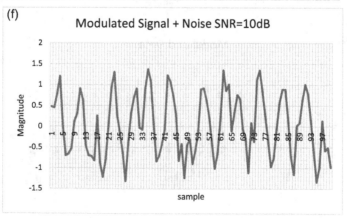

Figure 2-12. (*continued*)

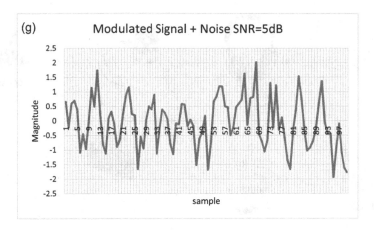

Figure 2-12. (*continued*)

Interference

Interference is a radio signal that either intentionally or unintentionally impairs the reception of the target transmitted signal at the receiver.

Like Signal-to-Noise ratio, we can incorporate the effects of interference into the Signal to Interference + Noise Ratio (SINR), where the denominator is the sum of both noise and interference that is seen at the receiver. The interference noise power is the sum of the Co-channel Interference (CCI) and Adjacent Channel Interference (ACI) noise powers.

SINR can also be inserted into the channel capacity expression that is discussed in the next section to determine the overall theoretical throughput of the system.

Figure 2-13. *Examples of interference affecting the transmission from the Point-of-Sale terminal to the Access Point*

Co-Channel Interference

Co-channel Interference (CCI) refers to noise that is within the desired signal's band that is caused by competing systems or devices that share the same band. Examples of CCI include Bluetooth signals interfering with Wi-Fi channels in the ISM band. Wireless protocols that share the ISM band should ideally check for signals already using a particular channel before sending data over that channel.

Co-channel Interference could also be caused by users from a different wireless system that shares the same frequency band such as the neighbor's Wi-Fi system.

Adjacent Channel Interference (ACI)

Ideally, all devices should ensure that their transmitted energy stays within their allocated channels. All devices should filter their transmitted energy so that it stays within its assigned channel. However, due to imperfect filtering, it is possible that there is spillover into neighboring channels. Adjacent Channel Interference (ACI) refers to noise from other devices that are transmitting in bands that are next to the desired signal's band but due to filter limitations some energy spills over.

Jamming

Jamming refers to radio transmissions from other devices in the same band as the IoT signal. The jamming can be classified as follows:

- Unintentional jamming: This category includes devices that exceed the allowed transmit power levels for the country where the device is located due to the combination of incorrect antenna and power settings of the radio. The local regulatory agency that is responsible for policing radio transmissions will enforce these types of issues.

- Intentional jamming: This category includes entities trying to illegally disrupt the network by generating energy in the IoT frequency band. This issue is mitigated by the local regulatory agency and service providers.

Fading and Multipath

In a real use case, objects in the environment impact the radio signal by blocking and reflecting the transmitted signal so that the received signal is distorted.

- Fading: Attenuation of the transmitted signal due to obstructions or cancellation or negative reinforcement of the signal (a reflected version that is inverted with respect to the original signal that when added to the original signal cancels it out).

- Multipath: Reflections of the transmitted signal that are delayed or otherwise modified versions of the target signal that arrive at the receiver and prevent optimal reception of the desired signal. These reflections are caused by buildings, vehicles, geological features, or vegetation. If either the transmitter or receiver are moving (such as in a car, truck, or train), the multipath will be time-varying.

Multipath results in a "smearing" of the received signal due to receiving all of the signal reflections with various delays, phase shifts, and amplitudes, making it difficult to determine if a "0" or "1" was sent.

Multipath is a critical issue for wireless communications, and a substantial effort has been made in communications theory to mitigate it. For example, *adaptive equalizers* were developed to detect and mitigate the effects of multipath. To assist in the effort of developing algorithms for mitigating multipath, the radio standards bodies maintain multipath models that represent typical scenarios. These models are used by communications engineers to test their mitigation algorithms.

Figure 2-14 illustrates some of the sources of multipath in a city environment, including reflections from buildings, trees, and vehicles.

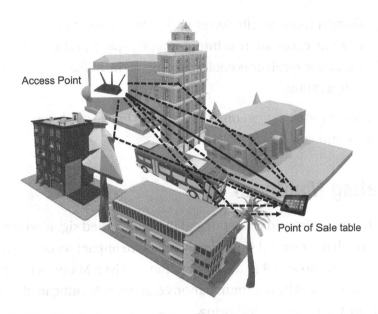

Access Point

Point of Sale table

Figure 2-14. *Depiction of multipath*

Techniques for Improving the Radio

In the previous section, we discussed some of the challenging aspects of wireless communications. In this section, we will focus on the techniques that have been developed for solving these issues.

Mitigating Noise

Earlier, we described how maximizing the Signal-to-Noise ratio will improve the overall capacity. The Signal-to-Noise ratio can be increased by

- Using *forward error correcting* codes that can correct bit errors and reduce the error rate for a given SNR.

- Designing and selecting a modulation scheme that is more immune to noise.

- Using a receiver with lower noise temperature; in extreme cases, such as interplanetary space probes, the entire receiver is cooled to reduce the noise temperature.

All these options require complex tradeoffs between system performance and cost.

Mitigating Multipath

Multipath creates delayed reflections of the transmitted signal which when combined with the original signal leads to severe impact on correctly recovering the radio signal at the destination receiver. Many techniques have been developed by communications engineers to mitigate the impact of multipath, including the following:[43]

- Adaptive equalizers: An equalizer is a filter that takes the distorted received signal that consists of the combination of the transmitted signal and delayed and attenuated replicas and effectively cancels out the replicas to recover the original signal. The filter is adaptive as it constant adjusts itself to minimize the error between the target signal and the processed signal.

- OFDM and Cyclic Prefix: Orthogonal Frequency Division Multiplexing (OFDM) is the modulation that is used in Wi-Fi and LTE and is based on forming a modulation symbol in the frequency domain and then using an *inverse Fast Fourier Transform* (IFFT) to generate the symbol in the time domain (see sidebar).

---

[43] Proakis, *Digital Communications*, 5th Edition, McGraw Hill, 2007.

Before sending the signal, a portion of the end of the symbol is pre-pended to the beginning of the symbol and is called the *Cyclic Prefix*. Multipath smears the signal from a preceding symbol into the next symbol and distorts the Cyclic Prefix which is simply removed at the receiver.

- Coded modulations: Coding is the process of adding redundant bits to the data to assist in detecting and correcting bit errors. Coding can be implemented purely on the bit stream. It can also be combined with the modulation technique (see sidebar) and the resulting coded modulation provides mitigation to multipath.

- Antenna diversity: Multipath is the combination of the reflected and transmitted signals at the antenna. The multipath will be different as seen by a second antenna a short distance away from the first antenna. By combining the signals from two or more suitably spaced antennas which is called *antenna diversity*, it is possible to cancel out the multipath.

COMPONENTS OF A DIGITAL RADIO

In the previous sections, we discussed some of the key considerations in selecting a radio technology, including how the throughput, range, number of devices, and security are important attributes. Next, we will describe the components of the radio and how these design choices affect the radio attributes.

In the case of wireless, the radio is the component that implements Layers 1 and 2 of the protocol stack.

Figure 2-15. *The radio includes the MAC and PHY, where the PHY includes the Digital Baseband and the Analog Front End (AFE)*

Key components of the physical layer are shown in Figure 2-16 and include

A digital radio includes both a Receiver (denoted as "RX") and a Transmitter (denoted as "TX"), and the combined device is called a transceiver.

The transmitter receives bits from Layer 2, prepares the data, and transmits a waveform. The transmitter functions include

- Packetizer: Receives data from Layer 2 and formats into packets.

- Scrambler: Randomizes the input data bits so the bit stream has a flat spectrum (add explanation on why this is necessary).

- Forward error correction (FEC) encoder: Adds bits that are used to detect and correct bit errors.

- Preamble: A pattern of bits called the preamble is prepended before the encoded data. This pattern of data is known by the receiver and is used by the receiver to quickly acquire and synchronize to the transmitted data.

- Symbol mapper: Maps the encoded bits to modulated symbols, either in the time domain (single carrier) or frequency domain (OFDM).

- Digital-to-analog converter: Converts the digital symbol to an analog value.

- Modulator: Upconverts the analog waveform to the target carrier frequency in the frequency band that is being used.

- Amplifier: Increases the amplitude of the waveform.

- Antenna: Radiates the waveform into free space.

The receiver processes the waveform that was sent by the transmitter, mitigate the effects of channel noise and distortions caused by fading and multipath, and provides the resulting data bits to Layer 2.

The receiver functions include

- Antenna

- Low noise amplifier

- Analog-to-digital converter

- Equalizer: Mitigates the effect of multipath and fading

- Demodulator

- Forward error correction (FEC) decoder

- Descrambler

- Depacketizer

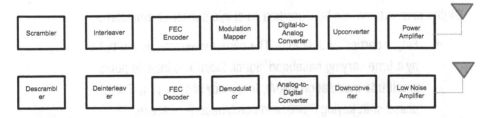

Figure 2-16. *Components of the physical layer*

ONE PAGER ON DIGITAL MODULATIONS

All of the radio techniques that are described in this book transmit digital data via RF waveforms. The process of converting a bit stream to a radio waveform is called **digital modulation**.

The data to be transmitted is called a *baseband waveform*. This is the binary sequence that is in the data frame that is received from Layer 2. The baseband waveform is characterized by the *symbol rate*.

Digital modulation is modifying the characteristics of the RF carrier with the baseband waveform: the amplitude, phase, or frequency of the carrier is modified by the baseband.

Digital modulations are designed to mitigate radio impairments, which may include the following:

- Channel noise.

- Interference.

- Multipath caused by the radio signal being reflected off obstacles and arriving at the receiver with a delay; if the transmitter and receiver are moving or if obstacles between the transmitter and receiver are moving (such as cars or people), the amplitude, phase, and delay of the multipath may be time varying.

Digital modulations can be classified as single carrier or multicarrier:

- Single carrier modulations: The carrier waveform is multiplied by a time varying baseband signal. Examples include pulse amplitude modulation (PAM), frequency shift keying (FSK), phase shift keying (PSK), and combinations of these.

- Multiple carrier modulations: The data bits are used to modulate subcarriers with frequency offsets; the resulting waveform modulates the carrier. Examples include Orthogonal Frequency Division Multiplexing (OFDM).

Selection of which digital modulation to use depends on many factors:

- The required data rate

- The allocated spectrum bandwidth

- The severity of the multipath

- The complexity, power consumption, and cost of the transmitter and receiver

Digital modulations can be characterized by their bandwidth efficiency and their energy efficiency. Modulations that are used in the wireless standards that we will discuss in this book are listed as follows:

- Wi-Fi: OFDM (Orthogonal Frequency Division Modulation), OFDMA (Orthogonal Frequency Division Multiple Access)

- Bluetooth: Gaussian Minimum Shift Keying (GMSK) and variations

- 802.15.4 (i.e., ZigBee): Gaussian Minimum Shift Keying (GMSK) and variations

- LTE: OFDMA, SC-FDMA

- LoRA: Chirp Z spread spectrum

ONE PAGER ON MIMO

Multiple Input Multiple Output (MIMO) techniques use multiple transmit and multiple receive antennas to increase the overall wireless throughput and increase robustness. These techniques were developed over the last few years and are now widely used in Wi-Fi and cellular systems.[44]

The fundamental concept is that both the transmitter and the receiver have multiple antennas. At the transmitter, the data stream is separated into multiple streams. Each stream is encoded (*MIMO precoding*) in a unique manner and sent over an antenna.

The coding is different for each transmit antenna and destination receiver. The coding is determined from Channel State Information (CSI) which are measurements of the communications channel between each transmit and receive antenna of each device in the network.

At the receiver, all of the streams are processed by each receive antenna, and the corresponding decoder is applied to the antenna streams which are then combined to produce the original data stream.

For Wi-Fi, the client device may have 2 receive and 2 transmit antennas and is called "2x2"; the Access Point may have 4 receive and 4 transmit antennas and is called "4x4."

For Wi-Fi, two MIMO implementations are as follows:

- Downlink Multi User MIMO (DL MU-MIMO): The Access Point sends uniquely coded data to each Station client device. In Wi-Fi, DL MU-MIMO is part of the Wi-Fi 5 standard.

---

[44] https://en.wikipedia.org/wiki/MIMO

- Uplink Multi User MIMO (UL MU-MIMO): Each client device in the network sends uniquely coded data to the Access Point. In Wi-Fi, UL MU-MIMO is part of the Wi-Fi 6 standard.

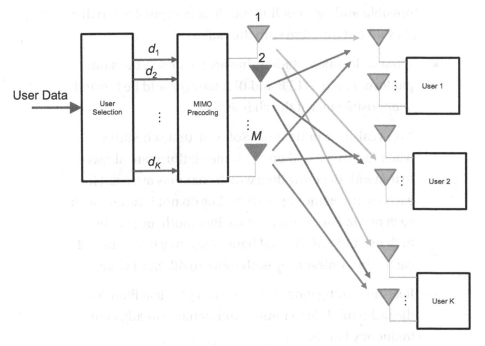

Figure 2-17. *Illustration of MIMO techniques*

Interference Mitigation

As we discussed earlier, interference is a crucial issue for overall performance of a wireless link. Some techniques for mitigating this interference include

- Radio design: The physical module should be shielded to prevent RF signals from the radio from interfering with other radios in the chassis or to stop other radios from interfering with it.

- Platform interference: Clock circuitry on the IoT platform may create spurs and harmonics that are seen as interference in the wireless bands. These harmonics can be mitigated by adjusting the clock frequency if possible and by shielding the clock components so that they do not interfere with the radio.

- Physical location: Radios that are located in the same platform (such as LTE and Bluetooth) could be located at opposite ends of the chassis.

- Non-real-time mitigation: Software that schedules when radios located on the same platform are allowed to transmit or controlling which channels are used for each radio technology so that they do not interfere with each other. For example, since Bluetooth and Wi-Fi both use the 2.4GHz ISM band, they may interfere with each other unless they each move to different channels.

- Real-time mitigation: Insertion of a physical filter into the radio module to remove interference in adjacent frequency bands.

Link Budget

The communications engineer designs a wireless system to reliably transport information from the transmitter to the receiver. One fundamental task is determining the Link Budget, which is the calculation of the Signal-to-Noise ratio of a communications system and incorporates all of the key impairments in one equation.

Consider the transmission of a signal from sensor A to Gateway B. As seen in the capacity equation, throughput or data rate *increases* as the Signal-to-Noise ratio at the receiver *increases*. Thus, one of the goals of the design of the radio system is to increase the Signal-to-Noise ratio S/N given the constraints of limited transmitter power, cost, etc.

To understand how we maximize the received Signal-to-Noise ratio, we consider the received signal power at Gateway B that is given by

$$P_{RX} = P_{TX} \times G_{TX} \times G_{RX} / L_{free} \tag{4}$$

where

P_{RX} is the received power at the output of the receive antenna

P_{TX} is the power transmitted

G_{TX} is the gain of the transmitter antenna

G_{RX} is the gain of the receive antenna

L_{free} is the free space loss which is determined by the distance D between the transmitter and receiver=$(4\pi fd/c)^2$

In decibel form, the link equation is given by

$$P_{RX}dB = P_{TX}dB + G_{TX}dB - L_{TX\,cable}dB + G_{RX}\ dB - L_{free}dB - L_{RX\,cable}dB \tag{5}$$

where

$P_{RX}dB$ is the received power in dB Watts (dBW) at the output of the receive antenna and is given by $10\times log_{10}(P_{RX})$

$P_{TX}dB$ is the power transmitted in dB Watts (dBW)

$G_{TX}dB$ is the gain of the transmitter antenna in dB

$L_{TX\,cable}dB$ includes losses in the cabling in the transmitter

$G_{RX}dB$ is the gain of the receive antenna in dB

$L_{RX\,cable}dB$ includes losses in the cabling in the receiver

$L_{free}dB$ is the free space loss in

dB= $10 \times log_{10}(4\pi fd/c)^2 = 20 \times log_{10}(d) + 20 \times log_{10}(f) + 20 \times log_{10}(4\pi/c)$

where c=3×10⁸m/s and f=2.45GHz for Bluetooth

The noise seen at the Gateway is given by $N=kTB$.

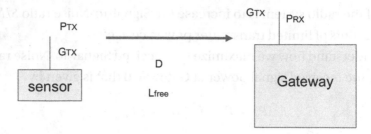

Figure 2-18. *Diagram showing the elements of the link equation*

In order for the Gateway to receive the signal from the sensor, the Signal-to-Noise ratio must be high enough so that the Gateway can recover the data that was sent by the sensor.

The value of SNR that is required is defined via the channel capacity.

Based upon the link equation, we can see that the receive power P_{RX} can be increased if

- The transmitter power P_{TX} is increased

- The transmit antenna gain G_{TX} is increased

- The receive antenna gain G_{RX} is increased

- The distance D between the transmitter and receiver is decreased so that free space loss L_{free} is decreased

To minimize noise power, the noise temperature and bandwidth should be reduced.

ONE PAGER ON LINK MARGIN

Often, the terms Link Budget and Link Margin are used interchangeably by wireless designers. We would like to differentiate these two terms.

Link Budget incorporates all the contributions and impairments on a radio link to determine if there is enough signal to power to receive the transmitted data reliably.

Key elements include

- Transmitted signal power in dBm (dB milliwatts)

- Transmitter antenna gain which is greater than 1 if the antenna is directional

- Receiver antenna gain which is greater than 1 if the antenna is directional

- Distance between the transmitter and receiver; signal strength decreases as distance squared in free space

- The frequency band that is used

- Boltzmann's constant k

- Receiver sensitivity: The minimum signal power in dBm at the receiver that is required to produce the target packet error rate

All of these components are included in the link equation in decibel form:

$$L_{free}dB = 20 \times log_{10}(d) + 20 \times log_{10}(f) + 20 \times log_{10}(4\pi/c)$$
$$= 20 \times log_{10}(d) + 20 \times log_{10}(f) + 147.55$$

Receiver sensitivity is an important performance parameter that appears on receiver data sheets. The receiver sensitivity is the received signal power level in dBm to produce a specified packet error rate.

Link margin is the difference between the received signal power and the receiver sensitivity in dB. If the link margin is greater than 0, their transmitted data can be received with the target packet error rate.

Note that the link margin can be reduced due to several factors:

- Attenuation of the radio signal due to obstacles such as walls, machinery, vegetation, people, etc.

- Misalignment of the transmit and receive antennas

As part of the deployment process, the site should be surveyed to identify potential impairments that could reduce the link margin and cause the system to fail.

Example: Bluetooth Link Calculation

It is helpful to go through an example of the link calculation for a real Bluetooth radio. Consider the *Texas Instruments CC2650MODA* Bluetooth Low Energy module.[45] From the data sheet for this module, we can find the following:

- The radio has an output transmit power of 5dBm.

- The sensitivity for BLE at 2Mbps is -97dBm to achieve a bit error rate of 1×10^{-3}.

- The gain of the integrated antenna is 1.26dBi.

BLE Transmission over an Open Field with Range of 50 Meters

Can we use this radio to transmit audio packets from a BLE sensor across an open field without obstructions from 50 meters? Let us solve for the link budget. Please refer to Table 2-5.

---

[45]www.ti.com/product/CC2650MODA

Table 2-5. *Link margin calculation for Bluetooth*

Component	Value	Units
$P_{TX}dB$	-25	dBW
$G_{TX}dB$	1.26	dBi
$L_{TX\ cable}dB$	0	dB
$G_{RX}dB$	1.26	dBi
$L_{RX\ cable}dB$	0	dB
$L_{free}dB$	74.03	dB

$L_{free}dB = 20 \times log_{10}(d) + 20 \times log_{10}(f) + 20 \times log_{10}(4\pi/c)$

$= 20 \times log_{10}(d) + 20 \times log_{10}(f) + 147.55$

$= 74.03dB$ for d=50m and $f=2.4 \times 10^9$

The received power is $P_{RX}dB = -96.5dBW = -66.5dBm$.

To achieve the BER of 1×10^{-3} requires a received signal power of -97dBm. Thus, on an open field there is approximately 30dB of link margin, and the signal should be received correctly.

Open Field with Distance of 1000 Meters Between TX and RX

Will the system work if there is a distance of 1000m between the TX and RX? Replacing $D=1000$ meters in the previous equation, the received power is now $P_{RX}dB = -92.5dBm$, and the link margin is 4.47dB as the receiver needs a received signal power of -97dBm to achieve a bit error rate of 1×10^{-3}. The system will work, but any obstruction between the TX and RX would likely cause enough attenuation to degrade the received signal strength.

How About Using LoRA?

Later we will discuss the LoRA wireless technology, which provides a means of transmitting data over 10km at data rates of 10.9kbits/s using the LoRA modulation. What is the link margin if we use LoRA instead of Bluetooth for this use case?

We will use the published values in the data sheet for the *MicroChip RN2843* LoRA module.[46] Please refer to Table 2-6.

Table 2-6. *Link margin calculation for LoRA*

Component	Value	Units
f	868	MHz
D	15 000	m
$P_{TX}dB$	14	dBm
$G_{TX}dB$	0	dBi
$L_{TX\,cable}dB$	0	dB
$G_{RX}dB$	0	dBi
$L_{RX\,cable}dB$	0	dB
$L_{free}dB$	114.7	dB
Receiver sensitivity to achieve PER=1e-3	-146	dBm

The calculated link margin is

$$P_{RX}dB = P_{TX}dB + G_{TX}dB - L_{TX\,cable}dB + G_{RX}\,dB - L_{free}dB - L_{RX\,cable}dB$$

---

[46] http://ww1.microchip.com/downloads/en/DeviceDoc/RN2483-Low-Power-Long-Range-LoRa-Technology-Transceiver-Module-Data-Sheet-DS50002346D.pdf

Plugging in values, the link margin is 57.3dB. This assumes no obstacles between the LoRA sensor and the gateway.

How does LoRA achieve this range? When compared to the Bluetooth receiver with a Rx sensitivity of -97dBm, the LoRA receiver has a sensitivity of -146dBm which is a difference of 50dB or 5 orders of magnitude. In terms of free space loss, this corresponds to 50dB improvement in free space loss.

Why Not Increase the Transmit Power?

You may ask yourself: why not just maximize your transmit power so as to maximize the receive power? This is problematic for several reasons:

- Regulatory agencies set a limit on the maximum transmitter power so that devices do not interfere with other devices who are part of the same system/ network.

- The device could generate out of band noise that affects other networks and systems that either share the same bands or are in adjacent bands.

- There are potential safety issues with the amount of microwave radiation that could affect people near the device.

Increasing the transmitter power beyond the manufacturer's specifications and regulatory requirements is illegal.

Why Not Increase the Antenna Gain?

You also may ask yourself: why not just use an antenna with more gain in order to increase the received power? This is problematic for several reasons:

- Using a higher gain antenna focuses the RF energy in a specific direction, which is fine for a point-to-point link where the source and destination devices are in fixed locations. The antennas need to be aligned to point at each other. If either device changes position, the antennas need to be realigned.

- The regulatory approval for the device is for a specific combination of module and antenna; changing the antenna may void the approval.

ONE PAGER ON ANTENNAS

Probably the most common question that we have gotten from customers is what type of antenna to use with their wireless module that is used in their product. In particular, the uniqueness of IoT product form factors (vs. PCs and phones) makes it challenging to prescribe a one-size-fits-all antenna solution for all IoT products.

Antennas are classified according to antenna gain and antenna pattern. The antenna gain is a figure of merit on the transmitted signal power. The antenna pattern is the distribution of the transmitted and received antenna gain over the x-y plane.

The type of antenna pattern that should be used depends upon the application. For a device that may need to receive and transmit to an access point in any direction, a uniform antenna pattern in all directions may be preferable.

For a device that is extending the range of Wi-Fi and is always pointed at the same access point, a more directional antenna may be required. On the other hand, a highly directional antenna would not receive signals very well from devices in other directions.

The type of antenna that is selected depends upon several considerations:

- Certification and regulatory constraints: Usually wireless modules are certified for a specific transmit power, and antenna as the total transmit power in a given frequency band is restricted to below a maximum value.

- Use case: Is the device moving or does it need to connect to other devices in different directions? Or is the device's location fixed and is it always sending or receiving data in the same direction? Is the device located far from its target?

- Cost.

- Device form factor: Can the antenna be located without the case of the device or does it need to be located externally?

- Size: How large should the antenna be and still meet the device form factor constraints?

- Number: How many antennas are required? If the wireless module supports 2x2 MIMO, then two antennas need to be used. In some cases, antennas can be shared for different wireless standards using the same band: for example, Wi-Fi and Bluetooth in 2.4 GHz ISM band.

Some commonly used antennas include the following:

- Dipole

- Ceramic

- Yagi Uda

- Grid

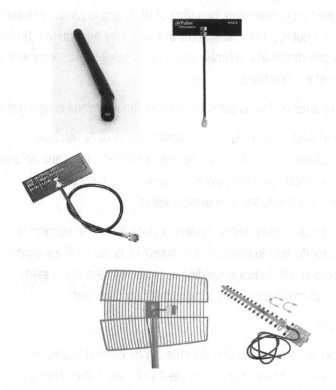

Figure 2-19. *Photos of commonly used IoT antennas. (a) Dipole, (b) patch, (c) PIFA, (d) Grid, and (e) Yagi*

Antenna Example for a Use Case

Consider a smart vending machine shown in Figure 2-20. This vending machine includes a cellular modem to connect it to the service center that will send out a supplier to replenish merchandise when it is low. What type of antenna should be used and where should the antenna be located? Consider that the vending machine may be located indoors and that the vending machine has a metal enclosure.

Figure 2-20. *Smart vending machine. Where should a cellular antenna be located?*

What Factors Affect How Fast We Can Send Data?

Most readers are probably aware from their personal experience with their smartphones or devices the limitations of their wireless connectivity technology which is characterized by how quickly (or slowly) they are sending and receiving their media content over the cellular network or Wi-Fi hot spots. The actual speed that they experience is the result of numerous factors including the radio technology that they are using, the radio environment, etc. Ultimately, the theoretical limitation on throughput is the channel capacity.

Channel Capacity

Given the numerous impairments that we discussed in the last section, is there a way of estimating the data rate that we can expect between the transmitter and receiver?

The famous Shannon-Hartley capacity theorem[47] from Information Theory expresses the maximum data rate C bits/second in terms of the channel bandwidth B Hertz and the Signal-to-Noise ratio S/N:

$$C = B \times \log_2\left(1 + \frac{S}{N}\right) \text{ bits/second} \qquad (6)$$

where

C is the maximum data rate in bits/second that can be achieved **with no errors**

B is the bandwidth in Hz

S is the signal power in Watts

N is the noise power of Additive White Gaussian Noise (AWGN) in Watts

The Shannon-Hartley equation expresses the theoretical limit of the achievable reliable data rate for a given bandwidth and Signal-to-Noise ratio. The key points of channel capacity

- The maximum data rate C of the wireless link depends on the **Signal-to-Noise ratio** and not just having high signal power is not sufficient to guarantee that the channel capacity can be achieved.

- It is worth reiterating this key point: Add any data rate below C, the data can be transmitted *without errors*. Conversely, at a data rate above C, error-free transmission is *not* possible.

---

[47] R. G. Gallager, "Information Theory and Reliable Communication," John Wiley & Sons, Inc., New York, 1968.

- The data rate C depends upon the allocated bandwidth B, and more bandwidth means a higher data rate.

- The Signal-to-Noise ratio is implicitly a function of the range between the wireless devices due to signal power decreasing with distance due to free space loss as we saw earlier in the discussion on the Link Budget; thus, the range also affects the throughput via the channel capacity expression.

- The channel capacity expression provides a theoretical limit but does not prescribe a method or technology that can be applied to achieve the capacity throughput.

Current radio technology has enabled many radio standards to come very close to channel capacity.

ONE PAGER ON THROUGHPUT AND BANDWIDTH

Data throughput or speed is an easily experienced Key Performance Indicator of a wireless protocol. We can perceive the effect of throughput when we download YouTube content to our device or phone and notice the amount of time it takes from when the media file download starts to when their video file starts playing on our device.

- What is bandwidth? Bandwidth is the width of the channel that is allocated to a user or device. The bandwidth is part of the wireless protocol and wireless standard and is allocated by a government agency in each country. For example, Wi-Fi uses channel bandwidths of 20, 40, 80, and 160MHz.

- How is speed or throughput related to bandwidth? As we will discuss later, the channel bandwidth establishes the bounds on the maximum symbol rate. The symbol rate × bits per symbol determines the maximum data rate. The bits per symbol is determined by the digital modulation that is used in the wireless standard.

- In practice, actual throughput is limited by overhead bits that are required to synchronize the destination with the source, error correction coding, acknowledgment packets, etc.

- How is throughput measured in practice? Throughput can be measured on a smartphone with an app that measures the amount of time it takes to upload and download a file of a specific size.

ONE PAGER ON INFORMATION THEORY

The theoretical foundation for computing the encoding and communication of data is Information Theory. The founder of Information Theory is Claude Shannon.[48] Some of the key concepts of information theory that are applicable to wireless communications for IoT are as follows:

Data compression: The *entropy* of a data source (randomness of the values of the data) determines the number of bits that are required to encode an information sequence such that it can be reproduced accurately. Intuitively, representing greater variations in information require more bits. This is important for IoT applications that are energy constrained because they are often battery powered or rely upon energy harvesting and have a limited

---

[48] Shannon, C.E. (1948) A Mathematical Theory of Communication. Bell System Technical Journal, 27, 379-423. https://doi.org/10.1002/j.1538-7305.1948.tb01338.x.

amount of power and bandwidth to send their sensor data back for analysis. An IoT use case would be an energy harvesting sensor that is measuring temperature of food that is being sent to a store.

Channel capacity: Channel capacity specifies the maximum data rate that can be used for a given Signal-to-Noise ratio with no errors. Channel capacity is relevant to IoT use cases where the IoT device is energy constrained and may be far from its target so that its received signal power at the destination is low and the Signal-to-Noise ratio is low. An example of an IoT use case where this is relevant is an agricultural sensor in a field that is far from the gateway located in the farmer's premises. Because of Shannon's work, we are now able to determine the lower bound for data throughput for a given SNR.

Figure 2-21. *Claude Shannon, founder of Information Theory.*[49]

---

[49] https://spectrum.ieee.org/tech-history/cyberspace/
celebrating-claude-shannon

Network Architecture Considerations

How Many Users/Devices Can I Connect to a Wireless Network?

In IoT applications, there may be a requirement to connect **many** wireless devices (sensors, Point-of-Sale terminals, surveillance cameras, etc.) and transfer data back to the Edge or Cloud. This connectivity scaling differentiates the "Do It Yourself" (DIY) IoT from Enterprise IoT.

Besides the capability of supporting a large number of devices, IoT applications may include additional challenging design constraints: the devices may be spread out over a large venue, such as an agricultural field, warehouse store, shopping mall, or industrial facility. The devices that are sending back data may be running off of batteries (perhaps not conveniently located near electrical wiring) and may be power limited.

As we noted earlier, the available spectrum is allocated by international and government standards agency and is a finite and scarce resource. There are many competing technologies vying to use the limited RF spectrum: phones, computers, TV, etc. Each service needs to then allocate its share of spectrum among multiple users and devices.

Because this is an important design consideration, we will describe the tradeoffs in wireless system topologies and access schemes.

Multiple Access Techniques

Most communications systems provide access to many users or devices concurrently by allocating the radio resources via Multiple-Access Techniques. We will describe the basics of multiple access techniques in this section mainly to point out how these methods affect the user or device experience in terms of latency and throughput.

Network resources can be visualized as a multi-dimensional entity:

- Frequency

- Time

- Space

- Code

- Space

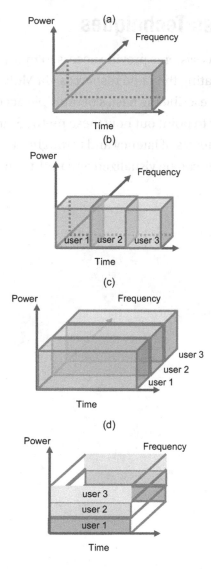

Figure 2-22. *Depiction of multiple access techniques for allocating radio resources among users: (a) total radio resource consists of frequency spectrum, power, and time; (b) time division multiple access divides users into time slots; (c) frequency division multiple access divides users into different frequency bands; and (d) code division multiple access divides users into unique spreading codes*

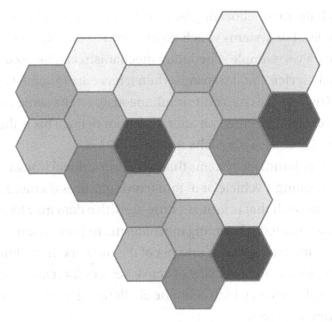

Figure 2-23. *Spatial multiplexing allocates different frequency bands for each cell. Shown here is the 7-frequency reuse pattern that is used by celular networks, where each color represents a frequency band. The cells are separated by sufficient distance so that there is not interference between cells that share the same frequency band*

These finite resources are distributed among competing devices and users. Each device would like to maximize its Quality of Service by either sending its data or receiving its data with minimal delay. Furthermore, each device would like to get enough resources to either upload or download its content as quickly as possible. Yet each device should be treated fairly by the network and given an opportunity to either send or receive data.

In the ideal case, each user would be able to be granted the bandwidth that it needs as soon as it needs it. In reality, other users are contending for the frequency resource. If the number of users exceeds the chunks of bandwidth that are available, then some users may have to wait to transmit their data which increases the latency that they experience.

The mechanism for allocating bandwidth to users can be very simple or very complex. For systems which do not need to meet low latency requirements, a very simple scheduling mechanism can be used. For example, each device could transmit when it has data to send. Collisions may occur if two devices transmit simultaneously on the same channel, but each device could retransmit after a random delay. This is the approach used in the classic Aloha net from 1971.[50]

On the other hand, for systems that have time critical transmissions, for example, controlling a vehicle or manufacturing process, a more complex scheduling approach that prioritizes time-sensitive data may be required.

More sophisticated scheduling mechanisms require a centralized controller that in turn increases the cost of the network. In addition, constant monitoring and checking of active devices increases the power consumption of devices, which could be challenging in use cases that have battery-powered devices.

MULTIPLE ACCESS TECHNIQUES

In many of the wireless system, there may be hundreds or thousands of devices that are attempting to access the network in order to transmit data. The wireless system must be designed to ensure that the devices receive a certain quality of service (QoS) that includes data throughput and latency.

Some considerations on selection of a multiple access technique include

- Total amount of bandwidth available to the network

- Bandwidth required for each device

- How often each device needs to send a message

---

[50] N. Abramson (1970). "The ALOHA System - Another Alternative for Computer Communications," *Proc. 1970 Fall Joint Computer Conference.* AFIPS Press.

- The amount of time for the message to be transmitted, received, processed, and a reply sent

- Network complexity and costs

Many different access schemes have been developed. These include

- Best effort schemes (Aloha): Devices in the network transmit data when they have a message to send; if the message is received correctly at the destination, an acknowledgment is sent from the destination back to the transmitter. If messages are sent simultaneously by multiple devices, a collision occurs, and the message is not received, and the acknowledgment is not sent. The device then resends its message until it is received correctly.

- Managed schemes: These schemes require that there is a central entity that schedules the transmissions from each device in the network. Examples include time division multiple access, frequency division multiple access, and orthogonal frequency division multiple access.

In later chapters of this book, we will discuss the bandwidth management schemes for popular wireless standards including the following:

- Wi-Fi 5

- Wi-Fi 6

- Bluetooth

- Cellular

Selection of Network Architectures and Topologies

The second key architecture consideration is the network topology which is the physical arrangement of devices in the network. The network topology establishes how nodes are added to the network as well as the number of devices that can be connected in the network.

We should point out that some wireless standards are able to support multiple network topologies: for example, Wi-Fi supports point-to-point Wi-Fi direct mode, the classic star topology (Access Points and Stations), and Wi-Fi mesh.

Point-to-Point

A point-to-point network consists of two network elements that connect directly. Examples include Bluetooth classic, RFID, and NFC.

Figure 2-24. *Depiction of a point-to-point network*

Mesh Network

As we will discuss on the section on different wireless standards, some standards enable devices to communicate directly with other devices without the intervention of a centralized infrastructure. In this topology, a device may use its nearest neighbor as a relay in order to send a message to another device that may be further away. This is an example of a *mesh network*.

Advantages: potentially greater distance coverage by sending packets across several hops; nodes do not need to be physically closer to a central access point and greater network reliability if there are multiple paths between nodes (if one node goes down, data can be routed around the failed node._

Disadvantages: potentially longer delay in sending messages across multiple hops and reduced energy efficiency as most nodes will need to stay active in order to relay data.

Examples: Bluetooth mesh, ZigBee, Wi-Fi mesh

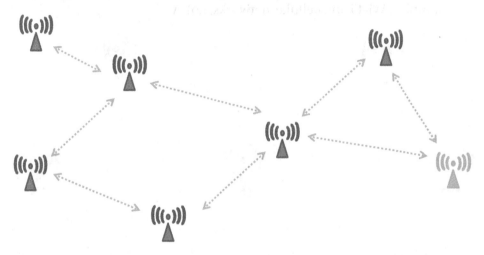

Figure 2-25. *Depiction of a mesh network*

Star Network

Other networks require a centralized controller in an Access Point or base station through which each device in the network needs to connect. In this case, the network is configured as a star network with a central access point through which all devices are connected directly.

Advantages: potentially lower delay in sending messages from a node to the center of the star; greater security as devices need to be granted access via the central access point; allows messages to be broadcast from the Access Point to all devices.

Disadvantages: maximum coverage is the potentially lower distance between the central hub and devices; greater complexity at the centralized controller which is responsible for scheduling transmissions to all of the network nodes; the centralized controller is a single point of failure and if the controller goes down the entire network goes down.

Examples: Wi-Fi and cellular networks, LoRA

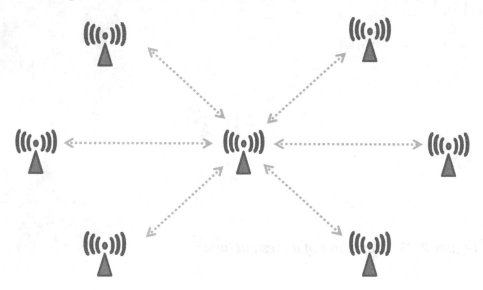

Figure 2-26. *Depiction of a star network*

Duplexing

For many IoT applications, a device in the system will both receive data from the central Access Point (Downlink) and transmit data to the Access Point (uplink). The uplink data and downlink data are separated so that the messages can be received correctly.

Time Division Duplex (TDD): the uplink and downlink transmissions share the same carrier frequency. Usage of the carrier is divided in time with uplink and downlink transmissions occurring during allocated time periods. TDD requires accurate timing among all of the devices in the network so that they transmit only during their allocated time slots.

Frequency division duplex (FDD): The uplink and downlink transmissions are in different frequency channels and can occur simultaneously. Each device needs to be able to accurately tune to the correct channel to send its data on the correct carrier frequency.

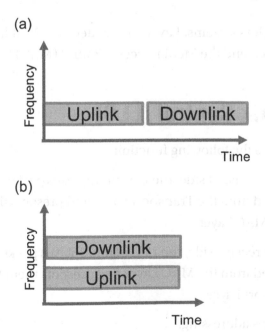

Figure 2-27. *Illustration of TDD and FDD*

Data Link Layer

The Data Link Layer is Layer 2 in the OSI model and sits between the Transport Layer and the Physical Layer in the OSI model. The Data Link Layer is responsible for ensuring that the transmitted data is (a) sent to the correct destination address and (b) received correctly at the destination.

On the source side, the Data Link Layer receives a datagram from the Transport Layer, processes it, and provides a frame to the Physical Layer that is to be sent to a destination node.

On the destination side, the Data Link Layer receives a frame of data from the Physical Layer and processes it so that an error-free datagram is passed to the Transport Layer. We have highlighted a key function that the Data Link Layer provides which is to provide error-free transmission of the datagrams from the Transport Layer; this means that the frames that are sent from the Data Link Layer to the Physical Layer are received error-free (eventually).

In many wireless systems, Layer 2 is divided into 2 sublayers: Logic Link Control (LLC) and the Media Access Control (MAC) Layer.

Logical Link Control (LLC)

The LLC performs the following functions:

- On the transmit side, the LLC multiplexes packets received from the Transport Layer and presents them to the MAC Layer.

- On the receive side, the LLC demultiplexes packets received from the MAC Layer and presents them to the Transport Layer.

- Provides addressing.

- Provides flow control.

- Provides acknowledgments upon the correct reception of a packet.

- Provides error notifications if a packet is not received correctly.

Media Access Control (MAC)

The MAC Layer performs the following functions:

- Receives packets from the LLC and presents them to the PHY.

- Receives packets from the PHY and presents them to the LLC.

- Ensures that packets are received without error from the PHY.

- Appends a packet header that contains the destination address and packet numbering.

- Reassembles the packets into the correct order.

- Performs frame synchronization.

Protocol and Network Complexity

The wireless protocol defines the mechanisms for how devices access and send messages across the network. The protocol includes a stack that defines the messages used by the components of the network (refer to OSI model). The protocol also allocates network resources such as bandwidth to devices that are sharing the network.

The protocol may use a scheduling mechanism to grant each device access to the network resources. The complexity of this scheduling mechanism depends on the Quality of Service requirements including latency and bandwidth.

Scheduling Transmissions

Scheduling refers to allocating network resources for each device to transmit its data without conflicts from other devices trying to send their data. The scheduling can be done by a centralized entity as in the case of a cellular system. Centralized scheduling or managed networks provide better Quality of Service which is essential for cellular applications such as voice calls.

On the other hand, the centralized scheduling that is provided by cellular operators requires an extensive network infrastructure of base stations, etc.

An alternative to managed networks is best effort scheduling which is used in Wi-Fi as discussed in Chapter 3.

ONE PAGER ON IP AND TCP VS. UDP

Internet Protocol (IP) is the network protocol used to packetize and route data on the Internet. IP is a connectionless, best effort protocol that routes a packet from source to destination by progressively moving the packet from source to a series of routers until it arrives at its destination.[51,52]

---

[51] www.networkworld.com/article/3338106/can-iot-networking-drive-adoption-of-ipv6.html

[52] www.ibm.com/support/knowledgecenter/SSLTBW_2.2.0/com.ibm.zos.v2r2.halc001/ipcicint_protocol.htm

As shown in Figure 2-28, Internet Protocol consists of Layers 3 and 4. The Transport Layer component of IP breaks a message from the Session Layer into smaller packets and sets up the delivery of the packet across the network from source to destination. The Transport Layer is implemented by either of two protocols, TCP or UDP:

- Transmission Control Protocol (TCP): A transport layer protocol that provides a virtual connection between the source and destination devices. TCP uses acknowledgments that flow from the destination back to the source to guarantee that the packets are received reliably at the destination and that the packets are received in the correct order.

- User Datagram Protocol (UDP): A transport layer protocol that provides a link-by-link and unreliable virtual connection between applications. UDP does not guarantee that packets will be received and are in order.

Layer 3 is implemented by the Internet Protocol. IP obtains the *IP address* of the destination device and enables data packets to be routed via connectionless link to the device. There are two versions of the IP address:

- Internet Protocol version 4 (IPv4) defines an IP address is 32 bits long. The total number of devices that can be distinguished with 32-bit address is $2^{32} = 4,294,967,296$.

- Internet Protocol version 6 (IPv6) defines an IP address is 128 bits long. The total number of devices that can be distinguished with 128-bit address is $2^{128} = 3.4028237 \times 10^{38}$ which is the total number of unique devices that can be supported in IP and is important as the number of IoT devices increases.

Why does UDP seem to produce a faster download data rate than TCP?
Suppose you are interested in measuring the speed or throughput of your
wireless link and use any of a number of PC smart phone apps such as iperf.[53]
When running download speed analysis on any number of phone apps, you
may observe that the download speed using UDP is faster than TCP. Note that
TCP uses acknowledgment packets to indicate that the data are received
correctly while UDP does not. Thus, UDP appears to be faster than UDP
because there is no delay caused by waiting for acknowledgments from the
destination to the source. However, TCP provides better data reliability at a
cost of lower apparent speed.

Why isn't TCP/IP used in all IoT applications? Some IoT protocols such as
Bluetooth or the LPWAN standards do not use IP. Bluetooth devices require a
hub that translates IP to the BLE 48-bit MAC addresses.[54] Because IPv4 used a
broadcast function to send messages all connected devices on a network, all
Bluetooth devices including those powered by batteries are required to turn on
which reduces their battery life. Therefore, IPv4 was not an efficient protocol
for Bluetooth applications.

IPv6 offers improvements that benefit IoT devices. The broadcast function was
replaced in IPv6 leading to more efficient battery usage for connected devices.
As we noted above, IPv6 supports 128-bit IP addresses. As we move towards
connecting billions of IoT devices, this address space becomes essential.

---

[53] https://iperf.fr/

[54] www.novelbits.io/bluetooth-address-privacy-ble/

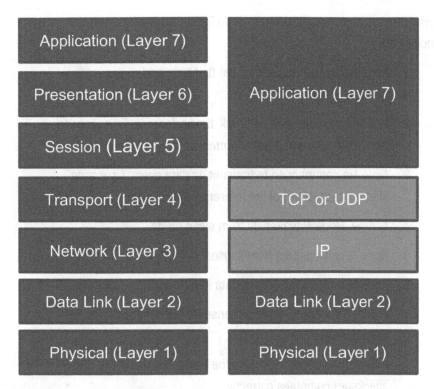

Figure 2-28. *TCP/IP implement Layers 3 and 4 of the OSI model*

ONE PAGER: WHAT HAPPENS WHEN A MESSAGE IS SENT BY A SENSOR?

In this chapter we have listed many of the considerations that go into selecting a wireless technology for an IoT use case. What is common across the different technologies that will be discussed in the remainder of this book is that messages are sent from IoT devices and sensors and are received at an Edge Gateway or Cloud device. The general process is the same across the different standards with differences in data rate, security, etc., that are defined by the specifics of the wireless standard.

Here are the steps for an example of an Edge Gateway and wireless sensor nodes N_i:

1. Node I joins the network for the first time and aligns to the network security that is in use.

2. Node I synchronizes to network-time reference T_R. It aligns to the frame start and duration time that is set by the gateway.

3. Node I is commanded to transmit its data every T_i seconds starting at an offset of the reference time T_R: time $T_R + T_i$.

4. At time, Node N_i wakes up from sleep mode.

5. Node N_i collects data from sensor.

6. Node N_i formats the sensor data into packet.

7. At time $T_R + N \times T_i$, Node N_i transmits the data packet to the Edge gateway.

8. If the Edge Gateway receives the packet correctly, the CRC checksum computes correctly.

9. The Edge Gateway sends an acknowledgment message back to node N_i.

10. If the CRC does not compute, then Node N_i must resend the packet.

11. Node N_i waits a random time T_{rand} and then resend the same message.

12. If the message is received at the Gateway, then the Node N_i goes to sleep.

IOT CONNECTIVITY VS. PC AND PHONE CONNECTIVITY

The same wireless connectivity issues that affect IoT devices are shared with PCs and cellphones that use similar wireless technologies. In fact, for some use cases, both PCs and cellphones can be considered as IoT platforms.

Why do we need to differentiate IoT wireless design from wireless design for these other devices?

In some IoT use cases such as retail Point of Sale (POS) devices and Thin Clients, the platforms are essentially PCs, and so the IoT wireless considerations are the same as for a PC:

- Phones typically support cellular bands, Wi-Fi, Bluetooth, and GPS/GNSS.

- PCs support cellular, Wi-Fi, and Bluetooth.

- IoT devices may support a combination of cellular, Wi-Fi, Bluetooth, GPS/GNSS, and ZigBee.

- PCs and phones are almost constantly attended to by the user. In some applications, IoT devices may be unattended for years. IoT devices may be mounted in different to access locations in a warehouse or factory.

- Phones are usually continuously connected to network and received notifications from the cellular base station that a call is incoming. The cellular network also monitors the signals from the phone to determine when to handoff the call to another base station.

- IoT devices may be in sleep mode and disconnected to the network until they have a message to send; this enables them to save power.

- PCs and phones are typically charged every day, and power consumption is important but not as critical as an IoT device.

- PCs and phones can receive software updates and patches relatively easily when compared to an IoT device.

There are a few key differences that can make the wireless design easier or harder:

IoT devices may be more energy constrained than either PCs or phones as the IoT device may be a physically smaller device with a limited battery size that may not be accessible to charging from the power mains. One example is a solar-powered sensor in a field on a farm.

IoT devices may be deployed for long periods of time measured in several years vs. PCs and phones which may have a 2- to 3-year lifespan as customers migrate to the "latest and greatest" and as a result need to have extended reliability.

Unlike phones and PCs, some IoT devices may be "headless" and not have a screen or display and user interface that are used to configure and commission the device (such as connecting to an Access Point for Wi-Fi). It is possible that an auxiliary technology such as Bluetooth could be used via smartphone to configure the device, but this adds to the cost, complexity, and security considerations of the device.

IoT devices may be deployed in harsh environments such as outdoors in the weather or in factories or vehicles and equipment such as utilities, oil rigs, etc., and may need to be ruggedized in order to survive a wide temperature range (called **extended temperature** such as -40 to 85C), humidity, shock, and vibration.

IoT devices may use a wider range of wireless standards in a single device such as cellular, Wi-Fi, Bluetooth ZigBee, LoRA, or Narrow Band IoT in an IoT Gateway.

In some cases, IoT devices do need to support the high data rates that are required by laptop PCs and cellphones that are used by consumers. For example, IoT sensors may need to send temperature or humidity data in packets every few minutes vs. downloading a large video file to a consumer tablet.

ONE PAGER ON SMART LIGHTING[55]

An example of an IoT technology that is available in the consumer space is Smart Lighting: LED lightbulbs that can be turned on/off and change colors via wireless technology. The smart bulbs are controlled via voice control through a smart speaker such as Amazon Echo, Google Home, or Apple Home Kit or directly via a smartphone app.

The bulbs include a LED bulb, microcontroller, and a wireless module and may or may not require a dedicated gateway platform to connect to the bulbs.

Control options: Color, on/off schedule, and remote control.

Wireless technologies: Smart bulbs can incorporate 2.4GHz Wi-Fi, Bluetooth, ZigBee, or Z-wave.

Hub: Bulbs that use ZigBee or Z-wave require a dedicated gateway or hub to send the commands to the bulb. An example is the Philips Hue lighting system that uses ZigBee technology and requires a bridge that can control up to 50 smart bulbs.

---

[55] www.amazon.com/ospublishing/story/433c92c2-cdc5-4b98-9b6e-192a5c
650cac/ref=sxin_8_osp22-433c92c2_cov?pd_rd_w=qjmA9&pf_rd_p=3494954a-
3e59-449e-91eb-b8736f013ede&pf_rd_r=ZWCR7493JD997CKOF5RX&pd_rd_r=
65cd9095-313a-4cad-8395-942db43dc061&pd_rd_wg=zfo6Z&cv_ct_pg=search&
cv_ct_wn=osp-search&ascsubtag=amzn1.osa.433c92c2-cdc5-4b98-9b6e-
192a5c650cac.ATVPDKIKX0DER.en_US&linkCode=oas&cv_ct_id=amzn1.osa.
433c92c2-cdc5-4b98-9b6e-192a5c650cac.ATVPDKIKX0DER.en_US&tag=reviewed
oap-20&qid=1586124428&cv_ct_cx=smart+bulb

Bulbs that use Wi-Fi or Bluetooth may not require a dedicated hub and can be controlled via a smart speaker or smart phone.

Figure 2-29. *Philips Hue starter kit*

Wireless Standards

Various industry or government consortia have defined standards to ensure interoperability and compatibility of devices. These standards have defined all of the key features that are necessary to design and build devices that can communicate effectively including allocation of spectrum (in many cases harmonized to be consistent in most countries of the world), power levels, mechanisms to prevent radio interference to other standards within the same frequency bands or adjacent frequency bands, security, and safety.

Fragmentation of Wireless Standards

As the reader is probably aware, there are a multitude of wireless standards that have been defined by industry standards bodies and consortia. Most of these standards are incompatible, and general IoT solutions are designed to support a small subset of these; for example, Wi-Fi and Bluetooth or cellular, Bluetooth, Wi-Fi, and GNSS.

The reason why there is no single radio technology is because each standard is defined for a given set of parameters: frequency band, data rate, range, network topology, cost structure, market segment, number of devices, set of use cases, and reliability.

Consider the following examples:

Use Case 1: A remote agricultural sensor monitors the temperature and moisture levels of crops and sends this data (a few bytes) every hour back to a gateway where the data are analyzed to control the irrigation system; there are thousands of sensors on a specific farm. The sensors are powered by solar cells, and the devices must be in the field under strenuous temperature and weather conditions for several years. The distance from the sensors to the gateway is 100 meters.

Use Case 2: A digital sign in a shopping mall displays the latest sales, and new products include video that engage the shoppers. The digital sign was added to an existing store, and thus it would have been expensive to run Ethernet cables to connect the sign to the network. Instead, the sign is connected via Wi-Fi to an Access Point. Content is refreshed wirelessly several times a day. The sign is connected to the power mains so power is not a concern.

Use Case 3: Sensors in a shipping container measure the temperature, humidity, acceleration, and location of the product that is being shipped. The data are sent periodically while the container is in transit on a truck, train, or ship or while stored in a warehouse. The data consists of a few bytes of data that are sent every few minutes. An alarm message is sent if the cargo is subject to extreme shock or temperature.

In the use cases that we have described, there is currently no single wireless standard that could be used to meet all of these requirements.

- For use case 1, possible solutions include 802.15.4 such as Zigbee.

- For use case 2, possible solutions include Wi-Fi.

- For use case 3, a possible solution is Narrow Band IoT, a cellular standard.

Classification of standards

One way of classifying wireless standards is based on the distance between devices that are transmitting and receiving data.[56]

- Wireless Body Area Networks (WBAN) are wireless standards that support a range of less than a meter between health monitoring sensors located on a person. An example of a WBAN is the IEEE 802.15.6 standard.

---

[56] https://cs.wmich.edu/~alfuqaha/fall13/cs6570/lectures/Bluetooth-ZigBee.pdf
https://er.yuvayana.org/types-of-wireless-networking-technology-and-comparison/
www.tpi1.com/solutions/wireless-infrastructure/wwan_wlan_wpan/
http://etutorials.org/Mobile+devices/mobile+wireless+design/Part+One+Introduction+to+the+Mobile+and+Wireless+Landscape/Chapter+3+Wireless+Networks/
www.researchgate.net/publication/320715773_A_Survey_on_Wireless_Technologies_for_Biomedical_Parameters
www.ittc.ku.edu/~jpgs/courses/intronets/lecture-mobilewireless-intronets-display.pdf
www.waves.intec.ugent.be/research/wireless-body-area-networks
https://standards.ieee.org/standard/802_15_6-2012.html

- Wireless Personal Area Networks (WPAN) are wireless standards that support a range of 10 meters between devices. Examples of WPANs include Bluetooth and ZigBee. WPAN networks do not require any infrastructure to connect devices as the connections are made directly between devices.

- WLAN: Wireless Local Area Networks (WLAN) are wireless standards that support a range of 100 meters between devices. WLAN systems include an infrastructure that provides access for devices on the network as well as a connection to the Internet. WLAN systems are located within an office, home, or facility. The infrastructure may provide the capability to enable devices to roam over different areas of the office building or campus. An example of WLAN is Wi-Fi based on the IEEE 802.11 standard.

- WMAN: Wireless Metropolitan Area Networks (WMAN) are wireless standards that support a range of 5 kilometers between devices. In this case, a single device is in a home or building. WMAN networks require an infrastructure to enable devices to connect to the network and provide Internet access. An example of WMAN is the defunct 802.16 WorldWide Interoperability for Microwave Access (WiMAX) standard.

- WWAN: Wireless Wide Area Networks (WWAN) are wireless standards that support a range of many kilometers between devices such as cities and countries and worldwide. WWAN systems require an extensive infrastructure of base stations that are connected over a network to enable device access. Examples of WWAN include cellular standards such as 3G and LTE and 5G.

129

- LPWAN: Low Power Wide Area Networks (LPWAN) are wireless standards that support a range of many kilometers between devices and sensors and gateways that receive their data. LPWAN systems are characterized by very low data rates, long latency, long battery life, and low power consumption; examples include LoRaWAN, SigFox, LTE-M, and NB-IoT.

Wireless Standard Bodies

The wireless standards that are used for IoT are depicted in Figure 2-30 and presented in Table 2-7.

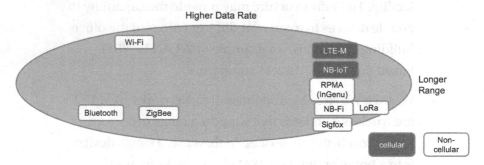

Figure 2-30. *Diagram depicting IoT wireless standards (from [])*

Table 2-7. *(Work in Progress) Summary of wireless standards that are used for IoT*[57,58,59,60,61,62]

Standard	Standards Body	Frequency Bands (GHz)	Maximum Throughput (Mbits/s)	Range	Type
WiGig 802.11ad	802.11	60	6750		WPAN
Bluetooth	Bluetooth SIG	2.4	2 (LE 2M PHY)	1500m (LE coded PHY)	WPAN

(continued)

[57] https://en.wikipedia.org/wiki/WiMedia_Alliance

[58] www.wimedia.org/en/specs.asp?id=specs

[59] www.link-labs.com/blog/complete-list-iot-network-protocols

[60] www.cnx-software.com/2020/04/06/mioty-silicon-vendor-agnostic-scalable-lpwan-standard-takes-on-lorawan-nb-iot/

[61] https://mioty-alliance.com/

[62] www.rfwireless-world.com/Terminology/difference-between-wifi-6-and-wifi-5.html#:~:text=The%20Standard%20IEEE%20802.11b,per%20mod%2Dcode%20rate%20viz.

Table 2-7. (*continued*)

Standard	Standards Body	Frequency Bands (GHz)	Maximum Throughput (Mbits/s)	Range	Type
802.15.4 (ZigBee)[63]	IEEE, ZigBee	0.868, 0.915, 2.4	0.02 (868MHz), 0.04 (915MHz), 0.25 (2.4GHz)	10m to 100m	WPAN
802.15.4 (Thread)[64]	IEEE, [65]	2.4	0.25 (2.4GHz)	10m to 100m	WPAN
802.15.4 (Wi-SUN)	IEEE, Wi-SUN [66]Alliance	2.4	0.3	10m to 100m	WPAN
RFID	ISO/IEC 18000-3	0.013		0.1m to 200m	WPAN

[63] www.sciencedirect.com/topics/engineering/zigbee-protocol/pdf
[64] www.threadgroup.org/
[65] Thread 1.1.1 Specification, February 13, 2017
[66] https://wi-sun.org/

NFC[67]	ISO/IEC 18000-3, NFC Forum	0.013	0.42375	10cm	WPAN
UWB Ultra Wideband	WiMedia Alliance[68]	3100 to 10600GHz	480	10m to 200m	WPAN
Wi-Fi 802.11b (Wi-Fi 1)	IEEE 802.11, Wi-Fi Alliance	2.4	11	38m indoor 140m outdoor	WLAN
Wi-Fi 802.11a (Wi-Fi 2)	IEEE 802.11, Wi-Fi Alliance	5	54	35m indoor 120m outdoor	WLAN
Wi-Fi 802.11g (Wi-Fi 3)	IEEE 802.11, Wi-Fi Alliance	2.4, 5	54	35m indoor 120m outdoor	WLAN
Wi-Fi 802.11n (Wi-Fi 4)	IEEE 802.11, Wi-Fi Alliance	2.4, 5	450	70m indoor 250m outdoor	WLAN
Wi-Fi 802.11ac (Wi-Fi 5)	IEEE 802.11, Wi-Fi Alliance	5	1300 (Wave 1) 2340 (Wave 2)	80m	WLAN

(continued)

[67] https://en.wikipedia.org/wiki/Near-field_communication#ISO/IEC
[68] www.wimedia.org/en/index.asp

Table 2-7. (*continued*)

Standard	Standards Body	Frequency Bands (GHz)	Maximum Throughput (Mbits/s)	Range	Type
Wi-Fi 802.11ax (Wi-Fi 6)	IEEE 802.11, Wi-Fi Alliance	2.4, 5	2400		WLAN
Wi-Fi 802.11ax (Wi-Fi 6E)	IEEE 802.11, Wi-Fi Alliance	2.4, 5, 6	2400		WLAN
Wi-Fi 802.11be (Wi-Fi 7)	IEEE 802.11, Wi-Fi Alliance	2.4, 5	30000		WLAN
DSRC					WLAN
802.11ah[69]	IEEE 802.11	0.9	347	1000m	WWAN
LTE (3GPP Release 8)	3GPP	Many[70]	100 downlink 50 uplink	5000m	WWAN

---

[69]www.mwrf.com/technologies/active-components/article/21846205/whats-the-difference-between-ieee-80211af-and-80211ah

[70]https://en.wikipedia.org/wiki/LTE_frequency_bands

5G (3GPP Release 13)	3GPP	Many	20000	500 (mmWave)	WWAN
LoRA	LoRA	0.433, 0.863, 0.9, 2.4	0.3	5km urban, 20km rural	LPWAN
NB IoT[71] (3GPP Release 13)	3GPP	0.882, 1.840	0.2	1km urban, 10km rural	LPWAN
LTE-M (3GPP Release 13)	3GPP	2.6	1		LPWAN
RPMA (Ingenu)	Ingenu	2.4	0.019	300 sq miles USA, 32 sq miles Europe	LPWAN
NB Fi	WAVIoT	0.430, 0.860	0.0256	10km urban, 40km rural	LPWAN
SigFox	SigFox	0.860, 0.900	0.0001 (uplink) 0.0006 (downlink)	10km urban, 40km rural	LPWAN

[71]https://en.wikipedia.org/wiki/Near-field_communication

135

Chapter Summary

It is important that the IoT solution developer is aware of the inherent limitations of wireless and take steps to mitigate the issues that we have described here. In particular, the developer needs to

- Understand the requirements of the application and key performance indicators (KPIs) in order to select the appropriate wired or wireless technology.

- Align the target Quality of Service (QoS) parameters (throughput and latency) for the target applications.

- Ensure that the IoT solution incorporates the necessary security and privacy requirements.

- Ensure that constraints of the wireless environment including signal attenuation, range limitations, noise, and interference are mitigated.

Choose and design components of the solution to maximize the effectiveness of the wireless solution including throughput, latency, reliability, etc.

In the upcoming chapters, we will explore the most prevalent wireless standards that are used for IoT applications.

Key Terminology for Chapter 2

- AWGN: Additive White Gaussian Noise

- Bandwidth: The amount of frequency spectrum allocated to a given wireless standard, which is in turn allocated to a specific application or user

- Capacity: maximum theoretical data rate.

- Channel: allocation of spectrum at a defined frequency and bandwidth.

- Cloud: collection of servers for storage and processing of data.

- Determinism: messages are received at a known time.

- Edge: computation on or near the site of the use case.

- Fading: reduction of signal strength due to multipath reflections.

- Latency: time between when a message is sent from the source until it is received at the destination.

- Licensed band: frequency band that must be purchased by the operator.

- Link Budget: required signal power to achieve the target performance.

- MAC Layer: layer above of the PHY layer that sends and receives data to and from the PHY.

- Modem: (modulator-demodulator) device that transmits and receives radio signals.

- Modulation: mapping of data bits to a signal waveform.

- Multipath: reflections of radio signals due to objects in the radio environment.

- Physical layer (PHY): section of the protocol stack related to the physical waveform.

- Quality of Service: measurement of the performance of a network, such as latency, determinism and error rate.

- Signal-to-Noise ratio (SNR): ratio of signal power to noise power, typically in dB.

- Signal to Interferer Noise Ratio (SINR): ratio of signal power to interference power, typically in dB.

- Throughput: available data rate at the user device.

- Unlicensed band: frequency band that is free to use.

Key Constants

The key constants that are used in this chapter are listed in Table 2-8.

Table 2-8. Table of key wireless constants

Constant	Description	Value–Linear	Units–Linear	Value–dB	Units–dB meters/s
c	Speed of light	3×10^8	meters/second	8.48E+01	dB meters/second
k	Boltzmann's constant	$1.38064852 \times 10^{-23}$	m^2 kg s^{-2} K^{-1}	-2.29E+02	dB m^2 kg s^{-2} K^{-1}

Chapter Problems

1. Discuss the motivation for following the OSI model when developing a protocol stack vs. creating a new stack from top-to-bottom.

2. Are there any disadvantages to following the OSI model?

3. What are the differences between TCP and UDP? When streaming a video to your phone, which should you use and why?

4. What is the advantage to using TCP over UDP?

5. Consider (a) a battery-powered moisture sensor in an agricultural field, (b) a Point-of-Sale terminal, and (c) an automatic robot in a factory. All are connected to the cloud. How would you design the OSI stacks to be optimal for each use case?

6. Our wireless robot is sent 128-bit command packets from a factory controller. If the factory requires four 9s of reliability, what is the required bit error rate that the radio needs to provide?

7. The SNR for an Additive White Gaussian Noise (AWGN) channel is 20dB. The channel bandwidth is 20MHz. What is the theoretical channel capacity of this channel?

8. You would like to send a video stream at 1Gbits/s through a 40MHz channel. What is the required SNR of an AWGN channel in order to achieve this theoretical data rate?

9. You would like to control an aerial drone using Bluetooth. Compute the Link Budget with following parameters:

    - If the drone is at an altitude of 1km directly overhead.

    - Receiver sensitivity is -97dB.

    - Transmitter power is 5.0 dBm.

    - Antenna gain is 1.26 dBi.

10. Repeat the Link Budget calculations for the case where the drone is 1Km away but behind a house which produces 20dB of attenuation.

11. The 802.11ac Wi-Fi standard defines 80MHz channels.

    - For an SNR of 50dB and a 1x1 link, calculate the channel capacity of Wi-Fi.

    - The standard defines a data rate of 433Mbps for this link. What do you think accounts for the difference?

12. Why is the MAC layer different for different wireless protocols?

13. What is the difference between error detecting and error correcting codes?

14. A system architect would like to use Wi-Fi to control a robot arm on a factory manufacturing line. The latency from the controller PC to the actuator on the robot arm must be less than 1msec. What issues do you see with using best effort Wi-Fi to control the arm?

15. You are designing a wireless communication network for a warehouse. The warehouse dimensions are 100meters x 100 meters x 20 meters. You need to transmit data at 500kbits/s from sensors that are uniformly deployed on machines deployed uniformly across the warehouse space. Which wireless standards would you consider using and why?

16. For the system that you designed in preceding problem, you now must incorporate real-time video from 10 cameras located uniformly around the warehouse. The data rate from each camera is 20Mbits/s. Which wireless standards should you consider using and why?

17. You are a consultant working with a city would like to transmit real-time video from traffic lights to a Network Video Recorder (NVR). The maximum distance from a camera to the NVR is 50meters. The data rate of compressed HD quality video is 80Mbps. To avoid installing cables, the city would like to use a wireless solution. Assume line-of-sight between the video camera and NVR with no obstruction between the camera and the NVR. What wireless solutions would you recommend?

References for Chapter 2

1. www.digikey.com/product-detail/en/pulselarsen-
    antennas/W3918B0100/1837-1007-ND/7667481?utm_
    adgroup=RF%20Antennas&utm_source=google&utm_
    medium=cpc&utm_campaign=Shopping_RF%2FIF%20
    and%20RFID_NEW&utm_term=&utm_content=RF%
    20Antennas&gclid=CjOKCQiAkKnyBRDwARIsALtxe7i
    D4hFX-Iq94RpELDx1b9J6ueIYXWhjc2SV9jk7zqoOd
    QqAjc4T7YoaArnkEALw_wcB

2. www.mouser.com/ProductDetail/Microchip-
    Technology/RN-SMA-4?qs=3vk7fz9CmNwMOuJP168ec
    g%3D%3D&gclid=CjOKCQiAkKnyBRDwARIsALtxe7jrXZ
    tRHwl2zADabnWLhg8xGhyVWdGRBRF6u5T46HHeRMEfyH
    75hFIaAhqZEALw_wcB

3. www.amazon.in/USR-ANT2G5G-S001-Embedded-
    Antenna-Serial-Dedicated/dp/B07MB9PNBV

4. www.solidsignal.com/pview.asp?p=GD5W-
    28P&utm_source=google&utm_medium=cse&utm_te
    rm=gd5w-28p&gclid=CjOKCQiAkKnyBRDwARIsA
    Ltxe7izx-15wJlh6ZqHWV383HyBNj7Njm8n-bS-
    RBLlV8AxBXuZXMsfBOaAuuREALw_wcB

CHAPTER 3

Wi-Fi

Chapter Overview

Because Wi-Fi is ubiquitous, the reader is already familiar with the everyday use of Wi-Fi for their laptops and phones.

It is hard to imagine how the world was before Wi-Fi appeared in the late 1990s and how it has revolutionized access to the Internet. As of 2019, approximately 13 billion Wi-Fi devices have been deployed worldwide.[1] While the majority of these applications are in smartphones and personal computers, Wi-Fi is also used for an increasing number of IoT applications. We will describe some of the IoT applications that use Wi-Fi and how the evolution of Wi-Fi makes it more amenable to IoT use cases.

What Do We Mean by Wi-Fi?

"Wi-Fi" refers to wireless products that are defined by IEEE 802.11 standards that are certified by the Wi-Fi Alliance (WFA).

Wi-Fi is also known as "Wireless Local Area Networks" (WLAN) and is the wireless analog of wired Local Area Networking (LAN) standards such as Ethernet.

---

[1] www.wi-fi.org/news-events/newsroom/wi-fi-alliance-celebrates-20-years-of-wi-fi

© Anil Kumar, Jafer Hussain, Anthony Chun 2023
A. Kumar et al., *Connecting the Internet of Things*,
https://doi.org/10.1007/978-1-4842-8897-9_3

Why Wi-Fi for IoT?

Since Wi-Fi is already everywhere for smartphone and PC applications, why not use it for IoT applications that require wireless connectivity? Here are some benefits for using Wi-Fi for IoT:

- Wi-Fi is a well-established technology that has been available for the past 20+ years.

- Wi-Fi is an industry standard from the IEEE and Wi-Fi Alliance (WFA); WFA has 858 members worldwide as of 2019.[2]

- The Wi-Fi Alliance certifies that the manufacturer's product complies with the standard which gives confidence to consumers that the product will work properly.

- There are many vendors providing components for the Wi-Fi ecosystem from access points and client silicon and modules.

- Because there are numerous vendors and many users, these products are in mass production which enabled the costs to be reduced.

- The 2.4GHz ISM band is standardized worldwide. This means that a Wi-Fi product will work in multiple countries (assuming that it passes the regulatory requirements for those countries).

- 5GHz is mostly available worldwide with a few exceptions.

---

[2] *Wi Fi Alliance ANNUAL REPORT 2019*, March 2020.

- As of 2020, the 6GHz is now available in the United States for unlicensed wireless including Wi-Fi; other countries to follow in 2021.

- High data rates (up to 2 G.4bits/s) for Wi-Fi 6 in 2x2 MIMO mode are sufficient for most use cases.

- Additional capabilities beyond basic data connectivity such as Voice Personal, Voice Enterprise, Miracast, mesh, etc.

- Wi-Fi is reliable enough for most applications.

- Operational costs: There are no additional monthly service charges for wireless access (vs. monthly charges for public cellular service).

- Reasonable installation and setup for most applications; enterprise installation requires more effort and cost.

- Requires no overall network management once it has been installed.

While it seems that Wi-Fi can be applied to many IoT use cases, there are also some considerations for *not* using Wi-Fi for IoT applications. Please see Table 3-1 for a comparison of Wi-Fi with other standards.

- High-end Wi-Fi 6/6E 2x2 MIMO modules are relatively expensive vs. Bluetooth and other low power wireless connectivity technologies.

- Security concerns: In comparison to LTE, LTE security is perceived as better; *however, the introduction of WPA3 security for Wi-Fi 6 has increased the robustness of Wi-Fi security.*

- Relatively higher power consumption of client devices vs. alternative standards such as LoRA and Zigbee which is an issue for battery-powered IoT devices.

- Limited range (~30m) between Access Points and client devices compared to other wireless standards such as cellular and LoRA.

- Bandwidth overhead limits real-world throughput to 50% of maximum (mitigated by 802.11ah or Wi-Fi HaLow[3]).

- Interference in the 2.4GHz unlicensed ISM band such as microwave ovens can reduce performance in comparison to cellular technologies in licensed bands (note: this applies to Bluetooth and 802.15.4 devices in this band also).

- Latency (best effort scheduling): In comparison to 5G, 5G uRLLC (Ultra Reliable Low Latency Communication) in the near future will provide lower latency (better for industrial use cases), better security, better management, immunity from interference, and easier to commission and deploy. However, Wi-Fi 7 may include the capability of improving determinism and reliability for mission critical applications.

- Wi-Fi's data rates are not aligned to low power and low data rate use cases (i.e., IoT sensors).

- Lack of centralized network management can lead to poorer quality of service. (*However, Wi-Fi 6 improves network management capabilities to improve the overall Quality of Service.*)

---

[3] https://en.wikipedia.org/wiki/IEEE_802.11ah

- It is possible for the end user or customer to install and manage the network. This is both a positive from the lower cost perspective and a negative from overall optimization of the network design.

Table 3-1. *Comparison of Wi-Fi with other IoT wireless connectivity standards*

Competing Wireless Technology	Feature
Cellular (LTE and 5G)	Cellular offers greater security than Wi-Fi 5
	Cellular offers better Quality of Service than Wi-Fi 5
	Managed cellular spectrum does not have the potential for interference as in the unlicensed bands used by Wi-Fi
802.15.4	802.15.4 offers greater range
	802.15.4 offers lower data rate
	802.15.4 offers lower power consumption
LoRA	LoRA has a longer range
	LoRA has substantially lower data rate
	LoRA has much higher latency
Ethernet	Ethernet offers higher reliability and determinism than Wi-Fi

Wi-Fi IoT Use Cases

Wi-Fi can be applied to IoT use cases that

- Require high upload and download throughput speeds on the order of tens of Megabits per second.

- Are not powered by batteries that are hard for the user to access and replace

- Have a range of <100 meters between devices
- Do not require extremely low latency and determinism
- Low mobility (platforms that are stationary or moving at most a few meters per second)

Some IoT examples that use Wi-Fi include

- Digital signage
- Digital surveillance
- Voice over IP
- Thin client (device that integrates GUI display with cloud compute)
- Point-of-Sale systems
- Industrial PCs
- Kiosks located in malls and transit centers that display information for users
- Automotive in-vehicle infotainment
- Smart lighting
- Smart speakers
- Smart appliances
- Human machine interface for automation
- Augmented reality/virtual reality

On the other hand, Wi-Fi may not be applicable for use cases that require

- High mobility such as from cars to a roadside infrastructure

- Very long range (>100 meters between devices) such as agricultural sensors

- Ultra-low power/very long battery life

- Low data rates

- Low duty cycles

Wi-Fi Standards Bodies

Wi-Fi is based on the IEEE 802.11 standards.[4]

The corresponding product certification and marketing is done through the Wi-Fi Alliance.[5]

Both global alignment on the technical standards and the mechanism for certifying that products meet these standards are necessary for developing the Wi-Fi ecosystem.

Wi-Fi Generations

Previously, different generations of Wi-Fi technology were denoted by the name of the IEEE 802.11 standard: 802.11a, b, g, n, ac, ax, etc. The association of the IEEE standard with Wi-Fi capabilities was not clear to the public outside of the technical community. In order to improve consumer recognition of Wi-Fi versions, the **Wi-Fi Alliance** has numerically designated each generation of Wi-Fi as shown in Table 3-2.

---

[4]www.ieee802.org/11/
[5]www.wi-fi.org/

Table 3-2. Summary of Wi-Fi standards[6]

Protocol	Frequency Bands (GHz)	Channel Widths (MHz)	Modulation	MIMO	Maximum Data Rate Mbps for 2x2 Client Device(Theoretical)	Year Introduced
802.11-1997	2.4	20	Frequency Hopped Spread Spectrum (FHSS)/Direct Sequence Spread Spectrum (DSSS)	N/A	2	1997
Wi-Fi 1 (802.11b)	2.4	20	Complementary Code Keying (CCK)	N/A	11	1999
Wi-Fi 2 (802.11a)	5	20	OFDM	N/A	54	1999
Wi-Fi 3 (802.11g)	2.4	20	OFDM	N/A	54	2003
Wi-Fi 4 (802.11n)	2.4 and 5	20 and 40	OFDM	Single User (SU-MIMO) 4x4	450 (3x3, 40MHz channel)[3]	2009
802.11ac Wave 1	5	20, 40, 80	OFDM	Downlink Multi User (MU-MIMO) 4x4	1300[2]	2014

Wi-Fi 5 802.11ac Wave 2	5	20, 40, 80, 160	OFDM	Downlink Multi User (MU-MIMO) 4x4	2340[2]	2016
Wi-Fi 6 (802.11ax)	2.4 and 5	20, 40, 80, 160	OFDMA	Downlink and Uplink Multi User (MU-MIMO)	2400[1]	2019
Wi-Fi 6E	2.4, 5, and 6	20, 40, 80, 160	OFDMA	Downlink and Uplink Multi User (MU-MIMO)	2400[1]	2020
Wi-Fi 7 (802.11be Extremely High Throughput)	2.4, 5, and 6	20, 40, 80, 160	OFDMA	Downlink and Uplink Multi User (MU-MIMO)	30000[1]	2024
Wi-Fi HaLow (802.11ah)	0.9	1, 2, 4, 8 and 16	OFDMA	Downlink and Uplink Multi User (MU-MIMO) 4x4	347	2017
WiGig (802.11ad)	60	2160	Single Carrier, Low Power Single Carrier, OFDM	N/A	6750	2012

[6]www.intel.com/content/www/us/en/support/articles/00005725/network-and-io/wireless-networking.html

Table 3-2 summarizes the different Wi-Fi generations in terms of key attributes: frequency bands that are supported, channel widths (which translate to data rates), modulation type, and MIMO (Multiple Input Multiple Output) type.

Figure 3-1 provides a similar perspective on the evolution of Wi-Fi data rate vs. the year that each Wi-Fi standard was launched. It is important to note that since the launch of Wi-Fi in 1999, the data rate has increased by 3 orders of magnitude over 20 years.

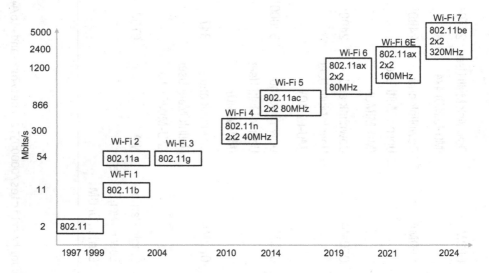

Figure 3-1. *Depiction of generations of Wi-Fi standards*

History of Wi-Fi: Aloha Network

The origins of Wi-Fi can be traced back to the **Aloha** network that was developed by Norman Abramson at the University of Hawaii in the 1970s.[7] The Aloha net was a packet-based radio network that was used to transmit

---

[7] Abramson, "THE ALOHA SYSTEM—Another alternative for computer communications*."

data between terminals located on campuses of the University of Hawaii distributed across the various Hawaiian Islands and a central time-shared computer.

The key contribution of the Aloha net was enabling the geographically scattered terminals to share a radio channel without a complex time multiplexing control system between terminals. Packets were sent by each terminal without any coordination; the received packets at the central computer were checked for accuracy using **parity check** bits attached to each packet and if they were received correctly an acknowledgment was sent back to the transmitting terminal. If no acknowledgment was received at the transmitting terminal from the central computer after a certain amount of time, it was assumed that the packet was not received due to network congestion (another packet sent at the same time) or noise and the packet was retransmitted. This scheme, with subsequent improvements, is still used today for Wi-Fi.

Other references on the invention of Wi-Fi include.[8,9,10]

Wi-Fi Standards of Interest

Certainly, there is overlap in the Wi-Fi standards and features that are used between consumer, enterprise, and IoT applications. In this section, we focus on the relevant Wi-Fi standards and features for IoT applications.

---

[8] www.thoughtco.com/who-invented-wifi-1992663
[9] https://airtame.com/blog/wifi-facts/
[10] www.roamingman.my/news/index/id/40

802.11bgn

The older generations of Wi-Fi include IEEE 802.11 b/g/n standards (i.e., Wi-Fi 1 to Wi-Fi 4) that are typically lumped together in *value* Wi-Fi products. These Wi-Fi modules have a price point in the $1 US range and are key ingredients in smart appliances, smart switches, smart bulbs, and other consumer applications.

These applications may be cost sensitive and are adequately served by data rates offered by the older generations of Wi-Fi standards. Support for only the 2.4GHz band is sufficient which reduces the cost of the radio. Because these devices may have been around for several years, they are less expensive to manufacture and have been well proven.

It is important to note that because succeeding generations of Wi-Fi APs (access points) are backwards compatible to the older standards, 802.11 b/g/n products will continue to be supported on Wi-Fi networks for years to come. In fact, IoT Wi-Fi market projections indicate that 802.11 b/g/n products will continue to be widely used through 2024.[11]

802.11ac or Wi-Fi 5

The 802.11ac standard, later denoted as "Wi-Fi 5" by the Wi-Fi Alliance, is an updated Wi-Fi standard in the 5GHz band. The standard was approved in two Waves:

- Wave 1, launched in 2013: Includes 80MHz channels, 256QAM modulation, and a maximum data rate of 1.3Gbps

---

[11] Andrew Zignani, "Wireless Connectivity Semiannual Update," ABIresearch, October 18, 2019.

- Wave 2, launched in 2016: Includes optional support for 160MHz bands, MIMO support for four spatial streams, Downlink Multi-User MIMO with support for up to four clients, and a maximum data rate of 2.34Gbps.

As of the end of 2020, Wi-Fi 5 products are still in wide use for IoT applications such as Point-of-Sale devices.

802.11ax or Wi-Fi 6 (2019)

The most current Wi-Fi standard is Wi-Fi 6 which is based on the IEEE 802.11ax specification and was approved in 2019.

Wi-Fi 6 is otherwise known as High Efficiency Wi-Fi and addresses the limitations of previous generations of Wi-Fi in supporting a large number of users.

Wi-Fi 6 offers key improvements over Wi-Fi 5 including maximum data rate of 9.6Gbps that is obtained via 160MHz channel bandwidths and 1024QAM modulation.

- Orthogonal Frequency Division Multiple Access (OFDMA) is a bandwidth allocation technique that is used in cellular standards. While Wi-Fi 5 divided bandwidth among users strictly by time, OFDMA enables channel resources to be allocated in both time and frequency. This results in more efficient allocation of bandwidth and gives each competing user a better chance of accessing the network.

- Uplink Multi User MIMO enables multiple client devices to simultaneously transmit their data to the Access Point without interfering with each other.

- Transmission Scheduling based on trigger frames enables centralized management of downlink and uplink transmissions and improved efficiency compared to the purely best effort scheduling techniques of previous versions of the Wi-Fi.

- BSS Colors enables spatial division multiplexing by specifying that user devices are associated with a specific color or Access Point; this becomes important when client devices are at the edge of the coverage area of one Access Point and close to the coverage area of an adjacent Access Point.

- Target Wake Time is a feature that is valuable for battery-powered IoT devices. Instead of remote devices keeping their Wi-Fi radios on continuously and draining their batteries, TWT enables the devices to sleep and wake up at pre-set intervals to send their data to the AP.

Wi-Fi 6E (2020)

Wi-Fi 6E is the Extended version of Wi-Fi 6 and adds the new 6GHz unlicensed band for Wi-Fi. This new band provides 1.2GHz of bandwidth for unlicensed radio technologies and is being approved in various countries around the world starting in 2020. The addition of this band increases the total bandwidth available to Wi-Fi to 2GHz and reduces Wi-Fi congestion in crowded networks and offers a tremendous advantage for high throughput applications.

A summary of Wi-Fi bands is shown in Table 3-1.

Table 3-3. *Wi-Fi bands*

Band	Lower Freq (MHz)	Upper Freq (MHz)	Total Bandwidth (MHz)
2.4	2400	2500	100
5	5150	5895	745
6 (USA and others)	5925	7125	1200
6 (European Union	5925	6425	500

While Wi-Fi 6 offers improvements in Quality of Service over Wi-Fi 5, Wi-Fi 6 still suffers the limitations of the 2.4 and 5GHz unlicensed bands. In particular, the 5GHz band offers limited support for 80 and 160MHz channels.

The Wi-Fi Alliance notes: "6GHz addresses Wi-Fi spectrum shortage by providing contiguous spectrum blocks to accommodate 14 additional 80 MHz channels and 7 additional 160 MHz channels which are needed for high-bandwidth applications that require faster data throughput such as high-definition video streaming and virtual reality."[12,13]

---

[12] www.testandmeasurementtips.com/what-you-should-know-about-wi-fi-6-and-the-6-ghz-band/

[13] www.techradar.com/uk/news/wi-fi-6e-looks-to-use-6ghz-spectrum-for-even-faster-wireless-connections

The country approvals for either all or part of the 6GHz band is continuing; through July 2021, the current update is shown as follows:[14]

- 5.925 to 7.125 GHz

  - Countries that have fully adopted this band include Brazil, Canada, Chile, Costa Rica, Guatemala, Honduras, Peru, Saudi Arabia, South Korea, and United States.

  - Countries that are considering this band include Australia, Colombia, Japan, Jordan, Kenya, Mexico, and Qatar.

- 5.925 to 6.425 GHz

  - Countries that have fully adopted this band include Argentina, European Union (*only adopting 5945-6425), Norway, Peru, United Arab Emirates, and United Kingdom.

  - Countries that are considering this band include CEPT (*only adopting 5945-6425), Egypt, Morocco, New Zealand, Oman, and Turkey.

Wi-Fi 6E Release 2 (2022)

The Wi-Fi Alliance recently announced the approval of Wi-Fi 6E Release 2.[15] The Release 2 standard includes Uplink Multi User MIMO. As noted earlier, UL-MIMO enables client devices to concurrently send their uplink data to the same access point. For IoT applications, this feature is important for time-critical applications like sensors or cameras that are uploading data to an Edge gateway.

---

[14] www.wi-fi.org/countries-enabling-wi-fi-6e

[15] www.wi-fi.org/news-events/newsroom/wi-fi-certified-6-release-2-adds-new-features-for-advanced-wi-fi-applications

The updated release also includes power optimization modes including Target Wake Time in which devices remain in sleep mode until waking up to transmit data at an agreed time. This feature is valuable for battery-powered sensors that must efficiently manage their power consumption.

Wi-Fi 7 (802.11be)

Even as Wi-Fi 6 is being rolled out, efforts are underway to develop Wi-Fi 7. Wi-Fi 7 corresponds to the IEEE 802.11be standard. The Wi-Fi 7 standard is targeted to be completed in 2024.

Wi-Fi 6 offered improvements in network efficiency and did not offer significant data rate upgrades vs. Wi-Fi 5. In contrast, Wi-Fi 7 will offer a maximum data rate of 46Gbps, a 5x improvement over Wi-Fi 6. This higher data rate is achieved through a combination of a higher order 4096QAM modulation, 320MHz channel bandwidth, and 16x16 Multi User-MIMO.[16]

Wi-Fi 7 will also offer lower latency, which is particularly beneficial for IoT applications such as machine controllers, robotics, and augmented and mobile reality.

Another key Wi-Fi 7 feature is Multi Link Operation which enables a client device to simultaneously connect to multiple APs using multiple client radios. This capability enables higher data rates as well as redundancy for use cases where the device is moving between APs such as mobile robots.

---

[16]www.fiercewireless.com/sponsored/wi-fi-7-next-generation-evolution-wi-fi

In January 2022, MediaTek announced publicly that it is testing its Wi-Fi 7 implementation.[17] It is expected that Wi-Fi vendors will start to launch their Wi-Fi 7 products in 2023.

Impact of Wi-Fi 6 Chip Shortages in 2021–2022

Silicon shortages impacted the Wi-Fi industry in 2021–2022: the combination of increased demand for Wi-Fi connectivity due to workers and families working and attending school from home due to Covid-19, inaccurate planning of silicon wafer quantities, and supply chain limitations.

The silicon shortages may stall the ramp up of Wi-Fi 6E products in 2022. Since Wi-Fi 7 products may launch in 2023, it is possible that customers may skip Wi-Fi 6E and go directly to Wi-Fi 7 products.[18]

Determining Which Wi-Fi Standards Are Supported by a Module

The design engineer considers which features are required for the product, which Wi-Fi standards are required to support the use case, and then which Wi-Fi standards are supported by a candidate module. The Wi-Fi Alliance maintains a list of modules that have been certified, and this list is readily available and is a valuable resource for the developer.[19]

---

[17] https://corp.mediatek.com/news-events/press-releases/mediatek-shows-the-worlds-first-live-demos-of-wi-fi-7-technology-to-customers-and-industry-leaders

[18] www.tomshardware.com/news/-wifi7-enroute-deloro

[19] www.wi-fi.org/

Wi-Fi System Architecture

The typical Wi-Fi system consists of

- One or more Wi-Fi Access Points (APs) that provide wireless coverage over the venue.

- The APs may be connected via an Ethernet switch to the Internet Service Provider.

- Multiple Client devices in Station (STA) mode that connect to the AP.

- The APs may be connected as a Wi-Fi mesh network in order to extend coverage of the venue.

- The Wi-Fi system operates in either the 2.4GHz, 5GHz, or the new 6GHz band. In some cases, the AP supports two or more of these bands concurrently. In this case, the client device can select which band to use.

- The Wi-Fi network is identified by its SSID (Service Set Identifier). The SSID can be a default name based on the AP manufacturer or it can be set by the owner of the network (e.g., *Anil_Network*).

- The SSID has an associated password that is set by the network owner.

- The network owner can create multiple Virtual LANs using one AP in order to partition the traffic.[20] For example, the network owner at a retail store may create a VLAN for employees and another VLAN for guests or customers. Each VLAN is designated by a different SSID.

---

[20] www.tp-link.com/us/support/faq/1607/

- The client device can scan for available SSIDs to connect to.

- Client devices need to be authenticated before they are given access to the Access Point.

- In some cases, a client device can connect directly to another client device in peer-to-peer (P2P) or Wi-Fi Direct mode. P2P mode can be used for direct file transfer or content sharing between two devices such a phone and a wireless printer.

- If the site is large enough to require multiple APs such as an office or factory and the client devices are mobile, then client devices and APs will need to support handoff.

Wi-Fi Stack

As seen in Figure 3-2, the 802.11 Wi-Fi standard implements Layers 1 (Physical Layer) and 2 (Data Link Layer).[21]

---

[21] https://blogs.arubanetworks.com/industries/layer-1-and-layer-2-wifi-basics/

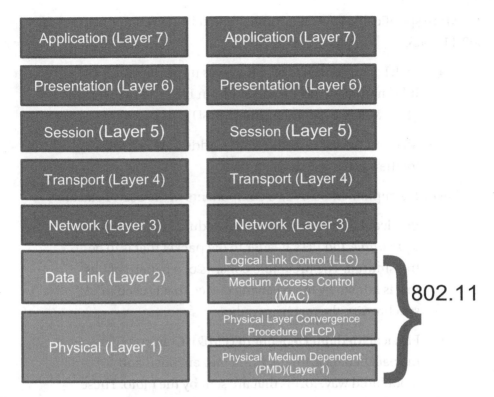

Figure 3-2. *Depiction of the Wi-Fi protocol stack. Layers 1 and 2 are implemented in the Wi-Fi stack*[22]

The Layers 3–7 are based on TCP/IP and are implemented in the host processor, the network, the gateway, and the cloud.

---

[22] www.google.com/search?q=drawing+of+OSI+model+wi-fi+802.11ac&tbm=isch
&ved=2ahUKEwj1urrjx_XoAhXVnJ4KHaVZCOOQ2-cCegQIABAA&oq=drawing+of+OSI+
model+wi-fi+802.11ac&gs_lcp=CgNpbWcQDFDf4wpY3e4KYPT6CmgAcAB4AIABRYgB-
AKSAQE2mAEAoAEBqgELZ3dzLXdpei1pbWc&sclient=img&ei=pNOcXvXYNdW5-gSls6H
oDg&bih=668&biw=1600#imgrc=f1YywTuRW5osnM

More specifically, Layer 2 is implemented by two components of the 802.11 stack:

- Link Layer Control (LLC): Receives upper layer information including packets from Layer 3 in the form of the Mac Service Data Unit (MDSU).

- Medium Access Control (MAC): Adds MAC addresses for the source and destination.

Layer 1 is implemented by two components of the 802.11 stack:

- Physical Layer Convergence Procedure (PLCP): Adds a *preamble* and PHY header to the packet that is to be transmitted. The preamble consists of a pattern of bits that is known by the receiving device that is used to synchronize the receiving radio.

- Physical Medium Dependent (PMD): Converts the packet data from the PLCP into encoded and modulated waveforms that are sent by the radio. These waveforms are designed to be reliably received at the other device.

Wi-Fi Software Stack

The OSI layers are implemented in hardware and software on the Access Point and client STA devices. We will describe the Wi-Fi software stack as implemented on open source Linux. We will discuss the Linux implementation since it is most widely used for IoT applications; a basic understanding is useful for most developers who need to integrate their device and software stack with the Wi-Fi stack.

We reference open source libraries where developers can find commands that can be used to customize the Wi-Fi stack for their applications.

The Wi-Fi stack is shown in Figure 3-3 and can be divided into three sections:

- User Space

- Kernel Space

- Wi-Fi Hardware

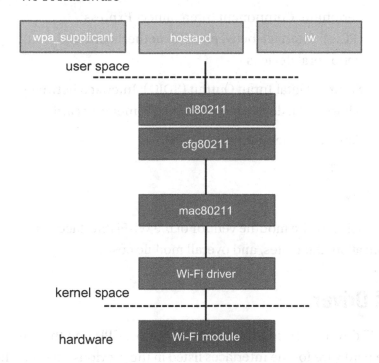

Figure 3-3. *Depiction of Wi-Fi software stack in Linux*

In an embedded device, the wireless architecture consists of a Wi-Fi module connected to the host CPU or microcontroller. In this architecture, the kernel space functions are implemented in the Linux operating system. The User Space is where IoT applications run, and these applications are integrated with the Wi-Fi stack via APIs.

167

Wi-Fi Module

The Wi-Fi module is the self-contained implementation of the Wi-Fi Physical and MAC layers. The host interfaces the Wi-Fi module via the Wi-Fi driver which provides both control and data to and from the Wi-Fi module.

The interfaces used on the Wi-Fi module are defined by specific standards. The most common Wi-Fi interfaces used by module vendors are shown as follows:

- Peripheral Component Interconnect Express (PCIe): Interface between a PC motherboard and peripheral devices

- Secure Digital Input Output (SDIO): Interface between a host and a device based on the SD memory card[23]

- Serial Peripheral Interface (SPI)

- UART

- USB

The choice by the module vendor of the Wi-Fi interface depends upon the application, data rates, and overall module costs.

Wi-Fi Driver

The Wi-Fi driver is the conduit between the host CPU and the Wi-Fi module hardware for the interfaces listed in the previous section. The Wi-Fi driver is developed by the Wi-Fi module vendor and is specifically developed for the operating system.

---

[23] https://en.wikipedia.org/wiki/SD_card#SDIO_cards

Wi-Fi drivers may be open source or proprietary. Some of the upstreamed Wi-Fi drivers can be found at linux.com.[24]

The Wi-Fi drivers that are available from kernel.org can be found here.[25]

The next sections list key aspects of the Linux Wi-Fi stack.

mac80211

The *mac80211* framework implements the API for software-based MAC implementations.

For additional details on mac80211, please see.[26]

cfg80211

The API for configuring the Wi-Fi module in Linux is *cfg80211*. Some of the key Wi-Fi parameters that set via *cfg80211* include whether 20, 40, 80, or 160 MHz bandwidths are allowed in a channel; channel definitions include center frequency, max antenna gain, max power, whether a beacon is found, and whether the Dynamic Frequency Selection (DFS) radar detection is required on a channel and many more parameters.

More details can be found here.[27]

---

[24] http://linuxwireless.sipsolutions.net/en/users/Drivers/

[25] https://mirrors.edge.kernel.org/pub/linux/network/wireless/

[26] https://wireless.wiki.kernel.org/en/developers/documentation/mac80211

[27] www.kernel.org/doc/html/latest/driver-api/80211/cfg80211.html

nl80211

nl80211 is the netlink interface public header and is used in conjunction with *cfg80211* and *iw* to configure the client Wi-Fi module.

nl80211 includes *testmode* that can be used for validation and factory testing of the Wi-Fi module.

Additional details on *nl80211* can be found here.[28]

iw

iw is a new command line interface utility that is used to configure a client Wi-Fi module. The *iw* utility replaces *iwconfig*.

Additional information on *iw* can be found here.[29]

wpa_supplicant

wpa_supplicant is the utility for connecting the client Wi-Fi device to an Access Point and includes authentication and encryption based upon WPA, WPA2, and WPA3 security standards and EAP (Extensible Authentication Protocols).

For more information on *wpa_supplicant*, please see this reference.[30]

hostapd

The *hostapd* software application is used to create a Wi-Fi hot spot or "Soft Access Point." For IoT applications, Soft AP can be used on an Edge Gateway to connect sensors or video cameras via Wi-Fi.

---

[28] https://wireless.wiki.kernel.org/en/developers/documentation/nl80211
[29] https://wireless.wiki.kernel.org/en/users/documentation/iw
[30] https://linux.die.net/man/8/wpa_supplicant

Authentication of client devices via wpa and wpa2 is also included in hostapd.

Additional information on *hostapd* can be found here.[31]

Virtualization: Connecting Containers to Wi-Fi

In traditional client devices, the host operating system includes kernel functions to interface to the Wi-Fi driver and the Wi-Fi radio and user applications that interface to Wi-Fi run in the user space and are scheduled by the host OS.

A more recent trend is to implement virtualization on the host machine in which virtual machines or containers run on top of the host operating system. These containers may implement another operating system called the Guest Operating System. The advantage of virtualization is to consolidate functions that run on a set of different processors which may require different operating systems and programming environments to run as virtual machines on a common processor.

In the next sections, we will shift gears and discuss some Wi-Fi's capabilities.

Wi-Fi Range

The effective range of Wi-Fi is a key consideration in IoT use cases. Can we use Wi-Fi to reliably transmit data from a Point-of-Sale terminal in a shopping mall back to the gateway? How about sending data to a smart switch at the other end of the office building?

---

[31] http://w1.fi/hostapd/

As we discussed in Chapter 2, the link equation is used to calculate the range of a Wi-Fi system. For Wi-Fi, we can use three bands in the link equation: 2.4, 5, and 6GHz. The channel bandwidths will vary from 20, 40, 80, and 160MHz.

The following examples discuss the effective range of Wi-Fi in the different bands that are available.

EXAMPLE 1: WI-FI RANGE IN THE 2.4GHZ BAND

Can Wi-Fi be used to transmit 4K 1080p video from a camera with a Wi-Fi 5 radio at a distance of 50 meters over an open field without obstructions in the 2.4GHz band with a 20MHz channel? Please refer to Table 3-4.

Let us assume that we need at least 25Mbits/s to stream 4K 1080p video over Wi-Fi.[32] Accounting for the difference between raw throughput and effective TCP throughput of 60%, we can use 802.11n MCS4 which has a data rate of 43Mbits/s with a 400ns Guard Interval.

We will perform the link calculation using the Texas Instruments WL1837 MOD Wi-Fi 5/Bluetooth module.[33] From the data sheet for this module, we can find the following:

- For Wi-Fi at 2.4GHz for MCS4 (43.3Mbits/s with 400ns Guard Interval and 20MHz bandwidth[34]) in SISO mode, the radio has an output transmit power of 15.3dBm.

- The sensitivity for Wi-Fi at 2.4GHz MCS4 in SISO mode is -78.0dBm in a 20MHz bandwidth with a packet error rate of <10%.

- Assume that the gain of the integrated antenna for both transmitter and receiver is 1.26dBi.

---

[32] www.usatoday.com/story/tech/columnist/2017/12/10/youre-buying-4-k-tv-how-much-internet-bandwidth-do-you-need/933989001/

[33] www.ti.com/document-viewer/WL1837MOD/datasheet

[34] https://en.wikipedia.org/wiki/IEEE_802.11n-2009

Table 3-4. Link margin calculation for Wi-Fi Example 1

Component	Value	Units
$P_{TX}dB$	15.3	dBm
$G_{TX}dB$	1.26	dBi
$L_{TX\,cable}dB$	0	dB
$G_{RX}dB$	1.26	dBi
$L_{RX\,cable}dB$	0	dB
$L_{free}dB$ (d=50m)	74.03	dB

$L_{free}dB = 20 \times log_{10}(d) + 20 \times log_{10}(f) + 20 \times log_{10}(4\pi/c)$
$= 20 \times log_{10}(d) + 20 \times log_{10}(f) + 147.55$
$= 74.03$dB for d=50m and f=2.4x10^{9}Hz
The received power is $P_{RX}dB$ =-56.2dBm.

To achieve the packet error rate of 1×10^{-1} requires a received signal power of -78dBm. Thus, on an open field, there is approximately -56.2- (-78)=22dB of link margin, and **the signal should be received correctly**.

EXAMPLE 2: WI-FI RANGE IN THE 5GHZ BAND

Can Wi-Fi be used to transmit 1080p video from a camera with a Wi-Fi 5 radio at a distance of 50 meters over an open field without obstructions in the 5GHz band with a 20MHz channel? Please refer to Table 3-5.

- For Wi-Fi at 5GHz for MCS4 (43.3Mbits/s with 400ns Guard Interval and 20MHz bandwidth) in SISO mode, the radio has an output transmit power of 16.5dBm.

173

- The sensitivity for Wi-Fi at 5GHz MCS4 in SISO mode is -79.8dBm in a 20MHz bandwidth with a packet error rate of <10%.

Table 3-5. *Link margin calculation for Wi-Fi Example 2*

Component	Value	Units
P_{TX}dB	16.5	dBm
G_{TX}dB	1.26	dBi
$L_{TX\ cable}$dB	0	dB
G_{RX}dB	1.26	dBi
$L_{RX\ cable}$dB	0	dB
L_{free}dB (d=50m)	80.7	dB

- $L_{free}dB = 20 \times log_{10}(d) + 20 \times log_{10}(f) + 20 \times log_{10}(4\pi/c)$

- $= 20 \times log_{10}(d) + 20 \times log_{10}(f) + 147.55$

- $= 80.7$dB for d=50m and f=5.2x10^{9}Hz

The received power is $P_{RX}dB$ =-61.7dBm.

To achieve the packet error rate of 1×10^{-1} requires a received signal power of -79.8dBm. Thus, on an open field there is approximately -61.7- (-79.8)=18dB of link margin and **the signal should be received correctly**. Note that the link margin has been reduced from 22 to 18 dB using the 5GHz mode instead of 2.4GHz.

EXAMPLE 3: WI-FI RANGE IN THE 6GHZ BAND

Can Wi-Fi be used to transmit 1080p video from a camera with a (hypothetical) Wi-Fi 6 radio at a distance of 50 meters over an open field without obstructions in the 6GHz band with a 20MHz channel? Please refer to Table 3-6.

- For Wi-Fi at 6GHz for MCS4 (43.3Mbits/s with 400ns Guard Interval and 20MHz bandwidth) in SISO mode, let us *assume* the radio has an output transmit power of 16.5dBm (at the time of this writing, there are only a small number of Wi-Fi 6E radios with published specs).

- The sensitivity for Wi-Fi at 6GHz MCS4 in SISO mode is -79.8dBm in a 20MHz bandwidth with a packet error rate of <10%. (Same comment applies.)

- Let us use the 20MHz channel at 6.775GHz for this analysis.

Table 3-6. Link margin calculation for Wi-Fi Example 3

Component	Value	Units
P_{TX}dB	16.5	dBm
G_{TX}dB	1.26	dBi
$L_{TX\,cable}$dB	0	dB
G_{RX}dB	1.26	dBi
$L_{RX\,cable}$dB	0	dB
L_{free}dB (d=50m)	83.0	dB

- $L_{free}dB = 20 \times log_{10}(d) + 20 \times log_{10}(f) + 20 \times log_{10}(4\pi/c)$

- $= 20 \times log_{10}(d) + 20 \times log_{10}(f) + 147.55$

- $= 83.0$dB for d=50m and f=6.775x10⁹Hz

The received power is $P_{RX}dB$ =-64.2dBm.

To achieve the packet error rate of 1×10^{-1} requires a received signal power of -79.8dBm. Thus, on an open field there is approximately -64.2- (-79.8)=15.8dB of link margin and **the signal should be received correctly**. Note that the link margin has been reduced from 18 to 15.8 dB using the 6GHz mode instead of 5GHz and from 22 to 15.8 dB using the 6GHz mode instead of 2.4GHz.

As we noted in Chapter 2, obstructions such as trees, walls, buildings, etc. can reduce the received signal power significantly. For example, drywall can attenuate the 2.4GHz signal by 5dB, and if there are three walls between the Access Point and the Client device, the link margin is severely reduced.

One method of mitigating the range limitations is via Wi-Fi mesh which is discussed in the next section.

DYNAMIC FREQUENCY SELECTION (DFS)

The 5GHz Wi-Fi band is not completely available all of the time as weather and military radars also use specific channels in this band. The channels that are used for radar depend upon the country and are shown in Table 3-7.

Wi-Fi Access Points in outdoor environments are designed to check for radar signals in the 5GHz band before using the channels shown in Table 3-7 using Dynamic Frequency Selection (DFS).

The tests that the AP needs to perform to detect radar signals are outlined in this reference[35] and require numerous trials; the tests can take anywhere from 1 to 10 minutes.[36] If radar is detected, the AP will send an announcement to connected STA devices that they are supposed to switch channels and then the BSSID is switched to an available channel.

---

[35] https://wireless.wiki.kernel.org/en/developers/dfs#dfs_requirements_world_wide

[36] www.tp-link.com/us/support/faq/763/

For the Wi-Fi system integrator, frequency planning in the 5GHz band includes weighing the risk of using the DFS channels for high priority traffic that might have to be switched if radar signals are detected by the AP.

Table 3-7. *DFS channels (after[37])*

Band	Channel	Frequency
U-NII-1	36	5180
	40	5200
	44	5220
	48	5240
U-NII-2 DFS Required	52	5260
	56	5280
	60	5300
	64	5320
U-NII-2e DFS Required	100	5500
	104	5520
	108	5540
	112	5560
	116	5580
	120	5600
	124	5620
	128	5640

(continued)

---

[37] www.tp-link.com/us/support/faq/763/

Table 3-7. (*continued*)

Band	Channel	Frequency
	132	5660
	136	5680
	140	5700
U-NII-3	149	5745
	153	5765
	157	5785
	161	5805
	165	5825

Wi-Fi Mesh

In the previous section, we calculated the Wi-Fi range in different frequency bands. In order to extend the coverage area of a Wi-Fi network to greater distances, we consider Wi-Fi mesh.

The most common Wi-Fi network topology is a star with the AP at the center and client devices that connect to the AP; the clients do not connect to one another directly.

In a mesh, the client devices are mesh nodes that are able to connect to other mesh modes. The mesh nodes are aware of other nearby mesh nodes and packets are sent from the source node to a nearby mesh node and forwarded between mesh nodes until they arrive at the destination node.

Wi-Fi mesh is defined by the 802.11s standard and is discussed in the sidebar. The size of the coverage area for the mesh network is defined by the number of hops from the end device on one side of the network and the mesh portal that connects to the Internet on the other side of the network. The system designer needs to understand the tradeoff between the number of mesh hops and the increase of delay and the reduction in bandwidth.

ONE PAGER ON WI-FI MESH

Given the prevalence of Wi-Fi mesh products from Google, Orbi, etc., it is worthwhile to send a little time discussing some of the key concepts. As shown in Figure 3-4, a Wi-Fi mesh consists of

- Mesh portal: Provides a conduit between the mesh and the Internet

- Mesh nodes: Implement the Wi-Fi mesh stack based on the 802.11s standard

- Mesh APs: Provide connectivity to non-mesh STA devices

Each mesh node can communicate with its nearest neighbors.

Any node that receives commands or sends data from/to the server needs to connect to the Mesh Portal (Node 0.) Nodes that have no direct connection to Node 0 due to distance or blockage may need to send its data over multiple mesh nodes. Each transmission path between two nodes is defined as a hop.

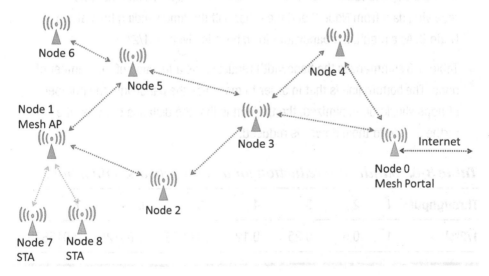

Figure 3-4. *Depiction of a Wi-Fi mesh network*

The mesh software stack incorporates (a) discovery of mesh nodes, (b) routing of data between two nodes, and (c) security to enable authorized nodes to join the network.

The Wi-Fi mesh radio operates on either 2.4 or 5GHz. More expensive radios can concurrently support both 2.4 and 5GHz. Let us consider a single radio example first.

Two potential issues with Wi-Fi mesh are (a) latency, the time it takes to traverse multiple hops in the network, and (b) bandwidth reduction over multiple hops.

For mesh nodes that have a single radio, the same channel is used for receiving data from one node and transmitting data to the next node. In this case, with two hops the bandwidth is reduced by ½ as the node spends half its time receiving and the other half its time transmitting.

Consider the process of sending data from Node 3 to Node 0 via Node 2 and Node 1. Node 2 spends half the time receiving data from Node 3 and the other half the time sending it to Node 1. With another hop from Node 1 to Node 0, the bandwidth is reduced by another ½ as Node 1 spends half the time receiving data from Node 2 and the other half the time sending the data to Node 0. As a result, the bandwidth for n hops is given by $1/2^{(n-1)}$.

Table 3-8 summarizes the bandwidth reduction as a function of the number of hops. The bottom line is that in order to maximize the bandwidth the number of hops should be minimized; the tradeoff is that the distance between the furthest node to the gateway is reduced.

Table 3-8. *Bandwidth reduction for a mesh network with n hops*

Throughput	1	2	3	4	5	6	7
$1/2^{(n-1)}$	1	0.5	0.25	0.125	0.0625	0.03125	0.015625

ONE PAGER: THE PROCESS OF CONNECTING A WI-FI DEVICE

Most readers are familiar with connecting their mobile device to a Wi-Fi network at home, school, work, hotel and airport terminal, etc.: open the "settings" window on their device which displays available Wi-Fi networks. They then select a network with sufficient "number of bars" (signal strength) and enter a password to gain access. What is happening behind the scenes? This section provides additional details on this process.

As noted in this reference,[38] a mobile device must be both authenticated and associated with the Access Point in order to send data to the Access Point. The mobile device and the AP exchange a series of management frames in order for the AP to authenticate the mobile device and then for the mobile device to associate with the AP.

The process of authentication begins with the mobile device sending probe requests to nearby networks. These probe requests indicate the data rates and 802.11 capabilities of the device.

In response, nearby APs reply with the SSID (wireless network name), supported data rates, encryption types, and 802.11 capabilities of the AP.

Smartphone users will see the available networks displayed including the network names. The next step will be for the user to select a network to use.

---

[38] https://documentation.meraki.com/MR/WiFi_Basics_and_Best_
Practices/802.11_Association_Process_Explained#:~:text=A%20mobile%20
station%20sends%20probe,802.11%20networks%20within%20its%20
proximity.&text=If%20they%20have%20compatible%20data,802.11%20
capabilities%20of%20the%20AP

The device sends an association request to the AP that it would like to connect with. If the device and AP have similar capabilities, then the AP creates an Association ID for the mobile device, and the mobile device is granted access to the network.

At this point, additional security authentication based on WPA/WPA2/WPA3 or 802.1X may be required.

Wi-Fi Authentication

Authentication is the process of validating that a device has credentials to access a network as well as validating the network for the device.[39] Of particular interest for this book is authenticating IoT devices on a Wi-Fi network.

For Wi-Fi networks, the 802.1X specification defines the authentication framework, and the Extensible Authentication Protocol (EAP) defines approximately 40 methods for authenticating a device.

The 802.1X specification defines three components in the authentication process:[40]

- Supplicant is the device attempting to access the network.

- Authenticator is the gatekeep to the network.

- Authentication server maintains a database of authorized devices.

---

[39] www.techrepublic.com/article/understanding-and-selecting-authentication-methods/

[40] www.arubanetworks.com/techdocs/ArubaOS_85_Web_Help/Content/arubaos-solutions/802-1x/unde-802_1x-auth.htm#802.1x_1833088626_1016891

Some EAP authentication methods are EAP-MD-5, EAP-TLS, EAP-PEAP, EAP-TTLS, EAP-Fast, and Cisco LEAP.[41]

Wi-Fi Security

Security is a critical enabling feature for Wi-Fi. As Wi-Fi devices are widely used in many public environments such transportation hubs, airports, and public buildings, they are an attractive target for adversaries.

A common perception is that Wi-Fi security is not as robust as licensed cellular standards such as LTE. This perception is due to security incidents due to rogue access points and the use of obsolete authentication protocols.[42]

Over the years, improved Wi-Fi security standards have been developed and incorporated into the WFA certification process and are summarized in Table 3-9.

---

[41] www.intel.com/content/www/us/en/support/articles/000006999/network-and-i-o/wireless.html

[42] https://us.norton.com/internetsecurity-wifi-public-wi-fi-security-101-what-makes-public-wi-fi-vulnerable-to-attack-and-how-to-stay-safe.html

Table 3-9. *Summary of Wi-Fi security standards*

Wi-Fi Security	Description	Comments
WEP[43] (Wired Equivalent Privacy)	Approved in September 1999. 64-bit encryption	Least secure method; retired in 2004
WPA[44] (Wi-Fi Protected Access)	256-bit WPA-PSK (Pre-Shared Key)	Superseded in 2006
WPA2	128-bit AES encryption keys	• Superseded WPA in 2006 • Vulnerable to the KRACK security attack
WPA3-Personal and WPA3-Enterprise[45]	• Protected Management Frames (PMF) for all network types • Dragonfly Key Exchange is resistant to dictionary-based attacks • Forward secrecy prevents an adversary from recording traffic for decryption later • 128-bit AES for WPA3-Personal • 192-bit security for WPA3-Enterprise	Required for all new Wi-Fi CERTIFIED™ devices on 1 July 2020

(continued)

[43] https://community.fs.com/blog/wep-vs-wpa-vs-wpa2-vs-wpa3.html
[44] www.makeuseof.com/tag/wep-wpa-wpa2-wpa3-explained/
[45] www.wi-fi.org/discover-wi-fi/security

Table 3-9. (*continued*)

Wi-Fi Security	Description	Comments
WAPI (WLAN Authentication and Privacy Infrastructure)	Has three independent elements: STA, AP, and Authentication Service Unit (ASU), to ensure authentication security. Encryption keys are generated after negotiation. WAPI authentication uses the SMS4 algorithm and supports 802.1X authentication applying to a large-scale network.[46]	Note that the standard is not available outside the People's Republic of China (PRC)[47]
Wi-Fi CERTIFIED Enhanced Open	Uses Opportunistic Wireless Encryption (OWE) to encrypt all communication, even on open networks	

As of this writing (2022), the WPA3 standard is required for all new Wi-Fi products that are being certified. WPA3 mitigates a key vulnerability in WPA2.

Readers are probably familiar with the temptation to use an open (unsecure) Wi-Fi network in an airport or hotel. Certainly, this practice is highly discouraged. If there are no safer alternatives, then it is recommended that the reader should use VPN to encrypt data to and from their device. In addition, the new Wi-Fi Enhanced Open standard that has been approved by the WFA in 2018 should be used to encrypt the traffic between the user's device and the AP, even on an open network.

---

[46] https://support.huawei.com/enterprise/en/doc/EDOC1000060368/80e6ae28/what-are-advantages-and-disadvantages-of-wapi-authentication
[47] www.wi-fi.org/download.php?file=/sites/default/files/private/Opportunistic_Wireless_Encryption_Specification_v1.0.pdf

---

MORE ON WPA3 SECURITY

Security is top-of-mind for IoT applications that use Wi-Fi to transport sensitive financial data in retail environments or manufacturing control data in industrial use cases.

As we have noted, the introduction of WPA3-Personal and WPA3-Enterprise improve upon WPA2 to provide improved network security.

Two areas of concern are (1) denial of service attacks that overwhelm a network and (2) brute force password attacks in order to gain access to the network.

WPA3 mitigates both of these areas of concern:

WPA3 defines a WPA3-Enterprise192-bit mode for applications that require increased security such as government and industrial operations.

Best Effort Wi-Fi

Wi-Fi is spoken of as a "best effort" protocol. What does this mean and how does this affect the user experience for Wi-Fi?

Earlier, we described the advantages of the original Aloha net: a simple approach for sending data from geographically dispersed terminals without the need for a complex and potentially expensive network management capability. If a device has a packet to send, it sends the packet over the shared radio channel and waits for an acknowledgment from the destination that the packet was received correctly; if the acknowledgment is not received over a specified period of time, the device assumes that its packet was affected by a collision with the packet from another device and resends the original packet.

Wi-Fi versions up to Wi-Fi 5 used this "best effort" approach called **Carrier Sense Multiple Access with Collision Avoidance** (CSMA-CA): a device with data to send listens to the shared radio channel to see if any other devices were sending packets and if the channel is clear, it sends its message; if another device is sending data, then wait a random time after the channel clears before sending a message.[48]

Note that Ethernet LAN uses a similar approach called **Carrier Sense Multiple Access with Collision Detection** (CSMA-CD). In the case of Ethernet, the device is able to monitor the shared medium and determine if its transmitted packet was affected by the packet from another device in the network.

It is apparent that the "best effort" approach, while simple and easy to implement, has limitations compared to a managed network: latency (the time the packet is sent to the time the packet is received correctly at the destination) is variable. This lack of determinism is an issue for time-sensitive applications such as controlling robots and production machinery in factories or augmented reality where data are overlaid on a real-time image. Later we will discuss techniques for mitigating these latency and determinism issues.

Bandwidth Allocation

As most people are aware, due to Covid-19 in 2020-2021, many workers and their families worked and attended school from home. For many households, this meant that family members were concurrently attending working and school voice and video calls over Skype, Microsoft Teams, Cisco Webex, and Zoom. Schoolchildren also had to watch YouTube videos as part of their classroom learning. Furthermore, the shelter in

---

[48] https://en.wikipedia.org/wiki/Carrier-sense_multiple_access_with_collision_avoidance

place meant that family members did additional entertainment and web surfing from home. As a result, most people experienced the direct effects of Wi-Fi network congestion on a daily basis.

It is helpful to understand how bandwidth is allocated among many users and devices, and the strategies for mitigating home network congestion due to the Covid-19 Work from Home mode can be applied to improving the overall performance of an IoT Wi-Fi-based network.

By default, all devices in a given BSSID have an equal opportunity to send their packets. This means that there is no priority to any specific types of traffic and that as network traffic increases there be a point at which packets are not received correctly on their first, second, third, etc. retransmission. In this situation, the users experience glitches in their video or audio as packets are dropped, leading to the common refrain: "My kids have started their online classes which is my important work presentation call dropped right in the middle of the key slide for my boss."

Quality of Service Improvements

We noted that originally Wi-Fi did not incorporate any capabilities for prioritizing traffic and all packets were treated the same. Later, the increasing use of video and voice over Wi-Fi created a need to support different levels of Quality of Service.

The 802.11e amendment that was added in 2005 provided QoS improvements for Wi-Fi.[49] In particular, 802.11e provides

- Transmit Opportunity (TXOP): Time interval that a station can use to send as much data as possible

- Specification of traffic into Access Categories: Voice, video, best effort, and background

---

[49] https://en.wikipedia.org/wiki/IEEE_802.11e-2005

Packets to be sent are prioritized from lowest to highest priority: background, best effort, video, and voice. Each packet type is assigned to a queue to await transmission. The highest priority voice and video packets are sent during a TXOP when the transmitting station is allocated time to send as much data as it can.

The Wi-Fi Alliance has certified the 802.11e feature as Wireless Multimedia (WMM).[50]

Key Wi-Fi Features

The following sections describe some of the key features of Wi-Fi that are applicable to IoT use cases.

Wi-Fi Roaming

Earlier we discussed the process of the client device authenticating and associating with the AP when joining a network. Consider IoT use cases where the client device uses Wi-Fi in a facility with multiple APs:

- A sales associate uses a mobile Point-of-Sale terminal to enter customer transactions that are uploaded to a gateway via Wi-Fi while roaming a large warehouse store

- An Autonomous Mobile Robot (AMR) traverses the floor of a distribution center while connected via Wi-Fi to a server that is providing instructions on which products to check.

---

[50] https://en.wikipedia.org/wiki/Wireless_Multimedia_Extensions

- A maintenance worker in a factory is connected via voice to her supervisor via her Wi-Fi enabled tablet using Voice over IP (VoIP).

Certainly, a disconnect during a voice or video call could be annoying while an interruption for an AMR could be catastrophic if it is fulfilling a critical task while moving between APs.

How It Works

In order to avoid a disconnect while roaming between APs, fast roaming capabilities that are certified by the WFA are required. These capabilities are based on the IEEE 802.11r, 802.11k, and 802.11v specifications:

- 802.11r: Fast BSS Transition defines procedures for the Wi-Fi device to quickly establish security and Quality of Service parameters with a neighbor AP.[51]

- 802.11k: Radio resource management – the Wi-Fi device measures the signal levels of the access point that it is connected to or it asks its current access point for a "neighbor report" on the signal levels of neighboring access points.[52] This process enables the Wi-Fi device to not waste time or energy scanning for neighbor APs.

- 802.11v: Includes capabilities for the AP to enable the Wi-Fi device to sleep longer by extending the idle period without the need to send "keep alive" packets to

---

[51] https://blogs.cisco.com/networking/what-is-802-11r-why-is-this-important
[52] https://blogs.cisco.com/networking/why-the-802-11k-and-neighbor-report-are-important

the AP and thus conserve battery power and transition messages to the Wi-Fi device on transitioning to the neighbor AP.[53,54]

Collectively known as "rkv," 802.11rkv enables rapid handoffs between APs and minimize glitches while the client devices are moving. These are part of the "Voice-Enterprise" WFA certification.

Soft Access Point or Wi-Fi Hot Spots

Many Wi-Fi client devices can also act a "Soft" Access Point (vs. a true hardware-based Access Point) or Wi-Fi Hot Spot. In some cases, the client device is capable of concurrently acting as both a client station and a soft AP – the device is connected to an Access Point as a station while also acting as a Soft AP for other devices.

There are natural limitations with the Soft AP mode when compared to a true Access Point:

- The number of client devices that can be supported by the Soft AP is limited to around 8 due to the software implementation of the AP functions.

- Because the device switches between client and soft AP mode, only a fraction of the frame is available which limits the number of slots that can be allocated among the client devices.

- Because the client device typically has 1 or 2 antennas, the MIMO capability is constrained when compared to a real AP that has four or more antennas.

---

[53] www.arubanetworks.com/techdocs/ArubaOS_6_5_3_X_Web_Help/Content/ArubaFrameStyles/VirtualAPs/BSS_Transition_Management_(80211v).htm
[54] www.cisco.com/c/en/us/td/docs/wireless/controller/9800/config-guide/b_wl_16_10_cg/802-11v.pdf

Enabling Soft AP

Earlier, we discussed using *hostapd* to turn on then Soft AP mode in Linux.

Applications of Soft AP for IoT

Soft AP has a number of applications, including the following:

- Enabling a small number of client devices to connect to a gateway via Wi-Fi Soft AP. The gateway may be connected to cloud via a wired Ethernet connection or a cellular connection, or it may also act as a Wi-Fi client device that is connected to an Access Point.

- Commissioning of a device via a smartphone can be done by first setting the device to be commissioned to soft AP mode, allowing the installer's phone to connect to it, configuring via the smartphone including connecting the device to the main access point, and then setting it to STA mode.

Wi-Fi Provisioning for IoT Devices

Provisioning of Wi-Fi on a user device means connecting the device to a Wi-Fi Access Point. Most readers are familiar with the process of connecting their phone or PC to an AP: go to the *Settings* menu, go to the Wi-Fi menu, search for networks, select the correct network, and enter a password. This method of provisioning Wi-Fi for a PC or phone relies on a Graphical User Interface and a display to enable the user to select the network and enter a password.

The challenge is for provisioning Wi-Fi for IoT devices that are *headless*: they have no user interface or display due to form factor and size constraints. Examples of headless devices include Smart Home light switches, light bulbs, thermostats, Smart Agriculture sensors, and Smart City video cameras.

For all of these use cases, the provisioning process has to be secure so that only the IoT device (vs. hacker adversaries who are trying to gain access to the network) is allowed to connect to the network. At the same time, the provisioning process has to be convenient and scalable to facilitate adding a large number of IoT devices to the network.

For headless devices, the following sections describe some methods for provisioning Wi-Fi. For additional details, please see this reference.[55]

Wi-Fi Protected Setup (WPS) Push Button Method

Wi-Fi Protected Setup (WPS) was developed by the Wi-Fi Alliance in 2006 to enable headless IoT devices to be provisioned. WPS defines two methods to provision Wi-Fi:

1) Enter a PIN that is printed on the AP exterior into the IoT device via a keypad on the IoT device.

2) Push button mode that is used if both the Access Point and the IoT device support the feature. When the buttons are pushed simultaneously on both the AP and the device, the IoT device has 2 minutes to connect to the AP. Please see Figure 3-5.

Advantages: Both the PIN and the Push Button methods are straightforward for installers to use to provision the network.

---

[55] Gil Reiter, "A primer to Wi-Fi ° provisioning for IoT applications," Texas Instruments.

Disadvantages: PIN method-a security flaw was uncovered in 2011 in which the PIN was susceptible to a brute force attack. Because of this flaw, the WPS PIN method is no longer supported. Push Button Method – since it requires the IT person to push the WPS button on the AP whenever a new device is added to the network, it might be physically challenging if the AP is permanently located on the ceiling or other difficult to access location. Also, when the button is pushed on the AP, there is a 2-minute window when any device, including an adversary, can access the network.

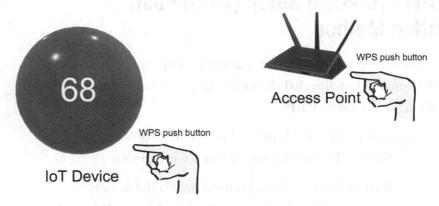

Figure 3-5. Depiction of WPS Push Button to provision the Wi-Fi network for the IoT Device. When the push buttons on both the AP and the IoT device are pressed, the IoT Device can join the network

Access Point Mode

In this method, the IoT device is initially configured as an Access Point after it has been reset. Resetting the device may require hitting a physical reset button.

The IoT AP name and the corresponding password may be in the product documentation or listed on the device packaging. The installer uses another device such as a phone or laptop and finds and connects to the device AP which brings up a webpage. The installer enters in the network name and password for the final network to connect the IoT device to the network. When the new configuration is enabled, the IoT device no longer appears as an AP and instead appears as a client device on the network.

Advantages: This method is secure as the installer, using his or her phone, enters in the information to connect the device to the network and at no time is security for the network compromised. Also, physical access to the IoT device is required to hit the reset button in order to enable the AP mode and to set its network connection. Note: this is also a disadvantage if the IoT device is installed in a difficult-to-reach location. Finally, physical access to the AP, which may be difficult if the AP is permanently installed on a ceiling, is not required as in the case of WPS.

Disadvantages: If the device needs to be reconfigured if there is a change to the Access Point infrastructure, then physically hitting the reset button may be challenging if the IoT device is installed in a difficult to access location. Also, the method does not lend itself to easy scaling as each device needs to be provisioned through the same process.

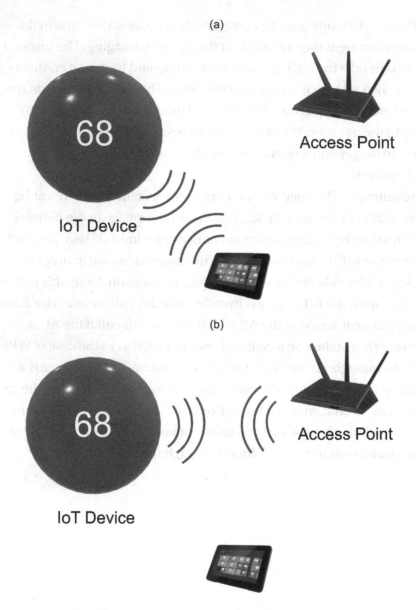

Figure 3-6. *Depiction of Access Point mode to provision the Wi-Fi network for the IoT Device: (a) IoT devices act as an AP that the user's tablet connects to; the user configures the connection to the AP; (b) the IoT device is reconfigured as a client device connected to the AP*

Wi-Fi Certified Easy Connect

The WFA launched Easy Connect in 2020 as a replacement for WPS.[56],[57]
Easy Connect was developed to enable provisioning of headless IoT
devices. Please see Figure 3-7.

Easy Connect defines a *Configurator* that is used to set up the network.
The Configurator can be implemented on a phone or tablet. Because of its
role in provisioning the network, the Configurator is backed up securely so
that it can be used to reconfigure the network in the future.

Easy Connect also defines *Enrollees* which are either Access Points and
client devices that are part of the network.

Provisioning the network requires the following steps:

1. Initial enrollment of AP: The Configurator enrolls an
   AP to establish the network.

2. Enrollment of additional devices: The Configurator
   enrolls other devices that are enabled to join the
   network.

In order to enroll a device to the Wi-Fi network, the Configurator
establishes mutually authenticates each Enrollee via a bootstrapping
process. Easy Connect devices include a QR code that could be a sticker on
the device that is readable by a camera on the Configurator. The app on the
Configurator uses this information, which includes a public key, in order
to authenticate the Enrollee which can then join the network.

---

[56] Wi-Fi CERTIFIED Easy Connect™ Technology Overview
[57] Wi-Fi Easy Connect™ Specification Version 2.0

Alternatively, the Configurator could display a QR code that can be read by a camera on the Enrollee. The example discussed in the Easy Connect Technology Overview is the display of the QR code on a display in a hotel room that the enrollee device could read in order to join the network.

Easy Connect also supports bootstrapping via NFC or BLE.

Advantages: When mutual authentication is used in the bootstrapping process, Easy Connect provides a secure connection between the Configurator and the Enrollee. Once each device is enrolled, it is easy to reconfigure them if the network changes. Physical access to the devices after they have been enrolled is not necessary.

Disadvantages: It seems that the process of enrolling numerous devices via the QR codes could be time consuming. However, Easy Connect supports using multiple Configurators that could speed this up.

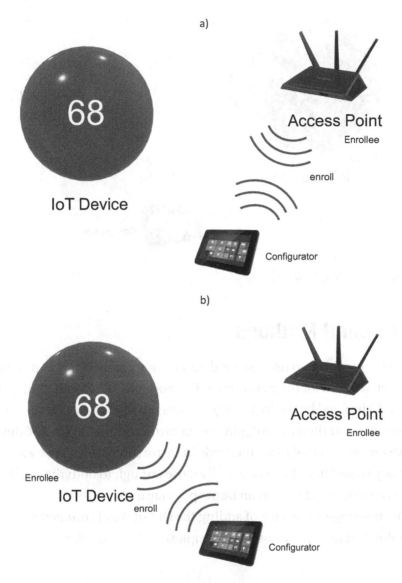

Figure 3-7. *Depiction of East Connect to provision the Wi-Fi network for the IoT Device. (a) The AP is enrolled by the Configurator that is hosted on a tablet, (b) the IoT device is enrolled by the Configurator, and (c) the IoT device and the AP are connected*

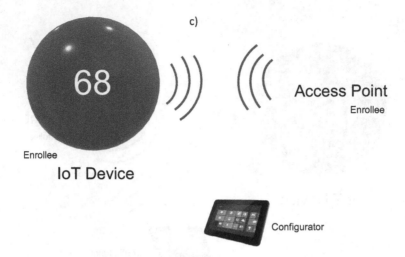

Figure 3-7. *(continued)*

Out of Band Methods

Another approach is to use a second connectivity technology to provision the Wi-Fi network for the new device. For example, Bluetooth, RFID, or USB could be used by the installer to connect to the IoT device via a phone or computer and then to configure the network settings on the IoT device.

Advantages: Out of Band methods increase security because an adversary would have to be physically close enough to both the device and AP to provision the device in an improper manner.

Disadvantages: The cost of adding the Out of Band connectivity technology increases the cost and complexity of the solution.

Proprietary Methods

Texas Instruments offers its proprietary SmartConfig technology that is used to provision TI IoT devices: an app on the installer's phone sends the SSID information of the network that the phone is connected to from the phone to the unprovisioned device.[58]

Advantages: As TI indicates, the SmartConfig technology can provision multiple devices simultaneously which makes it more scalable than the other methods that we have discussed.

Disadvantages: Only available for TI devices.

Wi-Fi Direct

In most cases, a Wi-Fi network requires an Access Point for client devices to connect to. The AP is connected to the Internet Service Provider via a backhaul; for example, the backhaul may be via a cable modem, satellite connection, or cellular modem.

Wi-Fi Direct is a feature that enables two client devices to connect directly without an Access Point. One application of Wi-Fi Direct for consumers is to use this capability are file or photo sharing between two people.

Applications

In the IoT space, potential applications include the following:

- Kiosk: Enabling a user to print a boarding pass or ticket from their smartphone at a kiosk at an airport or train station without the need to connect to the network.

---

[58] https://software-dl.ti.com/ecs/CC3200SDK/1_5_0/exports/cc3200-sdk/example/provisioning_smartconfig/README.htm

- Data download from a sensor or video camera: For a remote sensor that is out of regular wireless coverage that stores measurement data or video over a period of time, the data can be downloaded to a collection device via Wi-Fi Direct.

- Content download to a car: While stopped at a gas station or electric charging station, updated video, podcasts, audio, etc. can be downloaded from the facilities to the car via Wi-Fi Direct.

How It Works

The Wi-Fi Direct Specification from the Wi-Fi Alliance defines how this feature works.[59]

Miracast

Miracast is the name for the capability defined by the Wi-Fi Alliance for streaming content from one device to another via Wi-Fi.[60] IoT applications of Miracast include the following:

- Streaming videos to digital signage in a store

- Streaming content from the car Invehicle Infotainment (IVI) system to passengers with tablets

Miracast is built on other Wi-Fi capabilities including 802.11ac, Wi-Fi Direct, WMM, WPS, and WPA2. Wi-Fi Direct support is required on devices that are supporting Miracast.

---

[59] Wi-Fi Direct® Specification Version 1.8
[60] Wi-Fi CERTIFIED Miracast™ Technical Overview

Location Using Wi-Fi: 802.11mc Fine Time Measurement

Consider the use of Wi-Fi to measure the location of an object or person in a venue:

- Tracking the location of high value inventory in a warehouse or distribution center

- Tracking the location of specific patients (who accept being tracked) in a hospital

- Tracking the location and dwell time of consumers (who opt in to provide this data) in a store or shopping mall

- Tracking the location of workers (who accept being tracked by their employer) in an office to determine if socially distancing is maintained to mitigate Covid-19 issues

- Tracking the location of workers in a factory to ensure the manufacturing operation is safe and efficient

- Identifying locations in a stadium where people traffic is congested such as restrooms and snack bars

- Geofencing-sounding an alarm if a worker or asset leaves a specific area

There are many potential benefits to being able to track objects and people using Wi-Fi technologies. However, a key point is that in the case of people the privacy laws of the jurisdiction (city, state, and federal) must be enforced and that participants must opt in.

How Is It Done?

Estimating the location of an asset using wireless technology requires measuring the distance between the asset and at least three reference points, where the position coordinates (x, y, z, t) of the reference points are known.

The distance of the asset to the reference points can be estimated from the wireless signal by the received signal strength or the propagation time of a packet from the AP to the device.

RSSI measurements, while relatively simple, require calibration of the receiver and assume that there is a direct line of sight between the AP and the client device.

Time of Flight measurements using Fine Time Measurements as defined in the 802.11mc standard improve the accuracy of location estimates to approximately 1 meter.

802.11p DSRC

The rise of autonomous vehicles in the latter half of the 2010s has led to an increase in efforts to connect vehicles to other vehicles (V2V) and from vehicles to infrastructure (V2X).

Dedicated Short-Range Communications (DSRC) is wireless standard similar to Wi-Fi for communications from moving vehicles to roadside infrastructure and is based on the IEEE 802.11p standard.

In 2004, the FCC allocated 75MHz from 5.850 to 5.925 GHz for intelligent transportation systems which is divided up into seven 10 MHz channels.

DSRC uses 52 subcarrier OFDM with data rates from 3 to 27 Mb/s. The range is estimated to be up to about 300 meters.[61]

---

[61] www.mwrf.com/technologies/systems/article/21848325/the-battle-over-v2v-wireless-technologies

The original goals were to provide for wireless communication from vehicles with[62]

- Latency<0.02 seconds

- Limited interference

- Strong performance under adverse weather

One of the key use cases for DSRC is to communicate between vehicles for collision avoidance and to prevent accidents. For V2V applications, the transmitted data include the exact vehicle location and direction of travel, speed, and braking status. For V2X applications, the transmitted data might include weather, road, and traffic conditions.

Other DSRC use cases include toll collection, parking payment, and rental car payment.

While the Wi-Fi-based implementation was proven over the years since the DSRC spectrum was allocated, there was an increase in interest in a cellular-based implementation. As a result of this uncertainty on aligning the industry towards DSRC, the technology was never fully adopted.

As a result, at the end of 2020, the FCC effectively ended DSRC by allocating the lower 45 megahertz of the band for unlicensed use and the upper 30 megahertz for intelligent transportation systems that must use C-V2X technology.[63] The FCC argued that the auto industry in the United States has failed to use the DSRC spectrum in the 21 years that it had been available at that only 15,000 vehicles were equipped for DSRC in the United States.[64]

---

[62] https://connectedvehicle.devpost.com/details/understanding-dsrc
[63] www.rcrwireless.com/20201119/wireless/its-official-dsrc-is-out-c-v2x-and-wi-fi-sharing-is-in-at-5-9-ghz
[64] https://en.wikipedia.org/wiki/IEEE_802.11p

Wi-Fi Sensing

Imagine using the Wi-Fi signal to detect the presence and movement of people and pets in your house or apartment for "peace of mind" applications for home security. Furthermore, imagine if the Wi-Fi signal could non-invasively detect a person falling or breathing and potential applications for home health monitoring.

This is the promise of Wi-Fi sensing (being standardized as IEEE 802.11bf), which uses measurements of the properties of the Wi-Fi signal as it is affected by objects between the Access Point and a client device to detect movement and occupancy of an area. In contrast to cameras that capture and store images, Wi-Fi sensing techniques offer better privacy and perhaps would be more acceptable to residents of a home.

Technology

One approach to Wi-Fi sensing uses Channel State Information (CSI) that measures the multipath characteristics of the space between the Access Point and a client station. The CSI measurements will include people and their movements in this space and by storing and analyzing the CSI data with machine learning the correlation of the CSI with human characteristics can be determined.

Applications of Wi-Fi Sensing

Some of the key applications for Wi-Fi sensing include

- "Peace of Mind" – home security: Detecting the presence and movement of people in a home

- Elder care: Detecting if a person falls in a hospital room or home and triggering an alert to a caregiver

206

- PC wake and lock: Detecting whether a person in front of a PC moves and locking the device and waking up the PC when the person returns

- Traffic analysis: Detecting if people are congregating in front of a digital sign or display to determine if the digital ad is attracting eyeballs

Wi-Fi Reliability and Latency

Most Wi-Fi users can tolerate the occasion glitch and loss of connectivity during an online meeting or voice call that is made using Wi-Fi. However, for use cases that are either time sensitive or where human safety is at stake, providing robust reliability and minimal latency is essential. Some of the use cases are shown in Table 3-10.

Industry 4.0 is an effort to modernize manufacturing that combines Operational Technology with Information Technology and heavily defines the integration of computation and communications into the manufacturing infrastructure. Wireless technology is essential in this vision because it has the potential to enable rapid reconfigurability of the manufacturing line, reduces the expense of installing wired connectivity, and helps to accelerate the use of mobile robots that can improve efficiency.[65]

---

[65] https://avnu.org/wireless-tsn-paper/

Table 3-10. *Wi-Fi use cases and reliability and latency requirements (based upon Avnu)*[66]

Use Case	Reliability	Latency
Autonomous Mobile Robot	99 to 99.9%	10-100ms
Closed Loop Control (Programmable Logic Controllers)	99.9 to 99.9999%	1-10ms
Power Grid	99 to 99,8%	4-8ms
ProAV	99.99%	0.25-2ms

Putting Together an IoT Solution with Wi-Fi

We have covered some of the key Wi-Fi features and discussed the applicability of Wi-Fi as part of an IoT solution. To solidify the discussion, we will walk you through a solution that uses Wi-Fi.

Consider the following use case: the owner of a food truck would like to upgrade her connectivity. She would like to connect digital signage around the truck showing her menu, specials, future events, videos, etc. She would also like to enable customers to order using either a Point-of-Sale tablet mounted to the truck exterior or via an app that runs on phones. She would also like to position wireless webcams around the truck to gauge the crowds around the truck. To enable Wi-Fi access, she will also have a Wi-Fi hot spot enabled that customers can connect to. Preferred customers can connect to the Soft AP and she is notified when these customers connect and these customers could receive rewards. To handle the financial transactions, the Wi-Fi has to be secure.

---

[66] Cavalcanti, et al., *Avnu Alliance® White Paper Wireless TSN – Definitions, Use Cases & Standards Roadmap*, Version #1.0 – Mar 4, 2020.

Her solution is to add an Edge server into her truck with a Wi-Fi 6 client module and a 5G cellular modem. The 5G modem provides the backhaul from her Edge server to the network.

The Edge server runs Linux Ubuntu. Separate docker containers are used for the food ordering system and the digital signage content.

Figure 3-8 depicts the food truck solution. The key Wi-Fi features in her solution include

- Soft Access Point mode to connect to the Mobile Point of Sale terminal

- Soft Access Point mode to connect to customer devices that are used for ordering

- Miracast connections to her digital signage displays mounted to the sides of the truck

- Connections to webcams mounted on the sides of the truck

- WPA3 security

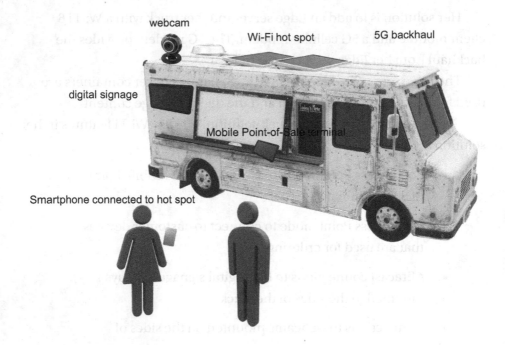

Figure 3-8. Food truck use case showing Wi-Fi connections

The Future of Wi-Fi

The rise of 5G (3GPP Release 16) cellular technologies has created the perception of an either-or conflict between Wi-Fi and 5G, particularly for IoT products. In a future edition of this book, we will discuss 5G technologies and the application of Private 5G devices for many IoT use cases.

In the meantime, some of these myths are listed as follows:[67]

- Cellular is more secure than Wi-Fi.

- Cellular is simpler to manage than Wi-Fi.

---

[67] https://spectrum.ieee.org/telecom/wireless/the-long-goodbye-of-wifi-has-begun

- 5G provides lower latency and better reliability than Wi-Fi.

Certainly, some of these perceptions may be valid based on earlier generations of Wi-Fi. However, ongoing improvements that are available in Wi-Fi 6/6E enable Wi-Fi to be as secure as cellular, improve Wi-Fi network management and reduce Wi-Fi latency, and improve Wi-Fi reliability with respect to 5G.

For many IoT use cases, we expect that deployments will incorporate cellular and Wi-Fi capabilities that play to the strengths of each technology:

- Large outdoor venues: How much area must be covered and how many Access Points are required?

- Infrastructure costs: What are the costs for client modules, Access Points, repeaters, and cabling if needed?

- Data rates: What is the bandwidth per device and the total number of devices? For example, will the devices be uploading HD video?

- Mobility: Will the devices be moving and if so what is the expected velocity and the frequency of handoffs between Access Points?

- Operating Costs: What are costs for network service, bandwidth, and management?

Wi-Fi beyond Wi-Fi 7 will continue to evolve, and we expect Wi-Fi to complement other wireless technologies including 5G.

Summary

In this chapter, we have presented an overview of Wi-Fi for IoT applications. Certainly, Wi-Fi can be applied to many use cases that require high throughput and a moderate range between a device and a gateway. Because Wi-Fi technology is mature and widely used, there are economies of scale that produce reduced prices for components.

For applications that use low data rates and have low power requirements, there are other technologies that are more applicable such as LoRA, Bluetooth, and 802.15.4. We will explore these technologies in subsequent chapters and versions of this book.

Problem Set

1. You are to design the connectivity solution for a battery-powered soil sensor that is 1km from a gateway that transmits 64bytes for 10 seconds every hour. Would you consider a Wi-Fi solution for this use case? Why or why not?

2. Consider a use case where you are assigned to provide diagnostics to a refrigerator. The refrigerator needs to connect to a network without any access to the home infrastructure. What technology would you recommend and why?

3. Now suppose that you have a means of provisioning the Wi-Fi in the refrigerator to enable it to attach to the customer's home Wi-Fi network. What technology would you select?

4. You are asked to implement the Wi-Fi network for a brand-new American football stadium that seats 50,000 fans. Suppose each fan is receiving a live video stream of different cameras on their smartphone via Wi-Fi 6 for the duration of the game and uploading photos and videos. Assuming that the fans are spaced uniformly throughout the stadium, what is the total network capacity required? How many access points would be required to cover the stadium?

CHAPTER 4

Bluetooth

Introduction

In a fast-moving digital world, it is hard to imagine our day-to-day lives without a smartphone. Thanks to the technological advancements that have made smartphones the center of attention and more than a necessity in our daily lives.

One of the key features that most smartphone users is familiar with is Bluetooth. Consumers benefit from Bluetooth technology by pairing and connecting the Bluetooth headset with smartphone for hands-free calling, by streaming music to their ear buds and Bluetooth speakers or car audio system from smartphone, by connecting smartphone to fitness tracker to collect vital signs, and so on.

In contrast to cellular and Wi-Fi which are primarily used to connect devices to Internet, Bluetooth is a *Wireless Personal Area Network* and is widely used for short-range wireless communication and for device-to-device communication in a number of Internet of Things applications demanding reliable, secure, scalable, low power, and low cost wireless communication.

A. Kumar et al., *Connecting the Internet of Things*,
https://doi.org/10.1007/978-1-4842-8897-9_4

This chapter will cover Bluetooth technology which is the most popular and widely used consumer technology for short-range wireless communication. We will discuss the two variants of Bluetooth technology: Bluetooth Classic and Bluetooth Low Energy (LE). However, the emphasis and focus will be Bluetooth LE as well as its application and suitability for various IoT use cases.

The goal of this chapter is to help the reader establish an understanding of the following aspects of Bluetooth technology:

- Basics of Bluetooth technology

- Bluetooth Classic vs. Bluetooth LE

- Key features of Bluetooth LE

- Suitability of Bluetooth LE for IoT applications

- Key considerations for building an IoT device with Bluetooth

- Getting started with Bluetooth LE

- Bluetooth Certification

Bluetooth Technology

Bluetooth is a short-range wireless communication technology that operates in 2.4 GHz unlicensed Industrial, Scientific, and Medical (ISM) frequency band. Wi-Fi and 802.15.4-based wireless standards also share this band.

Brief History

The name "Bluetooth" was proposed by Jim Kardach of Intel in 1997, and the development of this technology began in 1989 at Ericsson Mobile with the motivation to wirelessly connect a headset with a mobile phone.[1] The standard is named after Harold Bluetooth who was the second king of Denmark. At the time, the names that were being considered for the new standard were "MC-Link," "Biz-RF," and "Low Power RF." The name was selected because of the influence of Scandinavian companies (Nokia and Ericsson along with Intel) who were involved in the creation of the standard and most importantly had not been previously trademarked.

Bluetooth SIG

Bluetooth was initially standardized as IEEE 802.15.1 and later was adopted by Bluetooth Special Interest Group (SIG) in 1998. The Bluetooth SIG was founded in 1998 with five member companies including Intel, Ericsson, IBM, Nokia, and Toshiba.

Bluetooth is a global standard, and the Bluetooth SIG oversees the development of Bluetooth standard specification, drives Bluetooth interoperability through interoperability events and qualification program, and promotes the Bluetooth brand by increasing the adoption of Bluetooth technology.

The Bluetooth SIG maintains its own website (www.bluetooth.com) that provides information on Bluetooth-specific topics, links to standard specifications, and other technical details.

---

[1]https://blog.snapeda.com/2019/10/07/how-bluetooth-got-its-name-an-interview-with-jim-kardach/

Bluetooth Markets

Key Bluetooth markets include the following:

- Smart home

- Smart cities

- Smart buildings

- Smart industries, smart agriculture, smart farming

- Automotive

- Industrial automation

- Smart lighting

- Smart appliances

- Audio and entertainment

- Connected devices and IoT

- Phones, tablets, and PCs

ABI Research predicts that approx. 6.2 billion Bluetooth-enabled devices will ship in 2024 alone representing 8% CAGR since 2019.[2]

ABI Research also predicts that approx. 7.5 billion cumulative Bluetooth LE single-mode devices will ship from 2020 to 2024 with a 26% CAGR.[3]

---

[2] www.bluetooth.com/wp-content/uploads/2020/03/2020_Market_
Update-EN.pdf

[3] www.bluetooth.com/wp-content/uploads/2020/03/2020_Market_
Update-EN.pdf

Bluetooth Applications

In the beginning, Bluetooth was primarily used for the following applications:

- Connect a mobile phone with a Bluetooth headset for hands-free calling.

- Connect a mobile phone with a Bluetooth headset, ear buds, or Bluetooth speaker for wireless music streaming.

- Connect a mobile phone with a Bluetooth-enabled car audio system for hands-free calling and wireless music streaming.

- Connect peripherals like keyboard and mouse to a computer wirelessly.

- Connect a mobile phone to a printer, or connect a computer to a printer for wireless printing.

Today Bluetooth wireless technology is found in many consumer electronic devices such as smartphones, TVs, cameras, printers, digital picture frames, smart watches, fitness trackers, medical devices, and so on.

Bluetooth primarily supports two modes of operation:

1. Bluetooth Classic (Basic Rate/Enhanced Data Rate, or BR/EDR)

2. Bluetooth Low Energy (LE) formerly Bluetooth Smart

Bluetooth Classic

Bluetooth Classic,[4] or Bluetooth Basic Rate (BR)/Enhanced Data Rate (EDR), technology was originally developed as a short-range point-to-point wireless technology for mobile phones, computers, and accessories like Bluetooth headsets, Bluetooth speakers, keyboards, and mice. Bluetooth has become the de facto standard for wireless streaming of voice and audio with wireless speakers, wireless headphones, and in-car infotainment systems.

Bluetooth Classic leverages a robust Frequency Hopping Spread Spectrum (FHSS) approach and transmits data over 79 channels with 1MHz channel spacing. The Bluetooth Classic radio includes multiple PHY options that support data rates from 1 Mb/s to 3 Mb/s and supports multiple power levels, from 1mW to 100mW, multiple security options, and a point-to-point network topology.

Bluetooth Classic establishes a relatively short-range, continuous wireless connection, which makes it ideal for use cases such as streaming audio from a smartphone to a Bluetooth headset or speaker.

Bluetooth Classic technology was never optimized for low power applications requiring battery-powered devices for IoT such as 1-to-many, and machine-to-machine (M2M) communication in a secure, reliable, and scalable wireless network. To support these new use-cases, the Bluetooth SIG developed Bluetooth Low Energy (LE) technology and introduced it in Bluetooth specification version 4.0 released in 2010. Bluetooth LE enables short burst of wireless connections as well as data broadcast.

---

[4]www.bluetooth.com/learn-about-bluetooth/bluetooth-technology/radio-versions/

Bluetooth Low Energy (LE)

Bluetooth LE is a short-range low power version of Bluetooth technology for connecting devices wirelessly. Bluetooth LE technology allows exchange of short bursts of data, making it ideal for IoT applications requiring longer battery life. Bluetooth LE is meant for situations where long battery life is preferred over high data transfer speeds or longer range. Bluetooth LE is not suitable for use cases and applications requiring the transfer of large amounts of data.

Bluetooth LE was introduced in Bluetooth Specification version 4.0 released in 2010. The goal of Bluetooth LE is to provide low-power, low data rate, and reliable wireless communication which is a key requirement of many IoT use cases.

Like Bluetooth Classic, Bluetooth LE operates in 2.4 GHz ISM band but are not compatible with each other.

The Bluetooth LE radio leverages a robust Frequency Hopping Spread Spectrum (FHSS) approach that transmits data over 40 channels with 2MHz channel spacing as shown in Figure 4-1.

The Bluetooth LE radio offers more PHY flexibility than Bluetooth Classic, including multiple PHY options that support data rates from 125 Kbps to 2 Mbps, multiple power levels, from 1mW to 100mW. Bluetooth LE also supports multiple network topologies, including point-to-point, broadcast, and mesh networking.

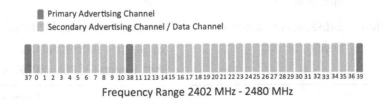

Figure 4-1. Depiction of BLE channels in the ISM band

After the introduction of Bluetooth LE in 2010, it was quickly adopted by smart phones and tablets, and it enabled new markets and applications like wearable devices, sports and fitness trackers, and beacon applications. Bluetooth LE-based sensors can run on coin-cell batteries for months and even years. Some of these sensors are so efficient that the kinetic energy from flipping a switch can provide operating power.

Comparison of Bluetooth Classic and Bluetooth LE

Table 4-1 provides a key comparison of the two versions of the Bluetooth technology.

Table 4-1. *Comparison of BLE and Bluetooth Classic*[5]

	Bluetooth Low Energy	Bluetooth Classic Basic Data Rate/ Enhanced Data Rate
Frequency band	2.4GHz ISM band (2.402 to 2.480GHz)	2.4GHz ISM band (2.402 to 2.480GHz)
Channels	40 channels with 2 MHz spacing (3 advertising channels/37 data channels)	79 channels with 1 MHz spacing
Channel usage	Frequency Hopped Spread Spectrum (FHSS)	Frequency Hopped Spread Spectrum (FHSS)
Modulation	Gaussian Frequency Shift Keying (GFSK)	Gaussian Frequency Shift Keying (GFSK), π/4 Differential Quadrature Shift, Keying (DQPSK). 8PQPSK

(*continued*)

---

[5]www.bluetooth.com/learn-about-bluetooth/radio-versions/

Table 4-1. (*continued*)

	Bluetooth Low Energy	Bluetooth Classic Basic Data Rate/ Enhanced Data Rate
Power consumption	~0.01 to 0.5x of Bluetooth Classic reference power	Bluetooth Classic reference power
Data rates	LE 2M PHY: 2Mbits/s LE 1M PHY: 1Mbits/s LE Coded PHY (*S*=2): 500kbits/s LE Coded PHY (*S*=8) LE 2M PHY: 125kbits/s	EDR PHY (8DPSK): 3Mbits/s EDR PHY (π/4 DPSK): 2Mbits/s BR PHY (GFSK): 1Mbits/s
Maximum TX power	Class 1: 100mW (+20dBm) Class 1.5: 10mW (+10dBm) Class 2: 2.5mW (+4dBm) Class 1: 1mW (0dBm)	Class 1: 100mW (+20dBm) Class 2: 2.5mW (+4dBm) Class 1: 1mW (0dBm)
Network topologies	Point-to-point (including piconet) Broadcast Mesh	Point-to-point (including piconet)

Bluetooth Network Topologies

Bluetooth technology supports multiple topologies. As shown in Figure 4-2, three examples of Bluetooth topologies include one-to-one (point-to-point), one-to-many (broadcast), and many-to-many (mesh).

Both Bluetooth Classic and BLE support point-to-point connections for streaming audio between a smartphone and speaker.

In addition, BLE supports broadcast connections (e.g., that can enable way-finding services at an airport) and to mesh connections (e.g., that support large-scale building automation).

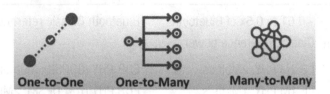

Figure 4-2. *Comparison of different Bluetooth network topologies*

Point-to-Point

Point-to-point is a network topology used for establishing one-to-one (1:1) device communication. The point-to-point topology in Bluetooth Classic is optimized for audio streaming and is ideally suited for a wide range of wireless devices, such as Bluetooth speakers, headsets, and hands-free car infotainment systems.

The point-to-point topology in Bluetooth Low Energy (LE) is optimized for data transfer and is well suited for connected device products, such as fitness trackers, health monitors, PC peripherals, and accessories.

Think of a smartphone that is connected to Bluetooth LE enabled smart watch over a point-to-point connection. Since Bluetooth also supports multiple connections, the same smartphone can also connect to a Bluetooth LE enabled heart rate monitor over a point-to-point connection. In such a scenario, smartphone can communicate directly with the smart watch and the heart rate monitor, but these two devices cannot communicate directly with each other.

Broadcast

Bluetooth LE supports broadcast network topology that used for establishing one-to-many (1:m) device communication. The broadcast topology in Bluetooth LE is optimized for localized information sharing and is ideal for location services such as retail point-of-interest information, indoor navigation and wayfinding, as well as item and asset tracking. A simple example is a Bluetooth LE beacon that broadcasts the advertising packets.

Bluetooth Classic doesn't support broadcast capabilities.

Mesh Networking

Mesh is a network topology used for establishing many-to-many (m:m) device communication. The mesh topology in Bluetooth LE enables the creation of low power, reliable, secure, robust, and scalable wireless networks containing hundreds and thousands of devices. Such Bluetooth LE mesh networks are suitable for large-scale IoT deployments such as commercial lighting, factory automation, wireless sensor networks, control, monitor, and automation systems where tens, hundreds, or thousands of devices need to reliably and securely communicate with one another.

Bluetooth LE mesh technology was defined in Bluetooth Core Specification version 4.0 and later was introduced by the Bluetooth SIG in late 2017; it is a separate specification that supports all versions of Bluetooth LE since version 4.0.[6]

Bluetooth Mesh uses the advertising and scanning states and does not require the radio to be in the connected state in order to relay messages in a mesh network. Bluetooth Mesh doesn't support Bluetooth 5 features such as extended advertisement and long-range communication.

---

[6] BT SIG reference

Contrary to point-to-point and point-to-multipoint topologies, a device in a Bluetooth Mesh network communicates with multiple devices or nodes in a mesh network.

The mesh topology available on Bluetooth LE enables the creation of large-scale M2M wireless network and is ideally suited for control, monitoring, and automation systems where tens, hundreds, or thousands of devices need to communicate reliably and securely with each another.

Target applications for Bluetooth mesh include the following:

- Wireless sensor networks

- Building automation

- Home automation

- Smart lighting

For example, the smart home use case for Bluetooth mesh can easily have 30 to 50 devices that measure temperature, humidity, motion, light levels, etc., and they are not necessarily in the direct range of each other.

Bluetooth mesh nodes will also support the existing Bluetooth LE topologies and use cases like point-to-point connectivity and Bluetooth beaconing, thus allowing smart phones to be connected to the Bluetooth mesh networks to control and monitor the Bluetooth mesh nodes as well as other uses cases like indoor positioning and asset tracking.

DEEPER DIVE INTO BLE MESH

- Most Bluetooth LE devices communicate with each other using a simple point-to-point network topology enabling one-to-one device communications. In the Bluetooth core specification, this is called a "**piconet**." Think of a mobile phone that has established a point-to-point connection with a heath monitor over which it can transfer data. Since Bluetooth allows devices to set up multiple connections, the same mobile phone will be able to establish a point-to-point connection with a fitness tracker. In this case, the mobile phone can communicate directly with both the health monitor and the fitness tracker, but the other devices cannot communicate directly with each other.

- In contrast, a mesh network has a many-to-many topology, with each device able to communicate with every other device in the mesh. Communication is achieved using messages, and devices can relay messages to other devices so that the end-to-end communication range is extended far beyond the radio range of each individual Bluetooth LE device.

- Bluetooth mesh also increases the range achievable by Bluetooth devices by hopping messages from one device to another until it reaches its destination. Applications for Bluetooth mesh range from building automation in an industrial environment, to consumer applications, such as home automation. To facilitate interoperability and accelerate time-to-market, the Bluetooth SIG has created a Bluetooth Mesh specification.

- Bluetooth mesh enables new applications in lighting, sensor networking, predictive maintenance, asset tracking, and positioning.

- Bluetooth mesh devices have a different host component, which contains the layers of the mesh protocol stack. Bluetooth mesh is a managed flooding mesh, which is a simple and reliable approach to distribute messages in a large dense network. Reliability is ensured with multiple paths from source to destination, and there is no single point of failure. Security permeates the technology: network and application security are completely separated, and protection against attacks is built in.

- Devices that are part of a mesh network are called nodes which are "provisioned devices." Devices that are not part of a mesh network are called "un-provisioned devices."

- The process that transforms an "un-provisioned device" into a "provisioned device" or a node is called "provisioning."

- An example of a Bluetooth mesh is shown in Figure 4-3. The diagram shows four types of mesh nodes: Relay, Low Power, Friend, and Proxy.

- Relay nodes support the "Relay" feature and can retransmit the received messages. "Relay" is a mechanism by which a message can traverse the entire mesh network, making multiple "hops" within the mesh network.

- Low Power Nodes (LPN) have a power constraint and need to conserve energy. Most of the time the Low Power Nodes send messages but sometimes have a need to receive messages as well. For example, think of a battery-powered Bluetooth temperature sensor. The temperature sensor sends the temperature measurements whenever the temperature crosses the preset threshold value. At the same time, the user is also able to send messages to the temperature sensor to reconfigure the temperature threshold value. Since the Low Power Node (temperature sensor) is not operating on 100% duty cycle to conserve power, it is possible that it would miss the configuration message. This is when Friend Nodes come into picture and work in tandem with the Low Power Nodes. Friend Nodes don't have a power constraint, and they assist in receiving and storing the configuration messages on behalf of the Low Power Nodes. The Low Power Nodes will check with the Friend Nodes infrequently if there is a pending configuration message to be processed.

- Proxy nodes expose a GATT interface to allow Bluetooth LE devices that do not possess a Bluetooth mesh stack to interact with the nodes in a Bluetooth LE mesh network.

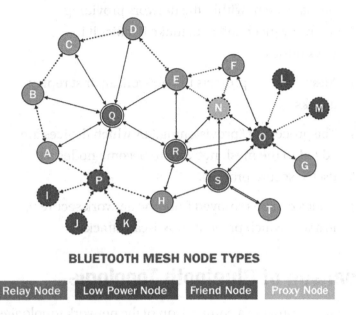

BLUETOOTH MESH NODE TYPES

| Relay Node | Low Power Node | Friend Node | Proxy Node |

Figure 4-3. *Illustration of a Bluetooth mesh*

Mesh Security

Security is mandatory in Bluetooth mesh. The following fundamental security statements apply to all Bluetooth mesh networks:

1) All mesh messages are encrypted and authenticated.

2) Network security, application security, and device security are addressed independently.

3) Security keys can be changed during the life of the
    mesh network via a Key Refresh procedure.

4) Message obfuscation makes it difficult to track
    messages sent within the network providing
    a privacy mechanism to make it difficult to
    track nodes.

5) Mesh security protects the network against replay
    attacks.

6) The process of "provisioning," by which devices are
    added to the mesh network to become nodes, is
    itself a secure process.

7) Nodes can be removed from the network securely,
    in a way which prevents trash-can attacks.

Comparison of Bluetooth Topologies

Tables 4-2 to 4-4 provide a comparison of the network topologies
supported by the two versions of the Bluetooth technology.[7]

---

[7] www.bluetooth.com/learn-about-bluetooth/bluetooth-technology/
topology-options/

Table 4-2. *Comparison of BLE and Bluetooth Classic for point-to-point communication*

Point-to-Point (1:1 Device Communications)	Bluetooth Low Energy	Bluetooth Classic Basic Data Rate/Enhanced Data Rate
Optimized for	Short burst data transmission	Continuous data streaming
Setup time	<6ms	100ms
Maximum connections/ device (piconet)	Unlimited (implementation specific)	7
Data rate	125kbits.s to 2Mbits/s	1Mbits/s to 3Mbits/s
Maximum payload size (bytes)	251	1021
Security	128-bit AES, user-defined application layer	64b/128b, user-defined application layer
Service definition	GATT Profiles	Traditional Profiles GATT Profiles

Table 4-3. *Comparison of BLE and Bluetooth Classic for broadcast communication*

Broadcast (1:m Device Communication)	Bluetooth Low Energy	Bluetooth Classic Basic Data Rate/Enhanced Data Rate
Maximum payload size (bytes)	Primary channel: 31 Secondary channel: 255 Chaining of packets for larger messages	Not applicable
Security	User-defined application layer	
Service definition	Beacon formats (not specified by Bluetooth SIG)	

Table 4-4. *Comparison of BLE and Bluetooth Classic for mesh communication*

Mesh (m:m Device Communications)	Bluetooth Low Energy	Bluetooth Classic Basic Data Rate/Enhanced Data Rate
Maximum number of nodes	32767	Not applicable
Maximum subnets	4096	
Message addressing	Unicast, Multicast, Broadcast Up to 16384 group address Supports publish/subscribe addressing	
Message forwarding	Managed flood	
Maximum payload size (bytes)	29	
Security	128-bit AES Device, network, and application levels	
Service definition	Mesh models, mesh properties	

Bluetooth LE Stack

The Bluetooth LE stack consists of two major architectural components, known as the **host** and **controller**, each of which contains various stack layers. The Host Controller Interface (HCI) defines a series of commands which the host can use to communicate with the controller and events which are used by the controller to communicate with the host as shown in Figure 4-4.

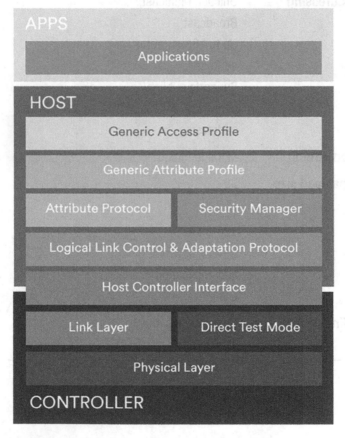

Figure 4-4. *Bluetooth LE stack with GATT and GAP*

Bluetooth LE PHY

PHY is the physical layer in the network model, and it is the interface between the Bluetooth radio and link layer and is shown in Figure 4-5.

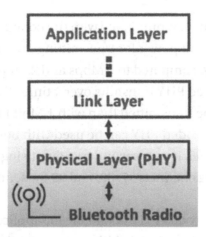

Figure 4-5. *Depiction of the Bluetooth stack*

Bluetooth LE supports three PHYs:

1. 1 Mbit PHY (introduced in version 4.0).

2. 2 Mbit PHY (introduced in version 5.0).

3. Coded or Long Range PHY (introduced in version 5.0). It offers up to 4 times the range as with 1 Mbit and 2 Mbit PHY at lower bit rates of 500kbps and 125kbps. Bluetooth LE coded PHY is an optional feature in version 5.0.

The Bluetooth LE coded PHY uses coding to achieve longer range and reliable communication without increasing the transmit power. Coding employs data redundancy that allows data recovery at the receiver without the need of data retransmission. In case if the transmitted data is corrupted, then the receiver can leverage data redundancy to recover the data by using **Forward Error Correction** (FEC).

235

Bluetooth LE coded PHY uses 1 mega symbol per second rate but uses multiple symbols (i.e., S=2 or S=8) to represent a single bit and add redundancy but reducing the effective data rate. This redundancy allows bit errors to be corrected. The effective data rate with $S=2$ is 500 kbps, and with $S=8$ is 125 kbps.

As a result of the data redundancy with the coded PHY, the radio consumes more transmit power for transmitting the same amount of data over 4 times the range compared to 1 Mbps and 2 Mbps PHY. For example, in case of $S=8$, LE coded PHY transmits over 4 times the range but requires 8 times more bits to be transmitted than with 1 Mbit PHY.

The Bluetooth LE coded PHY can be used with both advertising and data channels. However, it uses secondary advertising channels instead of primary advertising channels 37, 38, and 39 for sending the advertising packets.

The Bluetooth LE coded PHY is suitable for applications that require reliable long-range and low bandwidth communication. Practical demonstration has shown communication range of up to 1500 meters with Bluetooth LE coded PHY.

IoT applications such as smart sensors benefit from the Bluetooth LE coded PHY.

Bluetooth 5.0

The Bluetooth SIG introduced some key features and new enhancements since version 4.2 was released in 2014.

Bluetooth 5.0 was approved by the Bluetooth SIG in 2016[8] and provides four significant new features of Bluetooth 5.0 compared to version 4.2.

---

[8] https://en.wikipedia.org/wiki/Bluetooth#Bluetooth_5

1. Doubles the bit rate to 2 Mbps using the 2 Mbit PHY without increasing the transmit power. This feature helps save power by transmitting the same amount of data in half the time compared to version 4.2.

2. Four times the range with better sensitivity at bit rates of 500 kbps and 125 kbps using LE coded PHY.

3. Eight times improvement in broadcast capacity with advertising extensions. This feature allows the data channels to be used as secondary advertising channels in order to support advertising packets with payload size of up to 255 bytes as compared to 37 bytes in version 4.2. Secondary advertising channels can use any of the three PHYs, but primary channel can only use the 1Mbit or LE coded PHY.

4. Periodic advertising when scanner is synchronized with the advertiser to help save power.

5. Improved wireless coexistence by using an improved channel selection algorithm which enables improved channel coordination and coexistence efficiency in the 2.4 GHz frequency band.

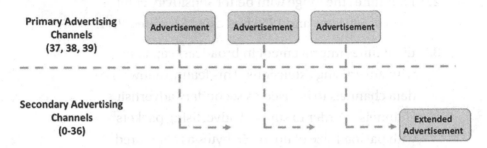

Figure 4-6. *Illustration of Bluetooth 5.0 Extended Advertisements*

In comparison with 1 Mbps PHY, the 2 Mbps PHY enables high bandwidth applications and has higher energy efficiency by consuming half the amount of energy per bit resulting in longer battery life for the device.

Advertising Extensions revolutionize the broadcasting capabilities of Bluetooth LE devices. Up to 8 times more advertising data can be included in an advertisement. Long Range connection establishment can be done directly. As shown in Figure 4-6, Advertisements can be chained together to broadcast larger advertising data sets.

Bluetooth 5.1

Bluetooth 5.1 was approved in 2019. Some of the key features in Bluetooth 5.1 include following:

- Direction Finding for asset tracking, item finding, path and way finding applications.

- Support for GATT caching (saves power consumption) for unbonded devices as well.

- Advertising enhancements.

- Advertising channel index randomization. Using advertising channels in random order reduces collisions, reduces retransmissions, and hence saves power.

- Periodic advertising sync transfer.

Bluetooth 5.2

Bluetooth 5.2 was approved at the end of 2019 and supports the following key features:

- Enhanced Attribute protocol (EATT): Enables concurrent transactions and allows multiple applications use the Bluetooth LE stack concurrently resulting in much lower end-to-end latency and improved responsiveness for better user experience

- LE Power Control

  - Reduces the power consumption using dynamic power management schemes between the connected devices

  - Improves the connection reliability by monitoring the receiver signal strength and requesting transmission power-level changes in connected devices in order to maintain an optimal signal strength

  - Improves the coexistence management with other wireless devices operating in the 2.4 GHz frequency band

- LE Audio: LE Isochronous Channels allow time-synchronized communication with connected devices or broadcast to an unlimited number of devices in a connectionless mode. An audio source can transmit audio for synchronized playback by multiple devices. This will benefit use cases like music sharing, theaters, lecture halls, and conferences.

Bluetooth Profiles

Bluetooth profiles make Bluetooth technology interoperable across devices.[9] **Profiles** are definitions of applications and specify general behaviors that Bluetooth-enabled devices use to communicate with other Bluetooth devices. Profiles that are built on the Bluetooth standard clearly define what kind of data a Bluetooth device is transmitting. The device's application determines which profiles it must support, from hands-free capabilities to heart rate sensors and more.

For two Bluetooth devices to be compatible, they must support the same profiles. And while profiles generally describe the same use case behaviors, they are different for Bluetooth Classic and Bluetooth LE implementations. Compatibility between Bluetooth Classic and Bluetooth LE implementations requires a dual-mode controller on at least one device.

For Bluetooth Classic, a wide range of adopted Bluetooth profiles describe many different, commonly used types of applications or use cases for devices.

For Bluetooth LE, developers can use a comprehensive set of adopted profiles, or they can use Generic Attribute Profile (GATT) to create new profiles. This flexibility helps support innovative new applications that maintain interoperability with other Bluetooth devices.

Bluetooth devices can be either dual mode, supporting both Bluetooth Classic and Bluetooth LE technology, or single mode, supporting either Bluetooth LE technology or Bluetooth Classic only.

---

[9]www.bluetooth.com/specifications/profiles-overview/

Bluetooth profiles typically contain information such as dependencies on other profiles and suggested user interface formats. For Bluetooth Classic, the profile will also specify the options and parameters at each layer of the Bluetooth protocol stack used to perform its task. This may include, if appropriate, an outline of the required service record.

Bluetooth Classic Profiles

Some of the most notable and widely used Bluetooth Classic profiles are discussed in the following sections. Note that while these profiles are applicable to PC and smartphone applications, they are also relevant to IoT applications such as the In Vehicle Experience (IVE) devices in cars.

Advanced Audio Distribution Profile (A2DP)

A2DP is used for the transmission of high-quality stereo audio. Most people are familiar with Bluetooth headphones and car stereo streaming that rely on this profile. Prior to the introduction of A2DP, the quality of Bluetooth audio was rather grainy and suitable only for phone calls using the Hands-Free Profile (HSP).

A2DP defines the protocols and procedures that realize distribution of audio content of high-quality in mono or stereo mode. A typical use case is the streaming of music content from a stereo music player to headphones or speakers. The audio data is compressed in a proper format for efficient use of the limited bandwidth.

Audio/Video Remote Control Profile (AVRCP)

AVRCP is used for remote control functionality such as playing and pausing music and is commonly used with headphones with volume and power buttons.

The AVRCP defines the features and procedures required in order to ensure interoperability between Bluetooth devices with audio/video control functions in the Audio/Video distribution scenarios.

Hands-Free Profile (HFP)

HFP enables calls to be answered, ended, and the volume level adjusted from a headset. This profile in conjunction with A2DP enables users switch between listening to music and making calls.

The HFP defines the protocols and procedures that shall be used by devices implementing the Hands-Free Profile. The most common examples of such devices are in-car Hands-Free units used together with cellular phones, or wearable wireless headsets. The HSP profile defines how two devices supporting the Hands-Free Profile shall interact with each other on a point-to-point basis. An implementation of the Hands-Free Profile typically enables a headset, or an embedded hands-free unit to connect, wirelessly, to a cellular phone for the purposes of acting as the cellular phone's audio input and output mechanism and allowing typical telephony functions to be performed without access to the actual phone.

Headset Profile (HSP)

The HSP defines the protocols and procedures that shall be used by devices requiring a full-duplex audio connection combined with minimal device control commands. The most common examples of such devices are headsets, personal computers, PDAs, and cellular phones, though most cellular phones will prefer to use a more advanced profile such as Hands-Free Profile. The headset can be wirelessly connected for the purposes of acting as the device's audio input and output mechanism, providing full duplex audio. The headset increases the user's mobility while maintaining call privacy.

File Transfer Protocol (FTP)

The FTP allows users to transfer files among Bluetooth devices. The FTP defines the requirements for the protocols and procedures that shall be used by the applications providing the File Transfer usage model.

Human Interface Device Protocol (HID)

HID provides support for peripherals added to Bluetooth devices, including keyboard and mouse.[10]

Bluetooth Classic Protocols

In addition to profiles, protocol specifications define the protocols that govern communication among devices on Bluetooth wireless networks such Audio Video Control Transport Protocol (AVCTP) and Audio Video Distribution Transport Protocol (AVDTP).

Bluetooth LE Profiles

Bluetooth LE supports GATT-based profiles and services. Each of these can be configured either as a GATT client or a GATT server. GATT profiles describe a use case, role, and general behavior based on the GATT functionality.[11]

GATT is built on top of the Attribute Protocol (ATT) and establishes common operations and a framework for the data transported and stored by the Attribute Protocol.

---

[10] www.bluetooth.com/specifications/protocol-specifications/
[11] www.bluetooth.com/specifications/gatt/

GATT provides profile discovery and description services for the BLE protocol. It defines how ATT attributes are grouped together into sets to form services.

Table 4-5 lists available BLE GATT profiles as of November 2020 along with a brief description of applicable use cases.

In the following sections, we describe the application of specific GATT profiles to IoT use cases.

Example: Smart Home Sensor Use Case

Example: Retail Proximity Use Case

Example: Covid-19 Contact Tracing Use Case

Table 4-5. *List of BLE GATT Profiles*[12]

Profile Specification		Version	Status	Adoption Date	Use Cases
ANP	Alert Notification Profile	1.0	Active	13 Sep 2011	
ANS	Alert Notification Service	1.0	Active	13 Sep 2011	
AIOP	Automation IO Profile	1.0	Active	14 Jul 2015	

(continued)

---

[12]www.bluetooth.com/specifications/gatt/

Table 4-5. (*continued*)

Profile Specification		Version	Status	Adoption Date	Use Cases
AIOS	Automation IO Service	1.0	Active	14 Jul 2015	
BAS	Battery Service	1.0	Active	27 Dec 2011	
BCS	Body Composition Service	1.0	Active	21 Oct 2014	
BLP	Blood Pressure Profile	1.0.1	Active	21 Jan 2019	
BLS	Blood Pressure Service	1.0	Active	25 Oct 2011	
BMS	Bond Management Service	1.0	Active	21 Oct 2014	
BSP	Binary Sensor Profile	1.0	Active	02 Jul 2019	
BSS	Binary Sensor Service	1.0	Active	02 Jul 2019	
CGMP	Continuous Glucose Monitoring Profile	1.0.1	Active	15 Dec 2015	
CGMS	Continuous Glucose Monitoring Service	1.0.1	Active	15 Dec 2015	
CHP	BR/EDR Connection Handover Profile	1.0	Active	11 Aug 2020	

(*continued*)

Table 4-5. (*continued*)

Profile Specification		Version	Status	Adoption Date	Use Cases
CPP	Cycling Power Profile	1.1	Active	03 May 2016	
CPS	Cycling Power Service	1.1	Active	03 May 2016	
CSCP	Cycling Speed and Cadence Profile	1.0	Active	21 Aug 2012	
CSCS	Cycling Speed and Cadence Service	1.0	Active	21 Aug 2012	
CTS	Current Time Service	1.1	Active	07 Oct 2014	
DIS	Device Information Service	1.1	Active	29 Nov 2011	
EMP	Emergency Profile	1.0	Active	02 Jul 2019	
EMCS	Emergency Configuration Service	1.0	Active	02 Jul 2019	
ESP	Environmental Sensing Profile	1.0	Active	18 Nov 2014	
ESS	Environmental Sensing Service	1.0	Active	18 Nov 2014	
FMP	Find Me Profile	1.0	Active	21 Jun 2011	

(*continued*)

Table 4-5. (*continued*)

Profile Specification		Version	Status	Adoption Date	Use Cases
FTMP	Fitness Machine Profile	1.0	Active	14 Feb 2017	
FTMS	Fitness Machine Service	1.0	Active	14 Feb 2017	
GSS	GATT Specification Supplement	2	Active	15 Sep 2020	
GLP	Glucose Profile	1.0	Active	10 Apr 2012	
GLS	Glucose Service	1.0	Active	10 Apr 2012	
HIDS	HID Service	1.0	Active	27 Dec 2011	
HOGP	HID over GATT Profile	1.0	Active	27 Dec 2011	
HPS	HTTP Proxy Service	1.0	Active	06 Oct 2015	
HRP	Heart Rate Profile	1.0	Active	12 Jul 2011	
HRS	Heart Rate Service	1.0	Active	12 Jul 2011	
HTP	Health Thermometer Profile	1.0	Active	24 May 2011	

(*continued*)

Table 4-5. (*continued*)

Profile Specification		Version	Status	Adoption Date	Use Cases
HTS	Health Thermometer Service	1.0	Active	24 May 2011	
IAS	Immediate Alert Service	1.0	Active	21 Jun 2011	
IDP	Insulin Delivery Profile	1.0	Active	24 Jul 2018	
IDS	Insulin Delivery Service	1.0	Active	24 Jul 2018	
IPS	Indoor Positioning Service	1.0	Active	19 May 2015	
IPSP	Internet Protocol Support Profile	1.0	Active	16 Dec 2014	
LLS	Link Loss Service	1.0.1	Active	14 Jul 2015	
LNP	Location and Navigation Profile	1.0	Active	30 Apr 2013	
LNS	Location and Navigation Service	1.0	Active	30 Apr 2013	
NDCS	Next DST Change Service	1.0	Active	13 Sep 2011	
OTP	Object Transfer Profile	1.0	Active	17 Nov 2015	

(*continued*)

Table 4-5. (*continued*)

Profile	Specification	Version	Status	Adoption Date	Use Cases
OTS	Object Transfer Service	1.0	Active	17 Nov 2015	
PASP	Phone Alert Status Profile	1.0	Active	13 Sep 2011	
PASS	Phone Alert Status Service	1.0	Active	13 Sep 2011	
PXP	Proximity Profile	1.0.1	Active	14 Jul 2015	
PLXP	Pulse Oximeter Profile	1.0	Active	14 Jul 2015	
PLXS	Pulse Oximeter Service	1.0	Active	14 Jul 2015	
RCP	Reconnection Configuration Profile	1.0	Active	05 Dec 2017	
RCS	Reconnection Configuration Service	1.0	Active	05 Dec 2017	
RSCP	Running Speed and Cadence Profile	1.0	Active	07 Aug 2012	
RSCS	Running Speed and Cadence Service	1.0	Active	07 Aug 2012	
RTUS	Reference Time Update Service	1.0	Active	13 Sep 2011	

(*continued*)

Table 4-5. (*continued*)

Profile Specification		Version	Status	Adoption Date	Use Cases
ScPP	Scan Parameters Profile	1.0	Active	27 Dec 2011	
ScPS	Scan Parameters Service	1.0	Active	27 Dec 2011	
TDS	Transport Discovery Service	1.1	Active	11 Aug 2020	
TIP	Time Profile	1.0	Active	13 Sep 2011	
TPS	Tx Power Service	1.0	Active	21 Jun 2011	
UDS	User Data Service	1.1	Active	15 Oct 2019	
WSP	Weight Scale Profile	1.0	Active	21 Oct 2014	
WSS	Weight Scale Service	1.0	Active	21 Oct 2014	

Bluetooth Applications and Product Categories

Bluetooth Application	Product Categories
Wireless Audio Streaming	Wireless headset, wireless speakers, hands-free, and wireless entertainment devices. Mobile phones, tablets, PCs, and peripherals like wireless USB mouse and keyboard, USB dongle. Cameras, digital picture frames, printers, TVs, and vehicles
Wireless Data Transfer	Wearables like smart watches and fitness trackers. Medical devices like health and wellness monitors like heart rate sensor, blood pressure sensor. Household appliances and toys
Proximity and Location Services	Proximity detection with Bluetooth beacons. Indoor positioning and real-time location-based services (Location-as-a-Service) for asset tracking, way finding, POI
M2M and Wireless Mesh Networking	Large-scale wireless networks. Control, monitor, and automate thousands of connected devices including lighting solutions, HVAC system, security system in a smart home, smart building, smart industry setting. Battery-powered sensors and gateway devices

Bluetooth Direction Finding

Bluetooth "Direction Finding" is one prominent feature introduced in Bluetooth 5.1 Core Specification that will enable devices to determine the direction of a Bluetooth device. This new feature will enable the Bluetooth proximity solutions to know the device direction and offer sub-1-meter level accuracy for location-based services.

Prior to the introduction of Direction Finding, received signal strength based mechanisms have been used for proximity solutions and location-based services using Bluetooth beacons providing meter level accuracy.

One key application of RSSI-based proximity detection mechanism is to find an item by using the battery-powered Bluetooth beacons or tags. For example, a user can attach a tiny Bluetooth tag (e.g., **Tile** tag) to a pair of keys, and then will be able to find the keys by using a smartphone app. The Bluetooth tag transmits beacon signal every few seconds, and when smartphone is within the reception range or close proximity of the Bluetooth tag, it indicates to the user that the keys are within close range; however, it doesn't know the direction of the keys.

Bluetooth Direction Finding enables new use cases and applications such as Real Time Location Systems (RTLS) for asset tracking in warehouses, tracking employees in factories, and tracking equipment, staff, and patients in hospitals. Direction Finding would also enable enhanced use cases such as pathfinding and way finding.

Bluetooth direction finding can be used to detect location in either two or three dimensions depending on the complexity of its implementation.

Proximity Detection vs. Direction Finding

Table 4-6 describes the differences between Proximity Detection and Direction Finding.

Table 4-6. *Differences between Proximity Detection and Direction Finding*

	Proximity	Direction Finding
Use of signal strength	Yes, leverages the Received Signal Strength Indicator (RSSI)	No
Antenna configuration	Single antenna at the transmitter and the receiver	Requires antenna array either at the receiver or at the transmitter
Can determine signal direction?	No	Yes, with an accuracy of up to 5 degrees
Determine elevation?	No	Yes, both 2D and 3D
Accuracy (distance calculation)	Meter level	Sub-1-meter level
Use cases	Beacon-based proximity solutions: Direct marketing to retail customers Item or asset finding Point of interest to enhance user experience	Real Time Location Services (RTLS) such as proximity solutions, item or asset finding, asset tracking Indoor Position Systems (IPS) such as indoor navigation and wayfinding

Bluetooth Direction Finding leverages the concept of Angle of Arrival (AoA) at Receiver and Angle of Departure (AoD) at Transmitter and makes use of the angular phase-shifts of the received signal between antennas as they receive (AoA) or transmit (AoD) RF signals to determine the direction of signal and calculate location.

AoA and AoD operate independently and have unique applications.

Angle of Arrival (AoA)

AoA is employed when the transmitter is moving, and the receiver is stationary. The transmitter needs a single antenna, and this can work with transmit only devices (i.e., advertising in the case of a Bluetooth beacon). The receiver has multiple antennas and it calculates the angle of arrival of the received signal at each antenna as well as the difference in phase shift of the received signal at each antenna. Using the known and fixed distance at each antenna, receiver calculates the direction of the moving or tracked device (see Figure 4-7).

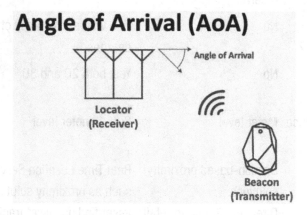

Figure 4-7. *Depiction of Angle of Arrival*

Angle of Departure (AoD)

Angle of Departure (AoD) uses antenna switching to transmit signal from each antenna one at a time and sends the sequence of signal transmission from each antenna as well as the antenna array information including the distance between the antennas at the transmitter. The receiver then uses all this information, calculates the angle of arrival of every received signal at the antenna, and determines the direction of the transmitter (see Figure 4-8).

Angle of Departure (AoD)

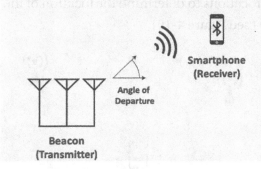

Figure 4-8. *Depiction of Angle of Departure*

Real-Time Location Services (RTLS)

Bluetooth direction finding also brings added user experiences in proximity-based scenarios for consumer awareness and contextual information.

Trilateration uses time of flight to determine distances from at least three transmitters installed at known locations to determine location (see Figure 4-9).

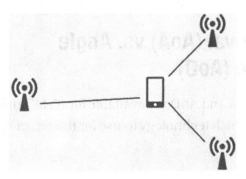

Figure 4-9. *Depiction of trilateration*

255

Triangulation uses angles of signals sent or received by devices installed at fixed locations to determine the location of the moving device or tracked device (see Figure 4-10).

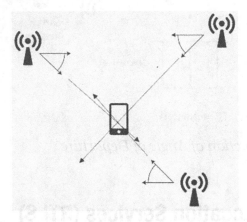

Figure 4-10. *Depiction of triangulation*

With the use of antenna arrays at either side of the communication link, phase shift data can be determined and from this, location can be calculated.

Bluetooth direction finding can be used to detect location in either 2D or 3D dependent on the complexity of its implementation.

Angle of Arrival (AoA) vs. Angle of Departure (AoD)

Given that both AoA and AoD are available for RTLS applications, how does one decide which technology to use for the target application?

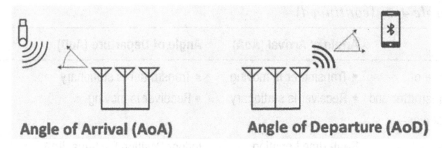

Angle of Arrival (AoA)   **Angle of Departure (AoD)**

Figure 4-11. Pictorial comparison of AoA and AoD

Table 4-7 summarizes the differences between using AoA and AoD for direction finding. A comparison of the differences between AoA and AoD is shown in Figure 4-11.

Table 4-7. Differences between using AoA and AoD for direction finding

	Angle of Arrival (AoA)	Angle of Departure (AoD)
Antenna configuration	Antenna array at receiver Single antenna at transmitter	Antenna array at transmitter Single antenna at receiver
Determination of signal direction	Calculates the angle of arrival of the received signal at each antenna and computes the angular phase-shifts in the signal received at each antenna to determine the direction of received signal, distance from the transmitter, and location of the transmitter	Calculates the angle of arrival of the received signal at the antenna. The received signal carries information about the antenna array at the transmitter (distance between antennas, and the angle at which the signal was transmitted) and the specific antenna that transmitted the signal. The receiver makes use of all this information to find the direction of the received signal, distance from the transmitter, and its own location

(continued)

Table 4-7. (*continued*)

	Angle of Arrival (AoA)	Angle of Departure (AoD)
State of transmitter and receiver	• Transmitter is moving • Receiver is stationary	• Transmitter is stationary • Receiver is moving
Use cases	Real-Time Location Services (RTLS) Item or asset finding along with the direction of the asset Asset tracking in a warehouse Employee tracking in a factory or in office building Equipment, staff, patient tracking in a hospital	Indoor Position Systems (IPS) Find your own location Indoor navigation like GPS is for outdoor navigation

Bluetooth Beacons

A beacon is a small Bluetooth radio transmitter, powered by batteries. Beacons are like a lighthouse in functionality. These small hardware devices incessantly transmit Bluetooth Low Energy (BLE) signals. The Bluetooth-enabled smartphones are capable of scanning and displaying these signals.

Beacons could be deployed on store-fronts, real estate properties, amusement parks, events, and other public venues to broadcast contextually relevant advertisements and notifications.

It is important to understand the difference between classic Bluetooth and Bluetooth Low Energy to appreciate BLE beacons. Classic Bluetooth consumes high power and transmits to long ranges, which is suited for Bluetooth headsets and speakers.

However, Bluetooth Low Energy transmits less data over a smaller range, hence consuming much less power. BLE beacons transfer small amounts of data at regular intervals of time.

Beacons transmit data packets. The components of these packets are slightly different for *iBeacons* to *Eddystone*. But in general, they just contain an ID with their spatial data, a component that indicates the status of the beacon (e.g., temperature, battery status, etc.) and a URL (only for Eddystone beacons) that would correspond to some data in the Nearby server.

A BLE beacon is a wireless device that periodically broadcasts a Bluetooth Low Energy advertising packet that is received by a smartphone and used to determine the user's position with respect to the beacon itself. This allows the beacon to provide "context-aware" information to the mobile user, opening up the possibility to connect the online (virtual) world with the offline (real) physical world.

Bluetooth Security

Like any other wireless technology, Bluetooth is prone to wireless security attacks such as replay attacks, passive eavesdropping, man-in-the-middle attacks, and so on.

The Bluetooth Core Specification defines the security features and capabilities of the core Bluetooth stack. Bluetooth profile specifications define how Bluetooth can be used for a product type or application. This includes stating security requirements and security considerations.

A basic Bluetooth LE security checklist should cover the following items:

1. Always assess and document the security requirements of your product as an explicit step in any product design project.

2. Base your product on the latest Bluetooth Core Specification.

3. Ensure your product or application meets the security requirements specified in applicable profiles at a minimum.

4. Use LE Security Mode 1 Level 4.

5. Use a pairing association model that includes Man-in-the-Middle (MITM) protection. Design your product so that it has I/O capabilities that make this possible.

6. If the use of LE Legacy Pairing is unavoidable, it is recommended that a secure OOB (out-of-band) mechanism is used for authentication.

7. Protect the privacy of users using private resolvable addresses.

8. Protect each attribute in your device's attribute table with access, encryption, and authentication permissions.

9. Verify through review and testing that your product meets the security requirements of applicable specifications, including those you defined for custom aspects of the product.

10.   Check the security of your implementation through security testing and techniques like security auditing.

There are several fundamental security concepts that must be understood before going into further details about detecting and preventing security attacks.

Confidentiality

When data is exchanged wirelessly, any device can intercept the transmitted data. Intercepting communication in this manner is known as passive eavesdropping that can compromise data privacy and confidentiality. The security measure to counter such a security vulnerability is to secure and encrypt the data before it is transmitted.

Authentication

Authentication is about asking for proof of identity to validate that the device you are communicating with is the actual device and not a device impersonating the actual device. Think of logging into your email account where you enter a username and password as part of the user authentication process. With added Two-Factor Authentication (2FA), email server may send a unique code to the registered mobile number as part of the authentication process and enhanced security measures.

Integrity

Data integrity is a key aspect of communication to ensure that the transmitted data has not been manipulated or tampered with and can be trusted even though sometimes data may get corrupted during transmission because of interference.

Security attacks such as Man-In-The-Middle (MITM) attacks in which the attacker intercepts the data exchanged between two devices can compromise data integrity by manipulating and modifying the data and also by leveraging replay attacks.

Authorization

Authorization is about permission and access control. Once the user is authenticated and logged in, the next level of security will engage authorization so that the authenticated user can only access the data for which it has permissions to read or modify.

Privacy

Data transmitted wirelessly would typically include the source and destination address which can easily be identified by an attacker with passive eavesdropping to track the location and movement of a device.

Security Attacks

Some of the commonly known security vulnerabilities and attacks include passive eavesdropping, Man-In-The-Middle (MITM) attack, Identity tracking, Daniel-of-Service (DoS) attack, trash-can attack in case of mesh networks, and so on.

Bluetooth LE Security

In the Bluetooth Core Specification, all the security features of Bluetooth LE are optional to implement. Some of the Bluetooth profile specifications do mandate minimum security requirements, and it is developers' responsibility to assess the security requirements of the product they are building and implement the Bluetooth security features needed to address those requirements. For example, security of the peripheral device is addressed by indicating appropriate parameters during pairing, setting an appropriate security level, and defining the right attribute permissions in the attribute table.

Security Levels and Modes

The Bluetooth Core Specification has introduced security mode and security level that refer to a combination of security attributes and requirements. A security mode may have several associated security levels as follows:

LE security mode 1 has the following security levels:

1. No security (no authentication and no encryption)

2. Unauthenticated pairing with encryption

3. Authenticated pairing with encryption

4. Authenticated LE Secure Connections pairing with encryption using a 128-bit strength encryption key

LE security mode 2 has two security levels:

1. Unauthenticated pairing with data signing

2. Authenticated pairing with data signing

LE security mode 3 has three security levels:

1. No security (no authentication and no encryption)

2. Use of unauthenticated Broadcast_Code

3. Use of authenticated Broadcast_Code

LE Secure Connections Only mode (LE security mode 1 level 4)

Security Manager

Bluetooth LE includes a component called the Security Manager and a protocol called the Security Manager Protocol (SMP). This protocol is involved in security procedures, such as pairing, and is illustrated in Figure 4-12.

The Security Manager component of Bluetooth LE architecture implements the security protocols to generate and exchange keys for authentication and data encryption.

Bluetooth LE supports increased level of security since version 4.2. Privacy is addressed via the use of private addresses that are randomly generated.

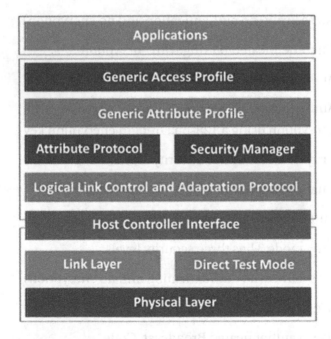

Figure 4-12. *Security Manager in Bluetooth LE architecture*

Most of the Bluetooth LE security features are applicable to devices that are in the connected state as compared to devices in connection-less state such as those communicating using GAP advertising and scanning.

All the transmitted Bluetooth LE packets include a Cyclic Redundancy Check (CRC) that is re-calculated and verified by the receiving device to detect changes in the received data. CRC verification checks do not offer protection against deliberate changes in data made with malicious intent.

Bluetooth Pairing and Bonding

Bluetooth devices form a secure trusted relationship through pairing. Pairing provides each device with security resources such as keys which are needed to allow other security features such as encryption to be used. If two Bluetooth devices have not paired, they will be unable to encrypt the link and unable to sign data. It will also be impossible to determine the identity of another device that is disguising itself using a privacy protection feature called resolvable private addresses.

Pairing is the foundation of Bluetooth security. There are a variety of ways in which pairing may proceed, to accommodate the capabilities of the two devices and their security requirements. When the security resources provided by pairing are stored for future reuse by the paired devices, they are said to be bonded.

There are several different ways in which pairing can proceed. This is apparent both in terms of variations in the user experience and in the messages exchanged between the two devices. Security requirements should be assessed for the pairing process itself separately from the security requirements for use of the device after pairing has been performed. The alternative ways in which pairing can proceed offer very different degrees of security.

The key to understanding Bluetooth pairing is to recognize what it must achieve as follows:

1) Keys that enable the use of required Bluetooth security features such as encryption, data signing, and privacy must be distributed to both devices for future use.

2) Distribution of up to three types of keys between the
    two devices must be accomplished with protection
    from passive eavesdroppers who may attempt to
    steal the keys being distributed.

3) It may be necessary to authenticate devices during
    pairing to protect against attacks, such as the
    MITM attack.

Pairing Methods

Devices running a Bluetooth LE stack compliant with Bluetooth Core
Specification version 4.2 or later may have two distinct pairing methods
available. The first is called LE Legacy Pairing, and the second, a newer
and substantially more secure method, is called LE Secure Connections.
In both cases, there are possible variations during each of the phases
of pairing according to several factors. Devices running a stack whose
version is earlier than Bluetooth 4.2 will only be able to use the LE Legacy
Pairing method.

The specification breaks pairing into the three phases as depicted
in Figure 4-13. There is a decision made in phase 1, resulting in either
LE Legacy Pairing or LE Secure Connections pairing being used. This is
followed by phase 2, which includes an optional authentication step, the
generation of a key with which to encrypt the link in all cases and then
initiation of link encryption. Phase 3 is then concerned with distribution
of the required keys which may include any one or more of the LTK, CSRK,
and IRK.

PHASE 1

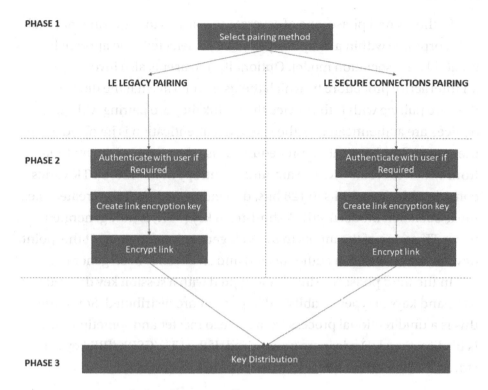

Figure 4-13. *High-level pairing flow*

Bluetooth LE Legacy Pairing

In the first phase, the two devices decide to use the Bluetooth LE Legacy Pairing by looking at the IO capabilities of the two devices and other pairing requirements that the devices express in the pairing feature exchange procedure. The types of keys which need to be generated and distributed, so that the devices can use the security features that they want to use (i.e., encryption, privacy, data signing), is also decided during this phase.

In the second phase, one of several approaches to acquiring material to incorporate within a temporary key (TK) is selected. The approach is called an association model. Optionally, the user is also involved in an interactive procedure by which the user confirms that the device they are pairing with is the device they think they are pairing with (i.e., devices are authenticated by the user). If authentication is involved, then the selected authentication procedure is also the source of the material from which to create TK. The amount of entropy in the 128-bit TK varies considerably, from 0 bits to 128 bits, depending on how TK is created (i.e., the association model used). A short-term key (STK) is now generated, using TK as one of the inputs to the STK generation function. At this point, devices may have been authenticated and an STK has been generated.

In the third phase, the link is encrypted with a session key derived from STK, and keys of types established in phase 1 are distributed. Sometimes this is a unidirectional process from slave to master and sometimes this is bi-directional. Devices are now paired. If the LTK/CSRK/IRK keys are stored for later reuse, the devices are said to be bonded.

Bluetooth LE Secure Connections

LE Secure Connections is an alternative and significantly more secure approach to pairing Bluetooth LE devices which was introduced in version 4.2 of the Bluetooth Core Specification.

LE Secure Connections pairing is also a three-phase process. Phases 1 and 3 play the same part as they do when LE Legacy Pairing is in use. Phase 2 in the LE Secure Connections pairing method is substantially different to Phase 2 in LE Legacy Pairing. Figure 4-14 shows the phases as they apply to LE Secure Connections pairing.

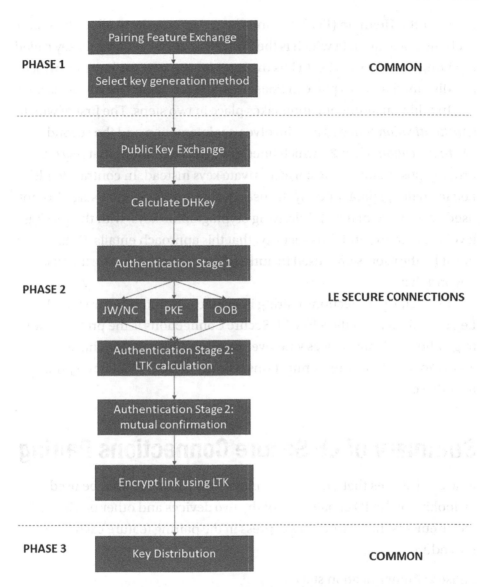

PHASE 1

Pairing Feature Exchange

Select key generation method

COMMON

Public Key Exchange

Calculate DHKey

Authentication Stage 1

PHASE 2

JW/NC   PKE   OOB

LE SECURE CONNECTIONS

Authentication Stage 2:
LTK calculation

Authentication Stage 2:
mutual confirmation

Encrypt link using LTK

PHASE 3

Key Distribution

COMMON

Figure 4-14. *Bluetooth LE Secure Connections pairing*

LE Secure Connections pairing uses public key cryptography. Phase 2 of LE Secure Connections pairing is very different to Phase 2 in LE Legacy Pairing in several ways. For example, LE Secure Connections uses Elliptic

Curve Diffie-Hellman (ECDH) public key cryptography to allow the secure exchange of data; data which is then used to create a symmetric key called the Long Term Key (LTK). LTK is then used to encrypt the link over which key distribution takes place in Phase 3, and it is retained for future use.

In addition, authentication takes place in two steps. The first of which (*Authentication Stage 1*) may involve user interaction and the second (*Authentication Stage 2*), which does not, uses techniques that rely on proving possession of the correct private keys instead. In contrast to LE Legacy pairing, data input by the user during authentication stage 1 is not used as a source of data for deriving cryptographic keys, with the varying levels of entropy, and thus security, that this approach entails. Data input by the user is only used in authentication and has no further use beyond that.

LE Secure Connections pairing is significantly more secure than LE Legacy Pairing, and therefore LE Secure Connections is the preferred way to go about pairing devices wherever possible. If two devices have the ability to use LE Secure Connections pairing, then it is mandatory that they do so.

Summary of LE Secure Connections Pairing

Phase 1: Decides that LE Secure Connections pairing should be used by looking at the IO capabilities of the two devices and other pairing requirements that the devices express in the pairing feature exchange procedure.

Phase 2: Authentication stage 1.

Step 1: The two devices possess Elliptic Curve public-private key pairs. They exchange their public keys during this phase. Their private keys are never disclosed.

Step 2: A shared secret called the DHKey is calculated by both devices using their own private keys and the public key of the other device, which is received in step 1.

Step 3: A confirmation procedure takes place using public keys and nonce values, exchanged in a strict sequence. This involves the Responder calculating and disclosing to the Initiator, a confirmation value that cannot be later changed (e.g., by an attacker).

Step 4: If MITM protection has been requested, the user is also involved in an interactive procedure by which the user confirms that the device they are pairing with is the device they think they are pairing with (i.e., devices are authenticated by the user).

Step 5: Authentication Stage 2 – The devices authenticate each other using a procedure that involves the private keys of the two devices. A key called the Long Term Key (LTK) is calculated.

Phase 3: The link is encrypted with a session key derived from LTK, and keys of types established in phase 1 are distributed. Sometimes this is a unidirectional process from slave to master and sometimes it is bi-directional.

Devices are now paired. If the LTK/CSRK/IRK keys are stored for later reuse, they are said to be bonded.

Association Models

Each pairing method offers several different ways in which pairing may proceed, including (where applicable) how authentication will be handled. These alternatives are called association models.

LE Legacy Pairing has three available association models, known as Just Works (JW), Passkey Entry (PKE), and Out of Band (OOB). LE Secure Connections pairing offers four association models:

Just Works, Numeric Comparison (NC), Passkey Entry, and OOB.

Difference Between LE Legacy Pairing and LE Secure Connections

The two pairing methods have the same fundamental goals. They differ from each other in two ways as shown in the following table.

	LE Legacy Pairing	LE Secure Connections
Confidentiality during keydistribution	Uses a simple process of exchanging secret data to derive a symmetric key with which to encrypt the link during the key distribution phase	Uses elliptic curve public key cryptography to allow a symmetric key to be securely derived. That key is then used to encrypt the link during the key distribution phase
Association models	Just Works, Passkey Entry, OOB	Just Works, Passkey Entry, Numeric Comparison, OOB

Security Keys and Security Capabilities

Bluetooth LE security features such as link encryption, privacy, and data signing need specific security keys to have been created and shared by pairs of devices before they can be used.

Key distribution and acquisition is the primary purpose of the Bluetooth security procedure known as pairing. There are three types of security key in Bluetooth LE.

- Long-Term Key (LTK) used in link encryption

- Connection Signature Resolving Key (CSRK) used in signing data sent over an unencrypted link

- Identity Resolving Key (IRK) used in the Bluetooth privacy feature

Each of these key types is optional. Devices may discard the keys created during pairing after they have been used during the lifespan of the initial connection. Alternatively, they may store the keys in a database, along with some identifying data. This allows the keys associated with a device previously paired with to be restored and used again with subsequent connections. Devices that store and reuse security keys across connections are said to be bonded.

Encrypted Connections

A Bluetooth connection between two devices may be encrypted so that all data passing across it in either direction retains its confidentiality and cannot be accessed by eavesdroppers. Bluetooth LE uses an authenticating encryption algorithm called AES-CCM, and, therefore, the authenticity of data exchanged using an encrypted connection is also assured.

Device Authentication

When devices are paired, authentication may be involved in the procedure. This means that an aspect of the pairing procedure will be concerned with verifying that the device the user thinks they are pairing with really is that device and not an imposter (a form of MITM attack).

Authentication of Data

Packets exchanged over an encrypted link have their authenticity safeguarded due to the use of the AES-CCM authenticating encryption algorithm by Bluetooth. Data signing may also be used with individual GATT write procedures via the ATT Signed Write command. This may be used to allow the receiving device to verify the authenticity of the attribute value in the ATT command but not of the packet as a whole.

Privacy and Device Tracking Protection

Devices may use a special form of address called a private address. An address of this type changes periodically and, as such, disguises the identity of the device that is transmitting it. This prevents that device from being tracked and helps to protects the privacy of the device user.

Attribute Permissions

The Generic Attribute Profile (GATT) allows devices to offer an interface to selected internal data and capabilities expressed in terms of a hierarchical structure that consists of services, characteristics, and descriptors. Services, characteristics, and descriptors are different types of attribute, and the collection of attributes a device has is organized in an internal table called the attribute table.

All attributes include a series of permissions governing the way they can be accessed and the rules that apply to access, including the degree to which the other device must be trusted. A device authenticated during pairing is deemed more trustworthy than one that was not. So, for example, an attribute permission may stipulate that only devices that were authenticated during pairing may read the attribute or write to it.

The White List

The Bluetooth LE link layer in the controller possesses a feature known as the white list. The white list is a list of device addresses and their type. Its purpose is to allow the link layer to perform device filtering of various types, referred to as filter policies. The white list is primarily aimed at reducing the amount of work performed by the stack in handling packets from devices of no interest and, therefore, reducing power consumption. It can also be used to thwart unsophisticated denial of service attacks.

GAP Peripherals can typically only accommodate one connection at a time. Therefore, an attacker could prevent another GAP Central device from connecting simply by connecting to the Peripheral device first. To address this issue, using the advertising filter policy, the white list can prevent devices that have not been paired from establishing a connection. All that is required to achieve this is to add an entry to the white list for each paired device and then enable the advertising filter policy. A connection request from any device not included in the white list will be ignored.

Isochronous Channels

Isochronous channels are used for the communication of data whose processing must be time synchronized by the devices receiving it (e.g., LE Audio). When used with connected devices, isochronous channels may use the same security features available in any other connected device scenario.

When isochronous channels are used in connectionless mode, devices are said to form a broadcast isochronous group (BIG). A BIG may use LE security mode 3, level 1, 2, or 3. Level 1 offers no security. Level 2 provides unauthenticated encryption, and level 3 provides authenticated encryption of all broadcast data to devices in the BIG. Encrypting data in a BIG requires the use of a broadcast code. This 16-octet value is obtained in a way which is defined by a profile specification and then passed from host to controller. An encryption key is generated from the broadcast code and used to encrypt all data broadcast to devices in the BIG.

Security and Implementation Issues

In simple terms, security issues can be said to arise from three fundamentally different sets of root causes:

1) **Specification Errors**

   If a security issue arises from the way a Bluetooth feature is defined in the applicable Bluetooth specification, then the root cause is the specification itself, and it is valid to describe the issue as a Bluetooth security issue. Issues of this type should be reported to the Bluetooth Special Interest Group for evaluation. If warranted, specification corrections that address the reported issue will be published.

2) **Implementation Errors**

   An implementation may be functionally correct and able to pass all the relevant Bluetooth qualification tests but still contain security vulnerabilities due to technical coding errors and issues that do not affect the observable behavior of the product with respect to its use of Bluetooth under test conditions. Issues of this sort are technical quality issues.

3) **Poor Implementation Choices**

   Implementors may make poor choices regarding the security features to be supported by a product but implement them quite correctly. This might be a result of security requirements not having been properly assessed for the product. A poor choice is a poor choice, regardless of how well it is implemented.

Specification Compliance

The Bluetooth Core Specification describes and defines the security features of a Bluetooth stack. Bluetooth profiles define the requirements for using those features in the context of a given set of use cases or product type. Like all specifications, they are just specifications, and it is incumbent on developers and other product development professionals to design and implement products correctly and in accordance with the applicable specifications. Bluetooth test cases seek to verify the correct implementation of and/or use of Bluetooth security features. A device exhibiting each of the expected outcomes defined for each of the associated test cases should be regarded as having demonstrated correct behaviors, as required for specification compliance and interoperability to be achieved. This should not be regarded as absolute assurance that the product is secure.

Technical Quality Issues

Writing secure code takes skill, experience, and an understanding of best practice. There are various ways poorly written code can introduce security vulnerabilities to a product. Common issues include a failure to check and enforce buffer length restrictions that can make buffer or stack overflow attacks possible and the inadvertent leaking of sensitive information.

Bluetooth test procedures cannot assess the internal quality of device code. It is, therefore, for the developer and his/her company's development and quality assurance practices to ensure that the technical quality of device code is fit for purpose and does not introduce security vulnerabilities.

Bluetooth LE includes a range of security features that can be used to meet requirements relating to confidentiality, authentication, privacy, and access to device data. Used properly and with a properly established and articulated understanding of product security requirements, secure Bluetooth products can be created. This is achieved through a combination of making the right choices of security features from the Bluetooth Core Specification, proper compliance with all applicable specifications, thorough testing (which includes testing of device security), and following best practice when it comes to writing code.

Bluetooth Qualification

The Bluetooth SIG is a global community of over 34,000 companies serving to unify, harmonize, and drive innovation in the vast range of connected devices all around us.

Through collective creation and shared technical standards, Bluetooth simplifies, secures, and enriches the technology experience of users worldwide.

Bluetooth SIG expands Bluetooth technology by fostering member collaboration to create new and improved specifications, drives global Bluetooth interoperability through a world class product qualification program, and grows the Bluetooth brand by increasing the awareness, understanding, and adoption of Bluetooth technology.

SPECIFICATION
We extend the capabilities of Bluetooth technology.

QUALIFICATION
We drive Bluetooth interoperability.

PROMOTION
We grow the Bluetooth brand.

Figure 4-15. *Bluetooth Qualification Process*

Bluetooth Qualification Process

The Bluetooth Qualification Process that is shown in Figure 4-15 promotes global product interoperability and reinforces the strength of the Bluetooth brand and ecosystem to the benefit of all Bluetooth SIG members. Qualification helps member companies ensure their Bluetooth products comply with the Bluetooth Patent and Copyright License Agreement and the Bluetooth Trademark License Agreement (collectively, the Bluetooth License Agreement) and Bluetooth specifications.

All Bluetooth products must complete the Bluetooth Qualification Process to be listed on the Bluetooth Product Listing Database.

Completing the Bluetooth Qualification Process

The Qualification Process applies to products incorporating Bluetooth designs. A design is a specific configuration of hardware and/or software implementation of adopted Bluetooth specifications. The design is assigned a Bluetooth product type per the definitions in the Compliance Requirements section of the Bluetooth specifications.

If an organization produces more than one product that incorporates the same Bluetooth design, those additional products can be listed within the same qualification at no additional cost.

Use the Bluetooth Qualification tool Launch Studio to complete the Bluetooth Qualification Process. There are two paths within Launch Studio.

- Qualification Process with No Required Testing
- Qualification Process with Required Testing

The path you use depends on whether your product uses a new or existing Bluetooth design.

Qualification Process with No Required Testing

This path applies to the following scenarios when you are

- Using another member organization's previously qualified Bluetooth End Product or Subsystem in your product with no changes or additions to the Bluetooth design

- Purchasing a Bluetooth product manufactured by a third party and distributing it with your organization's name or logo (also referred to as "white-labeling")

- Creating combinations involving only previously qualified Bluetooth End Products or Subsystems and you make no design changes

Qualification Process with Required Testing

This path applies to the following scenarios when you are

- Creating a new design or combination that does not involve only previously qualified Bluetooth End Products or Subsystems

    Altering a previously qualified Bluetooth design by changing the core configuration/functionality

- Qualifying a design that uses a previously qualified Bluetooth Component product type

Bluetooth Certification Labs

A Bluetooth Qualification Test Facility (BQTF) is recognized by the Bluetooth SIG as competent to execute qualification test cases identified within the Test Case Reference List (TCRL). The link provides a list of Bluetooth qualification test facilities

www.bluetooth.com/develop-with-bluetooth/qualification-listing/qualification-test-facilities/

Bluetooth Solutions

Bluetooth solutions are available as silicon chips (ICs) and as certified module. There are combinations of Bluetooth solutions with some only offering Bluetooth Classic while others offering Bluetooth LE only or Bluetooth Classic + Bluetooth LE combo also known as dual-mode Bluetooth solution. There are also solutions available as Wi-Fi and Bluetooth combo products suitable for products requiring both Wi-Fi and Bluetooth.

Selection Criteria

When it comes to selecting a Bluetooth solution, there are multiple options available. Decision to pick a specific solution would depend upon whether you require only Bluetooth LE, or both Bluetooth Classic and Bluetooth LE, or a combination of Bluetooth, Wi-Fi, ZigBee, Thread, Sub-1 GHz, etc. in a single solution.

Almost all the solutions are available in the form of a wireless SoC (System-on-Chip) and a wireless module.

A wireless module is a small PCB that is populated with the wireless SoC, crystal, RF components, RF shield, antenna matching circuit, antenna connector, etc.

In comparison with a wireless SoC, a wireless module offers following key advantages:

- Regulatory (FCC, IC, CE) and industry certifications (Bluetooth SIG).

- No RF expertise needed.

- Reduced wireless design cost.

- Faster time to market.

- Ready to use off-the-shelf.

- Optimized for optimal RF performance.

- Antenna matching circuit.

- Available with integrated or external antenna options.

- No capital expenditure on RF test equipment.

- No certification cost.

- Ideal for rapid prototyping.

- Ease of switching or upgrading to another wireless module.

- Wide availability of wireless module vendors.

- The end device can leverage the wireless module certification by following the PCB design and layout guidelines from the wireless module vendor.

Although a wireless module costs higher compared to a wireless SoC, it offers a range of benefits that outweigh the cost difference, hence making it a better choice for new IoT prototypes and designs from both product design cost and time to market standpoints.

It cannot be more convincing to state that all the generations of iPhone models have always used a wireless module.

Single Mode Bluetooth Solutions

Single mode Bluetooth solutions support either Bluetooth Classic or Bluetooth LE.

Single mode Bluetooth LE solutions are a good fit for building battery-powered sensor nodes and other IoT devices that demand low power consumption.

Bluetooth LE solutions are available in the form of self-contained wireless microcontrollers as they come integrated with an embedded processor running an RTOS and offer ample amount of memory, processing power, and other interfaces for application development.

Dual Mode Bluetooth Solutions

Dual mode Bluetooth solutions support both Bluetooth Classic and Bluetooth LE in a single silicon chip. Dual mode Bluetooth solutions would be suitable if you are building a device that needs to do music streaming to another Bluetooth device (e.g., Bluetooth speaker, Bluetooth headset) as well as also connect with a smartphone that is running an app that communicates with your device.

Dual mode Bluetooth solutions generally require a host processor running an RTOS or embedded Linux with Bluetooth host stack and application code.

Dual mode Bluetooth solutions use single antenna and cost more than the single mode Bluetooth solutions.

Multi-radio Solutions

In addition to Bluetooth-only solutions, there are multi-radio solutions available in the market that incorporate 802.11 and 802.15.4 radios and offer a mix of multi-protocols wireless capabilities including Bluetooth, Wi-Fi, ZigBee, Thread, and Sub-1 GHz.

The multi-radio solutions support concurrent wireless communication and coexistence management, and generally require a host processor that runs an RTOS or embedded Linux with Bluetooth host stack, networking stack, and application code.

The multi-radio solutions cost higher but are ideal for IoT devices like IoT gateways that need to communicate with other IoT devices over Wi-Fi, Bluetooth, ZigBee, Thread, etc.

Bluetooth Solution Vendors

There are several Bluetooth silicon vendors such as Intel, Nordic, Dialog, TI, NXP, Microchip, Cypress, Broadcom, Silicon Labs, Espressif, Marvell, MediaTek, Redpine Signals, STMicroelectronics, Qualcomm, Telink, etc. In addition, there are also Bluetooth module vendors such as Intel, u-blox, Sierra Wireless, Quectel, Telit, Raytac, Taiyo Yuden, Fanstel, Insight SiP, Laird, etc. who also build Bluetooth modules with integrated antenna.

Bluetooth Range

Bluetooth range in a system would depend on several factors including antenna design, antenna efficiency, antenna gain, antenna matching network, RF layout, ground plane clearance, transmit power, receiver sensitivity, PCB layout, enclosure, etc. It is common to have a wide variation in Bluetooth range in systems with same silicon and same parameter settings but a different RF layout and antenna-design. Bluetooth systems employ different types of antenna such as PCB antenna, chip antenna, wire antenna, whip antenna, etc.

The following is a reference to Bluetooth range estimator:

```
www.bluetooth.com/ja-jp/bluetooth-technology/range/?utm_
campaign=range&utm_source=internal&utm_medium=blog&utm_
content=3-common-myths-about%20-bluetooth
```

Improving Bluetooth LE Power Consumption

The battery life of Bluetooth LE IoT device needs to last for few years before replacement which means that low power consumption is a key requirement of battery-powered IoT device. Bluetooth LE power consumption can be reduced by limiting the transmit power and keeping the radio in sleep mode (or low power mode or idle mode) as much as possible. Lower power consumption can be achieved by adjusting certain parameters as shown in Table 4-8.

Table 4-8. *Summary of techniques that are used to reduce BLE Power Consumption.*

Parameter	Method to Reduce BLE Power Consumption
Transmit power	Lower the transmit power
Advertising interval	Increase the advertising interval
Connection interval	Increase the connection interval
Slave latency	Increase the slave latency
Connection supervision timeout	Increase the supervision timeout
Radio on and off duration	Reduce the radio on and off duration. Transmit data in one large chunk instead of multiple small chunks
Amount of data that needs to be processed	Limit the amount of data transmitted over the air
Receiver sensitivity	Higher receiver sensitivity means fewer dropped packets and less retransmission
Operating range	Make sure that the Bluetooth devices are within the operating range and there are no obstacles
Retransmissions	Reduce the number of retransmissions

Getting Started with Bluetooth

One good way to start working with Bluetooth is to get hold of a Bluetooth evaluation or development kit which is available from vendors such as Intel, Nordic, Espressif, Silicon Labs, Adafruit, etc. and use Arduino IDE or similar rapid prototyping platform.

Bluetooth Markets

Key Bluetooth markets include the following:

- Smart home

- Smart cities

- Smart buildings

- Smart industries, smart agriculture, smart farming

- Automotive

- Industrial automation

- Smart lighting

- Audio and entertainment

- Connected devices and IoT

- Phones, tablets, and PCs

ABI Research predicts that more than 5.4 billion Bluetooth-enabled devices will ship each year by 2023 representing 8% CAGR since 2018.

By 2023, more than 1.6 billion Bluetooth Low Energy devices will ship each year, and 90% of all Bluetooth devices will include Bluetooth Low Energy technology.

Chapter Questions

1. For a smart building application, we would like to relay temperature data from a BLE sensor to a hub. If the distance from the sensor to the gateway is 50 meters and the path loss from the sensor to the gateway is XXX dB, which BLE PHY would you recommend?

2. For a home security application, we would like to transmit a series of images from a camera to an edge server. If the image is 1Mbits and an image is sent from the camera every 30 seconds, could we use BLE for this use case?

References for Chapter 4

1. www.bluetooth.com/bluetooth-resources/ enhancing-bluetooth-location-services-with- direction-finding/

2. www.bluetooth.com/wp-content/ uploads/2020/03/2020_Market_Update-EN.pdf

3. www.silabs.com/products/wireless/learning- center/bluetooth/bluetooth-direction-finding

4. www.nordicsemi.com/Products/Low-power-short- range-wireless/Direction-finding

5. www.bluetooth.com/bluetooth-resources/le- securitystudy-guide/

CHAPTER 5

Low Power Wide Area Networks (LPWAN)

Chapter Overview

When you mention "Internet of Things," many people visualize billions of low power sensor nodes powered by energy harvesting that measure environmental data that are sent wirelessly to the edge and cloud for analysis via Artificial Intelligence and machine learning. These Wireless Sensor Networks (WSN) may use Low Power Wide Area Network (LPWAN) wireless standards to send this data.

IoT systems that use LPWAN are characterized by low duty cycles, very low data rates, relatively longer latencies, low power consumption, and coverage over several kilometers.

These wide area networks cover substantially more area than Wireless LAN (Wi-Fi) and Wireless PAN (Bluetooth) systems that we have discussed earlier.

© Anil Kumar, Jafer Hussain, Anthony Chun 2023
A. Kumar et al., *Connecting the Internet of Things*,
https://doi.org/10.1007/978-1-4842-8897-9_5

These systems are ideal for applications such as smart agriculture, smart cities, smart buildings, smart energy, environmental monitoring, industrial manufacturing and process control, and asset tracking. In contrast to IoT applications in which humans are sending the information such as in Point-of-Sale terminals, many of these use cases are purely machine-to-machine (M2M), and thus these wireless standards are also designated as Machine Type Communications (MTC).

The wireless requirements are lower data rates, longer coverage distances, and lower power requirements than the Wireless LAN and Wireless PAN protocols that we have discussed up to now and complement the Wi-Fi and Bluetooth standards that are in your IoT wireless connectivity toolbox.

LPWAN Use Cases

LPWAN systems are utilized to provide data to solve key customer pain points. Some of these key use cases and customer pain points are as follows (please see Figure 5-1):

- Environmental monitoring

  - *Pain point: Ensure the safety of the population in the event of natural disasters, emergencies, and climate change.*

  - Wireless sensors measure temperature, humidity, air pressure, pollution wind speed, precipitation, chemicals, radiation, etc. to determine short-term and long-term environmental trends.

- Smart agriculture

  - *Pain point: Optimize crop yields in times of climate change, limited resources, and growing populations.*

- Wireless sensors can monitor soil moisture levels, humidity, temperature, and light conditions and optimize crop irrigation.[1]

- Smart cities

  - Pain point: *Ensure the safety of the city's citizens and the city's resources are being used effectively.*

  - Wireless sensors are deployed around a city for weather and earthquake monitoring, water quality, waste and water management,[2] energy meters, smart lighting, traffic and parking management, and health monitoring.[3]

- Smart buildings

  - Pain point: *Ensure the safety of building occupants and productivity of workers and that buildings are operated in a clean, safe, and sustainable manner.*

  - Wireless sensors detect intruders, room occupancy, temperature, humidity, lighting levels, air quality, smoke detection, building disinfection (in these Covid-19 times), and energy usage.

[1] G. Santos, G. Vicente, T. Salvado, C. Gonçalves, F. Caetano and C. Silveira, "Agro Smart: IoT Autonomous Irrigation System," 2022 17th Iberian Conference on Information Systems and Technologies (CISTI), 2022, pp. 1-6, doi: 10.23919/CISTI54924.2022.9820014.

[2] F. Solano, S. Krause and C. Wöllgens, "An Internet-of-Things Enabled Smart System for Wastewater Monitoring," in IEEE Access, vol. 10, pp. 4666-4685, 2022, doi: 10.1109/ACCESS.2022.3140391.

[3] N. Kaushik and T. Bagga, "Smart Cities Using IoT," 2021 9th International Conference on Reliability, Infocom Technologies and Optimization (Trends and Future Directions) (ICRITO), 2021, pp. 1-6, doi: 10.1109/ICRITO51393.2021.9596386.

- Smart energy

  - Pain point: *Ensure that energy is produced and distributed efficiently and economically to meet demand.*

  - Wireless sensors measure energy usage and generation and detect energy theft and loss.

- Asset tracking

  - Pain point: *Track the location and status of items being shipped to ensure delivery to optimize a supply chain and manufacturing costs.*

  - Wireless sensors locate high value equipment and goods as they are being moved and transported through a supply chain or a facility and ensure that they are delivered intact by measuring temperature (for food items) and acceleration/shock.

- Industrial manufacturing and process control

  - Pain point: *Ensure that a manufacturing process is optimized, safe, and cost efficient.*

  - Wireless sensors monitor equipment status, location of components that are required for manufacturing, and safety conditions such as temperature, pressure, chemicals, etc.

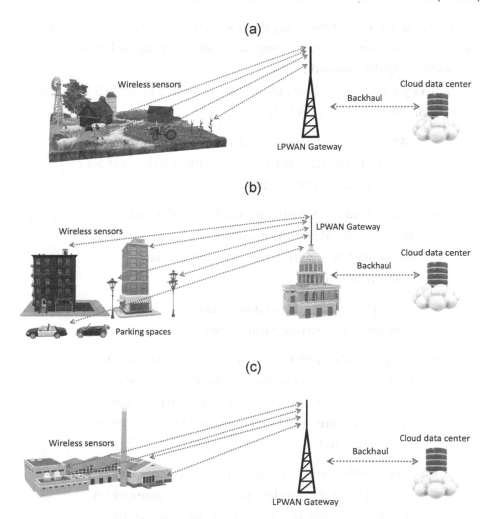

Figure 5-1. *Examples of wireless sensor network use cases. (a) Smart agriculture, (b) smart city, and (c) smart factory*

As we have noted earlier, these key use cases for LPWAN networks are applications that require low data rates, low power, low duty cycle, longer latency, and long range between sensors and the edge server. These applications do not require real-time video, audio, and voice. Wireless connectivity is a necessity because of the large coverage area.

Because these use cases may deploy many sensors, low cost of the sensors is also a key attribute along with low operating and maintenance costs for the entire network.

The key aspects of LPWAN use cases are shown in Table 5-1. Common aspects of these use cases include

- Massive scaling: Connecting a very large number of sensors to the network and ensuring that traffic from the nodes is received reliably.

- Ruggedization: Sensors must withstand extreme environmental conditions when deployed outdoors for smart city, smart agriculture, factory, and environmental use cases.

- Small packet size: Small amounts of data are sent with long intervals between transmission.

- Long latency: Non-mission critical latencies when environmental measurements are collected but potentially mission critical requirements when real-time alarms are being presented or real-time controls being activated.

- Mostly uplink only: In many of the use cases, data are sent from the wireless sensors to the gateway on the uplink, and there is very little downlink traffic. Note that there could be exceptions as there might be downlink signals needed to control an actuator or switch.

- Long product life: Sensors need to be deployed for years without servicing, for example, in difficult to reach locations which require hardware hardening and software and security upgrades that can be delivered over the air.

- Robust security and authentication: Essential to ensure that the transmitting sensors are legitimate, that the gateway is legitimate, that the transmitted data are valid, and to prevent intruders from accessing the data.

- Low power: Battery-powered sensors have requirements for low power consumption, long battery life, and recharging via energy harvesting so that sensor batteries do not need to be replaced in the field.

- Economically viability: Operating and maintenance and servicing costs of the network infrastructure and sensor nodes have to be low to ensure positive return on investment. The challenge is a tight operating margin because of the huge number of sensors that are built and deployed and will eventually require servicing.

Table 5-1. LPWAN use case summary (to be filled in)

Use Case	Typical Data	Throughput	Message Frequency	Uplink (UL) (Sensor to Gateway) / Downlink (DL) (Gateway to Sensor) or Uplink Only	Mobility	Mission Critical Latency	Real-Time Location Coordinates	Security Requirements
Smart agriculture	*Temperature, humidity, moisture*	*Low*	*Low*	*UL/DL if watering valves are activated*	*None*	*Low*	*No*	*Medium*
Environmental monitoring	*Temperature, humidity, moisture*	*Low*	*Low*	*UL*	*None*	*Low*	*No*	*Medium*

Asset tracking	Location coordinates	Medium	Medium	UL	Yes	Medium	Yes	High
Smart buildings	Temperature, moisture, smoke detectors, intruder detection, security alarms	Low	Low	UL	None	Medium	No	High

(continued)

Table 5-1. (*continued*)

Use Case	Typical Data	Throughput	Message Frequency	Uplink (UL) (Sensor to Gateway) / Downlink (DL) (Gateway to Sensor) or Uplink Only	Mobility	Mission Critical Latency	Real-Time Location Coordinates	Security Requirements
Smart cities	Parking space availability, street light control, trash collection status, water leaks	Low	Low	UL	None	Medium	No	Medium

Smart energy	Energy usage	Low	Low	UL	None	Medium	No	High
Industrial manufacturing	Sensor data	Low	High	UL	None	Mission Critical	No	High
Industrial process control	Sensor data	Low	High	UL/DL	None	Mission Critical	No	High

LPWAN Systems in 2022

In this section, we will provide an overview of the LPWAN systems that are available in 2022. Much of the information presented here is based on industry forecasts, technical literature, or documentation from LPWAN vendors.

For the IoT product developer, selection of a LPWAN technology depends upon both the alignment of technical capabilities to the use case and the industry momentum behind the technology.

Open Standard or Proprietary

In contrast to Wi-Fi and Bluetooth, which are based on publicly published specifications, LPWAN systems that are available in 2022 are comprised of both semi-proprietary systems developed by vendors and open specifications and standards.

In some cases, a vendor developed the technology and then opened parts of their proprietary protocol into an industry standard to build a new ecosystem. LoRa is based on a proprietary PHY layer (from Semtech) and public MAC, Sigfox is based on a publicly published standard, and RPMA is based on a proprietary specification.

On the other hand, LTE-M and NB-IoT are based on the 3GPP cellular standards.

For the purposes of this discussion, we will focus on de facto standard LPWAN systems and will omit descriptions of purely proprietary protocols.

Spectrum Selection

The choice of LPWAN spectrum depends on whether the LPWAN system is based on a cellular standard or a non-cellular standard that uses unlicensed wireless spectrum.

If you decide to use an LPWAN system that is based on a cellular standard, then you will use licensed spectrum corresponding to the country and carrier who own that specific band, and the device certifications will be for all of the bands in the countries where the device will be deployed.

An advantage of using a licensed band is that interference is tightly controlled by the carrier who owns that band, in contrast to an unlicensed band in which there may be multiple standards competing for access.

If you select a non-cellular LPWAN system using unlicensed spectrum, then the choices include the following:[4]

- Worldwide: 2.4GHz (also used for Wi-Fi, Bluetooth, and 802.15.4)

- North America: 902-928MHz

- South America: 902-928MHz, 915-928MHz

- Europe: 433MHz, 863-870MHz

- Africa: 433MHz, 863-870MHz

- China: 470-510MHz, 779-787MHz

- Japan: 920-923MHz

- India: 865-867MHz

- Australia: 915-928MHz

---

[4]www.thethingsnetwork.org/docs/lorawan/frequencies-by-country/

The sub-1GHz bands are also subject to duty cycle requirements that control the amount of time the device is allowed to transmit in order to avoid interference with other devices. Examples of list of duty cycles for the 863MHz band can be found in this paper.[5] The duty cycle requirements limit the amount of data that the device is allowed to send. The 868MHz band that is used by SigFox and LoRa has a 1% duty cycle.

The sub-1GHz bands offer potential longer range than the 2.4GHz band due to lower path loss. Another issue is potential interference in the 2.4GHz band due to competing standards that share this band including Wi-Fi and Bluetooth.

Spectrum fragmentation is an issue in a LPWAN implementation. To operate the WSN device in a specific country means that the radio needs to be designed and certified to operate using the spectrum that is available in that country. For a device that will be deployed in multiple countries or will roam between countries (e.g., for an asset tracking use case) means that a variation of the device with the appropriate RF front end (SKU) needs to be developed and certified for that country; this process adds complexity to the product mix and inventory management and increases time to market and development costs.

Public or Private Network

A LPWAN network can be operated by a public cellular carrier or service provider or as a private network that is operated by the customer.

Using a public carrier to operate the LPWAN system (whether cellular or non-cellular) has several advantages: setup, configuration, maintenance, and network support are provided by the carrier, and it frees up the customer's resources for analyzing and monetizing the collected

---

[5] Saelens, Martijn & Hoebeke, Jeroen & Shahid, Adnan & De Poorter, Eli. (2019). Impact of EU duty cycle and transmission power limitations for sub-GHz LPWAN SRDs: an overview and future challenges. EURASIP Journal on Wireless Communications and Networking. 2019. 10.1186/s13638-019-1502-5.

data. In addition, the customer does not need to have the in-house LPWAN expertise and purchase and build out the network infrastructure. However, the customer (or subscribers) will pay the network operator to run the LPWAN network and reduce the return on investment.

If the customer operates the network on their own as a private network, then they need to have the in-house capabilities to purchase, build install, operate, and maintain the LPWAN infrastructure themselves and will have to invest in the necessary skills and resources. However, they will save on the service fees that would have been paid to a carrier to run the network.

System Design Tradeoffs

The wish list for the requirements for a wireless sensor network goes like this:

- Coverage over tens of kilometers.

- Support for billions of sensors in the network.

- Low battery consumption.

- Untended operation for 10 years.

- Operates under any weather conditions.

- Works both outdoors and indoors deep within buildings.

- Transmits data with minimum delay to the destination.

- Ensures that transmitted data packets are received reliably at the destination.

- Transmission is robust from effects of interference and impairments in the radio environment such as multipath.

- Physically secure and tamper proof.

- Transmitted information is securely encrypted.

- Wireless sensors and network access require authentication.

- Able to operate in multiple countries seamlessly.

- Able to support mobility if the sensor is attached to a moving shipment.

- Simple and inexpensive terminals.

These ideal requirements are conflicting and require tradeoffs. For example, the large coverage area means higher transmit power which increases the battery size and cost of the wireless sensor. Support for indoor coverage with high signal attenuation due to walls means either increasing the transmit power or repeating a transmission multiple times to ensure that the message is received, which increases battery consumption meaning that a larger battery is required. Mobility requires continuous connectivity to the network as the wireless sensor moves between cells which reduces battery life. Supporting many wireless sensors concurrently requires a means of allocating bandwidth to each user which increases the complexity of the network and the wireless sensor and increases the cost of the network.

The LPWAN designers have addressed these tradeoffs, and there are compromises in their implementations – in other words, there is no single optimal solution that is available today.

Ecosystem Viability

Given the substantial investment that would be required to deploy and build out a large-scale IoT system comprised of sensor nodes, gateways, edge servers, and LPWAN radios over a large site, the developer should be confident that industry and vendor support will be there for a number of years, as is the case of Wi-Fi, Bluetooth, and 3GPP.

The LPWAN ecosystem needs

- Multiple vendors to provide the sensor radio components (modules and transceivers) and infrastructure radios and gateways

- Developer and reference kits that enable potential customers to try out the technology quickly for their applications

- Software drivers and stacks for the most popular operating systems

- Documentation including hardware and software specifications that enable vendors to create products and developers to create applications

- A process of certifying that products meet the specifications and standards and are compatible with other products

- Training materials including videos, case studies, and white papers

- Partner labs who can aid in device certifications and testing and apply a logo indicating that the device is officially certified

- Support staff and forums to support developers and partners when they run into technical issues

Creating an industry alliance to bring together all of these components (such as the LoRa Alliance) is essential to formalizing this ecosystem. Indicators of a healthy LPWAN ecosystem is an industry alliance with key industry players along with an increasing number of products, vendors, partners, developers, and deployments covering multiple use cases.

Key LPWAN System Parameters

Various assessments of LPWAN systems have been published in the literature[6,7]; we will reference these works and summarize the results in the next section. Note that we have used a combination of independent research papers, industry forecasts with material published by LPWAN vendors where the LPWAN vendor material in some cases emphasizes the capabilities of their system vs. competitors.

We have summarized the key parameters of LPWAN systems in Table 5-2; note that there was conflicting information between the various sources that we used.

Common aspects of these systems include

- Star of stars network topology: The end server is connected to Gateways that are connected to the wireless sensors. This simplifies the architecture but leaves the end server is a single point failure for the network.

---

[6] M. Chochul and P. Ševčík, "A Survey of Low Power Wide Area Network Technologies," 2020 18th International Conference on Emerging eLearning Technologies and Applications (ICETA), 2020, pp. 69-73, doi: 10.1109/ICETA51985.2020.9379213.

[7] A. Ikpehai et al., "Low-Power Wide Area Network Technologies for Internet-of-Things: A Comparative Review," in IEEE Internet of Things Journal, vol. 6, no. 2, pp. 2225-2240, April 2019, doi: 10.1109/JIOT.2018.2883728.

- Methods for increasing Link Margin/MCL: Either repeating transmissions or using spread spectrum to take advantage of processing gain in order to improve performance.

- Methods of simplifying wireless sensor end devices: Most of the standards have limited downlink capability; the transceivers generally do not support concurrent uplink and downlink.

Table 5-2. *Key parameters of LPWAN systems that are available in 2022. Note: Maximum Coupling Loss (MCL) is a figure of merit that is used to compare cellular systems*

Protocol	Type	Frequency Band	Channel Width	Data Rate	Message Size	Transmit Power	Topology	Receive Sensitivity	Range from Device and Gateway/MCL	Number of Deployed Systems
LoRA	Proprietary PHY and open association	863-870MHz (Europe)[8] 433MHz (Asia) 2.4GHz	125kHz	Up to 300kbits/s	Up to 222bytes	2-20dBm (Uplink) 14dBm (Downlink)	Star	-148dBm -137dBm for end device -142dBm for gateway	5km urban 20km rural	173 network operators

SigFox	Open standard and proprietary deployment	860MHz [9](Europe) 900MHz (USA) 433MHz (Asia)	100bits/s (Uplink) 600 bits/s (Downlink)	12bytes/message 140 messages per day from node 8 bytes/message 4 messages per day from base station	14dBm (Europe)	Star	-125dBm -142dBm for end device at 100bps -134dBm for end device at 600bps	10km urban 40km	111 customers listed[10]

(continued)

[8] Y. Lykov, A. Paniotova, V. Shatalova and A. Lykova, "Energy Efficiency Comparison LPWANs: LoRaWAN vs Sigfox," 2020 IEEE International Conference on Problems of Infocommunications. Science and Technology (PIC S&T), 2020, pp. 485-490, doi: 10.1109/PICST51311.2020.9468026.

[9] A. I. PETRARIU and A. LAVRIC, "SigFox Wireless Communication Enhancement for Internet of Things: A study," 2021 12th International Symposium on Advanced Topics in Electrical Engineering (ATEE), 2021, pp. 1-4, doi: 10.1109/ATEE52255.2021.9425213.

[10] www.sigfox.com/en/customers

Table 5-2. (*continued*)

Protocol	Type	Frequency Band	Channel Width	Data Rate	Message Size	Transmit Power	Topology	Receive Sensitivity	Range from Device and Gateway/MCL	Number of Deployed Systems
NB Fi[11]	Proprietary system developed by WAVIoT	430-500 MHz and 860-925	50kHz (uplink) 100kHz (downlink)	50, 400, bits/s, 3.200 25.600 kbits/s	8 bytes Uplink: up to 20Mbit per base station per day Downlink: up to 10Mbit per base station per day	Downlink: 30dBm	Star	-148 dBm (for 50 bps)	10km urban 40km rural	Unknown

| RPMA[12,13] | Ingenu | 2.4GHz | 1000kHz | 19kbits/s | 100kBytes per day | Europe Uplink and Downlink: 21dBm USA Uplink 21dBm Downlink 30dBm | Downlink: -133dBm Uplink: -142dBm | USA: 300miles² per Access Point Europe: 32miles² per Access Point | 35 |

(continued)

[11] https://waviot.com/faq/
[12] www.ingenu.com/
[13] www.ingenu.com/wp-content/uploads/dlm_uploads/2015/08/How-RPMA-Works.pdf

311

Table 5-2. (*continued*)

Protocol	Type	Frequency Band	Channel Width	Data Rate	Message Size	Transmit Power	Topology	Receive Sensitivity	Range from Device and Gateway/MCL	Number of Deployed Systems
NB-IoT	Open standard from 3GPP	Licensed LTE frequency bands 882MHz, 1840MHz	180kHz	200kbits/s	1600bytes	23dBm	Star	-141dBm	1km urban 10km rural	110[14]
LTE-M	Open standard from 3GPP	Licensed LTE frequency bands 2.6GHz	1400kHz	1Mbits/s			40dBm		-141dBm	70

[14] www.gsma.com/iot/mobile-iot-commercial-launches/

WHAT IS MAXIMUM COUPLING LOSS (MCL) AND HOW DOES IT DIFFER FROM LINK MARGIN?

3GPP defines the term **Maximum Coupling Loss (MCL)** in order to easily compare different systems and standards.[15] MCL is defined as the difference between the transmitted power from the source at the input port to the transmit antenna $P_{TX\,port}dB$ and the received power at the destination at the output of the receive antenna port $P_{RX\,port}dB$ that is required to achieve the target error rate at the receiver:

$$MCLdB = P_{TX\,port}dB - P_{RX\,port}dB$$

The MCL is a rearranging of the Link Margin calculation that we discussed earlier in Chapter 2:

$$P_{RX}dB = P_{TX}dB + G_{TX}dB - L_{TX\,cable}dB + G_{RX}\,dB - L_{free}dB - L_{RX\,cable}dB$$

The MCL is defined at the input port to the transmit antenna and the output port of the receive antenna and so the $G_{TX}dB$, $G_{RX}dB$, $L_{TX\,cable}dB$ and $L_{RX\,cable}dB$ are not included in the expression.

$SINR_{target}dB$ is the target Signal-to-Interference + Noise ratio at the receiver that is needed to achieve a target error rate.

The target $SINR_{target}dB$ at the receiver is the difference between the received power at the antenna port and the received noise

$$SINR_{target}dB = P_{RX\,port}dB - Noise\_dB$$

$$= P_{RX\,port}dB - \left(NoiseFigure_{dB} + NoiseFloor_{dB}\right)$$

where

NoiseFigure_dB is the figure of merit of the receiver,

---

[15] www.techplayon.com/maximum-coupling-loss-mcl-and-maximum-path-loss-mpl/

and *NoiseFloor_dB* is =*kTB* as discussed in Chapter 2. As a reminder, the noise is a function of the bandwidth *B* and temperature *T*.

Rearranging

$$P_{RX\,port}dB = \text{SINR}_{target}dB - \left(NoiseFigure_{dB} + NoiseFloor_{dB}\right)$$

From the definition of MCL:

$$\text{MCL}dB = P_{TX\,port}dB - P_{RX\,port}dB$$

$$\text{MCL}dB = P_{TX\,port}dB - \left(\text{SINR}_{target}dB + NoiseFigure_{dB} + NoiseFloor_{dB}\right)$$

To summarize, MCL is a function of the transmit power, the target SINR, and the noise performance of the receiver. The advantage of using MCL as a measure of performance is that the path loss due to distance, frequency, and penetration loss are combined together into this single term.

LoRaWAN

Of the LPWAN systems that we discussed in this chapter, LoRaWAN is the most widely deployed.

The LoRaWAN ecosystem, including a wealth of information and collaterals, is accessible via the Semtech website.[16]

LoRaWAN: History

Semtech created the LoRa proprietary PHY in 2012 and manufactures the LoRa transceiver and RF chips. Semtech also founded the LoRa Alliance[17] in 2015 that created the LoRaWAN open standard drive this ecosystem.

---

[16]www.semtech.com/

[17]https://lora-alliance.org/

LoRaWAN: Technical Summary

LoRaWAN is based on the "star of stars" topology that is shown in Figure 5-2. The network consists of the LoRaWAN network server that is connected to multiple LoRaWAN gateways, and each gateway is connected to multiple LoRaWAN devices. Depending upon its location and the radio environment, a LoRaWAN device may be connected to more than one gateway.

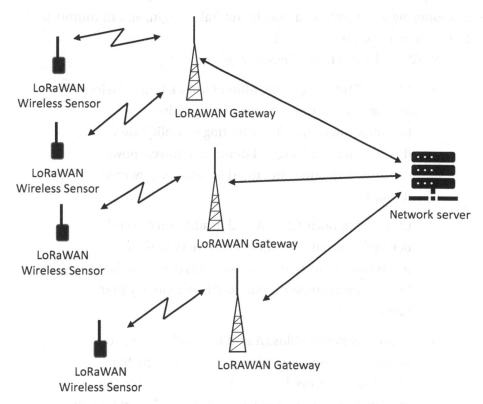

Figure 5-2. *LoRaWAN architecture*

The LoRA PHY uses *chirp spread spectrum* to modulate each sensor's data.[18] A chirp is a linear change of frequency across the allocated frequency band.

Spreading factors SF from 7 to 12 are supported, where the spreading factor and the bandwidth (which is 125, 250, or 500kHz) determine the actual data rate. The Semtech reference describes the advantages of using Chirp Spread Spectrum vs. narrowband techniques including constant envelope, higher overall data rate, better link margin, and immunity to channel impairments.

LoRaWAN defines three classes of devices[19]:

- Class A: The end device initiates uplink transmissions and has two windows to receive downlink transmissions only after initiating an uplink signal; this class has the longest latency and lowest power consumption and is intended for battery-powered devices.

- Class B: Supports Class A and in addition the end device can open windows to receive downlink transmissions from the gateway; this class has the higher power consumption and lower latency than Class A.

- Class C: Supports Class A and in addition the end device keeps windows open to receive immediate downlink transmissions from the gateway; this class has the highest power consumption and lowest latency.

---

[18]www.semtech.com/uploads/documents/an1200.22.pdf
[19]www.thethingsnetwork.org/docs/lorawan/classes/

Semtech is the only vendor of the proprietary LoRa PHY. Both sub-1GHz and 2.4GHz versions are available.

The sub-1GHz RF transceiver components are denoted as *LoRa Core*. Use of Frequency Hopped Spread Spectrum modulations is a key feature as the spread spectrum modulation improves the receiver sensitivity after despreading. Signal bandwidth is up to 500kHz and TX power is up to 22dBm, Rx sensitivity for the LoRa modulation down to -148dBm, and range is up to 30miles.

The *LoRa 2.4GHz* version supports the 2.4GHz ISM band that is available worldwide. These radios support Rx sensitivity to -132dBm, 12.5dBm output, link budget of 144.5dB, 3km range, and data rates up to 250kbps. These radios also support location estimation based on Time-of-Flight measurements which is valuable for asset tracking use cases as an addition GPS receiver to determine location is not needed.

As we have noted, the LoRa PHY is proprietary, and the implementations are only available from Semtech. In contrast, the upper part of the stack above the PHY is included in the LoRaWAN open standard including the Link Layer, Back End interfaces, and regional frequency channel plans and certification process.[20]

LoRaWAN: Key Ecosystem Partners and Deployments

The LoRa Alliance includes ~378 members. The benefits of membership include being able to participate and contribute in technical and user groups, access to certification tools and support, technical assistance, and marketing access. LoRa alliance offers various membership tiers and fees.

---

[20] https://lora-alliance.org/lorawan-for-developers/

LoRaWAN ecosystem includes 173 network operators.[21] Coverage is most of the world with parts of Africa not currently being supported.

LoRaWAN: Assessment

The LoRa ecosystem appears to be vibrant with numerous members, products, network operators, and deployments covering a range of IoT use cases. The developer environment includes readily available kits and software tools to facilitate creating of applications.

Based on the number of stakeholders, products, and collaterals, LoRaWAN is a viable LPWAN technology.

SigFox
Sigfox: History

Sigfox was founded in 2010 in France with a goal of connecting every object in the physical world and is available in 75 countries with 20Million registered devices with 79Million messages sent per day.[22] The Sigfox network is depicted in Figure 5-3.

Sigfox: Overview

Sigfox is currently rolling out its global *0G* network with the following key attributes:

- Star of star network: Devices connect to Sigfox base stations that are connected to the Sigfox cloud in the Sigfox Network (SNW).

---

[21] www.semtech.com/lora/ecosystem/networks
[22] www.sigfox.com/en/sigfox-story

- Small payload: Extends battery life.

- Lightweight protocol.

- Ultra-narrowband modulation: Increases network capacity.

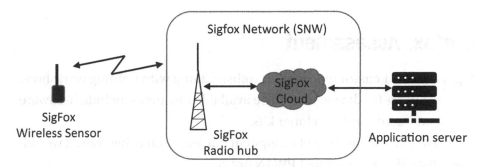

Figure 5-3. *Depiction of the Sigfox 0G network*

Sigfox: Technical Summary

- 100Hz channels in Europe.

- 600Hz channels in FCC.

- 12-byte payload.

- Randomized in time and frequency.

- Uplink signals are repeated 3 times to improve reliability.

Currently, because the Sigfox system does not support downlink messages, there is no capability to acknowledge that an uplink message was received correctly at the gateway. In addition, there is no means to perform over the air firmware updates that may be required to mitigate security issues.

Sigfox: Key Ecosystem Partners and Deployments

The Sigfox website lists 801 total service providers, module and product suppliers, and a total of 876 end products.[23]

Sigfox: Assessment

Sigfox lists 111 customers on their website along with training workshops and resources for developers.[24] The available resources include hardware breakout boards and developer kits.

Based on the number of ecosystem partners and collaterals, it would seem that Sigfox is a viable LPWAN option.

RPMA (Ingenu)
RPMA: History

Ingenu was formerly known as *On-Ramp Wireless* and was founded in 2008. The company headquarters is in San Diego, CA. Ingenu is a privately held company.

While the focus of discussion in on Ingenu's LPWAN system, Ingenu made an announcement in 2021 about a satellite-based version of RPMA using 72 satellites.[25]

---

[23] https://partners.sigfox.com/search/companies?sort=_date_desc

[24] www.sigfox.com/en/sigfox-developers

[25] www.prnewswire.com/news-releases/phantom-space-announces-agreement-to-build-and-launch-72-satellite-constellation-for-ingenu-301387668.html

RPMA: Technical Summary

The RPMA architecture is depicted in Figure 5-4. Key technical parameters are as follows:

- Random phase multiple access (RPMA): Direct sequence spread spectrum supports 1200 users per antenna. It is not clear from the available documentation the details on the code type, length, and how it is selected for a specific sensor.

- Channel allocation: 1MHz channels with 1MHz buffers on either side of each channel for a total of 40 channels in the 80MHz wide spectrum in the 2.4GHz band.

- Data rate of 19kbits/s per 1MHz of channel bandwidth

- 2.4GHz band advantage: Worldwide availability of this unlicensed spectrum vs. separate sub 1GHz unlicensed bands in the United States, Europe, Asia, etc.

- 2.4GHz band disadvantages: Interference from the standards in this band including Bluetooth, Wi-Fi, and 802.15.4 along with decreased range when compared to the 800MHz band.

- Direct sequence spread spectrum is used: Differential Binary Phase Shift Keying (D-BPSK) modulation with Gold Codes, 8192 chips per symbol and 39dB of processing gain.[26]

---

[26] How RPMA Works -The Making of RPMA, eBook by Ingenue

- Time division duplexing is used to separate downlink and uplink transmissions in time; the total frame length is 4.64 seconds divided by 2.2 seconds for the downlink and 2.1 seconds for the uplink.

- Downlink uses both a broadcast channel and data channels.

- Antenna Gain is listed as 17dB in the United States which is key to achieving the link budget that is required to support the long range.

- Link budget 176dB (as indicated in the SARA-S200 product summary).

- Channel coding using Viterbi decoder, guaranteed message arrival with 50% packet error rate.

- Coverage: Ingenu's white paper claims a coverage area of 300+ square miles in the United States. This range is attributed to the 17dB antenna gain in the United States combined with the RX sensitivity of 142dB (Uplink) and 133dB (Downlink). However, the results in [] indicate that because it uses the 2.4GHz band, RPMA suffers greater losses than other LPWAN systems due to obstructions that are in the path between the sensor and the edge gateway, especially in urban areas.

- Security uses 128-bit encryption with two-way authentication and 16-byte hash.

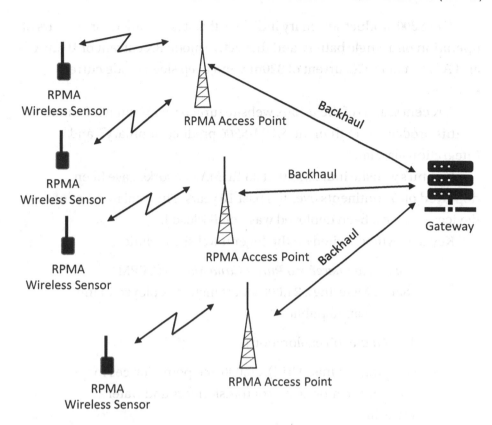

Figure 5-4. *RPMA architecture*

RPMA: Key Ecosystem Partners and Deployments

u-blox announced the availability of the *SARA-S200* RPMA module in 2017.[27] This module, which is the second-generation u-blox RPMA module, has dimensions 16mm x 26mm x 2.3mm, and was intended the sensors for Smart meter, Smart Building, Oil and Gas, and Agriculture applications.

---

[27] www.ingenu.com/2017/05/u-blox-announces-ultra-small-rpma-module-the-sara-s200/

The *S200* product summary indicates that it is intended for 10 years of operation on a single battery and that active mode RX current of 105mA and Active mode TX current of 320mA and deep sleep mode current of 19uA.

A recent search of the u-blox website turned up minimal information on this product other than the *SARA-S200* product summary[28] and integration manual.[29]

Ingenu's website indicates that 35 RDMA networks have been deployed on 5 continents over the past 10 years. The total number of devices that have been deployed was not disclosed.

Key deployments cited on the Ingenu website include

- *Consorcio Energético Punta Cana Macao* (CEPM) (Smart Metering): 24,000 smart meters deployed in the Dominican Republic

- *WellAware* (oil exploration)

- *N.V. Elmar* (Smart Grid): 50,000 end point devices for oil pressure monitoring of transformers and water metering

RPMA: Assessment

We were not able to find much comprehensive information on RPMA technology, ecosystem, developer kits, and other collaterals from our recent search of the Ingenu website. While the u-blox SARA-S200 RPMA module was launched in 2017, we were not able to find a successor product from u-blox. In addition, we could not find information on a manufacturer of the RPMA gateway hardware.

---

[28] https://content.u-blox.com/sites/default/files/SARA-S200_ProductSumm ary_%28UBX-17013042%29.pdf

[29] https://content.u-blox.com/sites/default/files/SARA-S200_SystemInteg rationManual_%28UBX-17048719%29.pdf

The lack of recent information on the RPMA ecosystem would give us pause on using this technology for a new deployment.

NB-Fi

NB-Fi (Narrow Band Fidelity) is a LPWAN standard that was developed by WAVIoT. Details can be found on the WAVIoT website.[30]

NB-Fi: History

WAVIoT was founded in 2016 with offices in Moscow, Russia, and South Dakota, United States. In 2019, Federal Agency for Technical Regulation and Metrology of the Russian Federation approved NB-Fi as a national standard.

NB-Fi: Technical Summary

NB-Fi is an ultra-narrow band LPWAN system that is shown in Figure 5-5. Key parameters for the NB-Fi system are[31,32]

- Topology: Star.

- Full duplex for base stations and half duplex for devices.

- 32-bit ID per device.

---

[30] https://waviot.com/

[31] https://waviot.com/technology/nb-fi-specification/

[32] www.akgec.ac.in/wp-content/uploads/2020/10/1-Satya_N_CORRECTED_26_SEPT.pdf

- Non-IP implementation.

- 8bytes per NB-Fi packet.

- Channel bandwidth from 50Hz to 25600Hz.

- Uplink data rates 50, 400, 3200, 25600bps.

- Time and frequency separation of devices: The method of bandwidth allocation is not described on the WAVIoT website.

- AES-256 encryption.

- DBPSK modulation.

- Base Station Receiver sensitivity ranges from -148dm (50bps) to -123dBm (25600bps).

- Uplink capacity 20Mbits per day per base station.

- Downlink capacity 100kbits to 10Mbits per day per base station.

- Range: 10km urban and 40km rural.

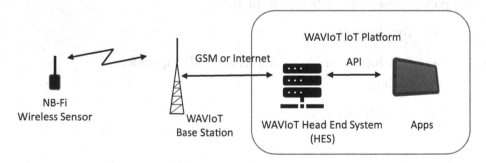

Figure 5-5. *NB-Fi architecture (after[33])*

---

[33] https://waviot.com/solutions/smart-cities/

NB-Fi: Key Ecosystem Partners and Deployments

We were not able to find information on actual NB-Fi deployments.

NB-Fi: Assessment

NB-Fi is a recent entry into the LPWAN competition. Its claimed range of 10km in urban environments and 40km in rural scenarios puts it at the higher end of LPWAN systems.

Information on the NB-Fi open standard is very limited as of 2022 and can only be found on the WAVIoT website. The company lists 12 employees, primarily in Russia. Details on NB-Fi products and solutions also appear to be limited to those provided directly by WAVIoT[34].

Given the uncertain geopolitical situation with Russia in 2022, the viability of the NB-Fi system outside of Russia would be questionable.

WHAT IS MOBILE IOT (MIOT)?

GSMA classifies both NB-IoT and LTE-M as standards as Mobile IoT (MIoT) standards. MIoT emphasizes that NB-IoT and LTE-M support true mobility as defined in the 3GPP LTE standards. True mobility differentiates NB-IoT and LTE-M from the other LPWAN standards that presume that the wireless sensors are mostly fixed and opens up use cases such as transportation and logistics.

3GPP Mobility includes the following:

- The extensive LTE signaling infrastructure for handoffs as the wireless sensors move between cell base stations.

---

[34] https://waviot.com/catalog/

- Use of LTE frequency bands that are globally supported so that wireless sensors can communicate as shipments move across borders.

- Roaming between service providers as the wireless sensor moves between countries is supported by the established LTE infrastructure.

To accelerate the adoption of its LPWAN standards for mobile applications, GSMA has established its Mobile IoT Innovators forum.[35]

NB-IoT
NB-IoT: History

Both NB-IoT and LTE-M are based on 3GPP cellular standards. GSMA (GSM Association) is the industry association of cellular operators, and members include 750 full members and 400 associate members.[36]

Like LTE-M, NB-IoT was defined in the3GPP Release 13 specification and was rolled out in 2017.[37]

---

[35] www.gsma.com/iot/mobile-iot-innovators/
[36] https://en.wikipedia.org/wiki/GSMA
[37] www.gsma.com/iot/narrow-band-internet-of-things-nb-iot/

NB-IoT: Technical Summary

A comprehensive discussion of the NB-IoT PHY can be found in this tutorial paper.[38] Some of the key aspects of NB-IoT include

- NB-IoT is defined in the 3GPP Release 13 specification with subsequent updates in the Release 14 and 15 specifications.

- The implementation is based on LTE with changes to accommodate IoT requirements of low power and long range. This reuse means that existing cellular networks can support NB-IoT.

- NB-IoT supports IP traffic over the Control Plane.

- 3GPP has defined a set of 21 frequency bands for NB-IoT to ensure global coverage; based on the frequency allocations in different countries, in actuality, there are a total of ten bands that are available globally for NB-IoT.

- NB-IoT shares the Frequency Division Duplex (FDD) feature of LTE with separate bands for the uplink and downlink.

- A total of 180kHz is allocated for the NB-IoT downlink at a different frequency from the uplink with 12 subcarriers of width 15kHz each. As in LTE, OFDMA is used as the downlink modulation.

---

[38] M. Kanj, V. Savaux and M. Le Guen, "A Tutorial on NB-IoT Physical Layer Design," in IEEE Communications Surveys & Tutorials, vol. 22, no. 4, pp. 2408-2446, Fourthquarter 2020, doi: 10.1109/COMST.2020.3022751.

- A total of 180kHz is allocated for NB-IoT uplink at a different frequency from the downlink with subcarrier spacings of either 15kHz of 3.75kHz are used As in LTE, SC-FDMA is used as the uplink modulation.

- The UE (i.e., Wireless Sensor) transmits on the uplink in half duplex mode where it either transmits or receives at different times.

- The eNB can transmit the downlink and receive the uplink simultaneously.

- NB-IoT supports a maximum of 250kbps.[39]

- Power Save Mode (PSM) is a feature that enables the IoT device to conserve power and achieve a 10-year battery life by reducing the amount of time that the radio searches for Paging messages from the network. This feature is supported on LTE-M also.

- Extended Discontinuous Reception (eDRX) is a feature that saves battery power by turning off the radio receiver between 5.12 seconds to 43.69 minutes. This feature is supported on LTE-M also.

- Cat NB1: Support for Class 3 (23dBm).

- Each cell can support 200,000 NB-IoT devices.

- Like cellular devices, NB-IoT devices use a SIM card that ensures end-to-end security.

---

[39] ABI, "Best Fit Use Cases for LPWANs," available at www.ingenu.com/portfolio/best-fit-use-cases-for-lpwans/?doing_wp_cron=166198024 4.2210021018981933593750

The depiction of the NB-IoT system that is shown in Figure 5-6 shows that much of the infrastructure is the same as the 3GPP for cellular applications.

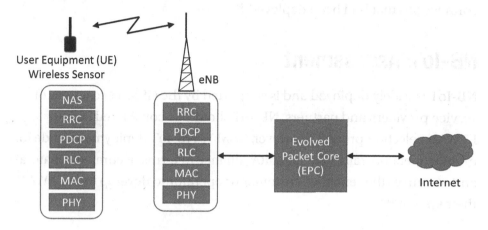

Figure 5-6. *Depiction of the NB-IoT system (after [Kani]) that follows the LTE system architecture. The UE (User Equipment) represents the wireless sensor, and the eNB is the LPWAN cellular basestation*

NB-IoT: Key Ecosystem Partners and Deployments

The GSMA NB-IoT Forum is the industry forum that is accelerating adoption of NB-IoT.[40]

GSMA lists 110 deployed NB-IoT networks.[41] The deployment map for both NB-IoT and LTE-M is available from GSMA and can be found here.[42] NB-IoT is available in most of the world with the exception of Africa (other than South Africa).

---

[40] www.gsma.com/iot/mobile-iot-technology-nb-iot/

[41] www.gsma.com/iot/mobile-iot-commercial-launches/

[42] www.gsma.com/iot/deployment-map/

GSMA also lists numerous NB-IoT and LTE-M modules that are currently available along with links to vendors.[43]

Finally, in 2020 GSMA announced that there were 100Million NB-IoT connections that had been deployed.[44]

NB-IoT: Assessment

NB-IoT is widely deployed and is supported by the GSMA ecosystem of service providers and partners. NB-IoT should be considered in your LPWAN selection process. However, GSMA's NB-IoT deployment guide for mobile operators falls short of LoRA Alliance in terms of curated collaterals and resources that enable a customer or operator to develop their LPWAN their system.[45]

LTE-M

LTE-M: History

LTE-M was defined in the 3GPP Release 13 specification in March 2016.[46]

LTE-M: Technical Summary

LTE-M, otherwise known as Category M1 in Release 13 to 15, introduces key features to support Mobile IoT devices which have different requirements from Smartphones.

---

[43] www.gsma.com/iot/mobile-iot-modules/

[44] www.gsma.com/iot/news/nb-iot-now-exceeds-100-million-connections-and-will-prove-an-essential-tool-in-adapting-to-covid-19/

[45] www.gsma.com/iot/wp-content/uploads/2019/07/201906-GSMA-NB-IoT-Deployment-Guide-v3.pdf

[46] www.3gpp.org/release-13

These features are summarized in this document.[47]

- LTE-M supports IP traffic over the User Plane as other LTE devices.

- 3GPP has defined a set of 11 frequency bands for LTE-M to ensure global coverage.

- Release 13 defines LTE-M with a bandwidth of 1MHz and maximum of 1Mbps for both the uplink and downlink.

- Release 14 adds category M2 with a bandwidth of and a DL data rate of 4Mbps and UL data rate of 7Mbps, both of which are significantly higher than the other LPWAN systems that we are discussing in this chapter.

- Power Save Mode (PSM) is a feature that enables the IoT device to conserve power and achieve a 10-year battery life by reducing the amount of time that the radio searches for Paging messages from the network.

- Extended Discontinuous Reception (eDRX) is a feature that saves battery power by turning off the radio receiver between 5.12 seconds and 43.69 minutes.

- Support for extended coverage mode A: Enables the repletion of data channels by up to 32 times to improve the reception of signals and increase signal coverage further from the eNB or in a building.

---

[47] www.gsma.com/iot/wp-content/uploads/2019/08/201906-GSMA-LTE-M-Deployment-Guide-v3.pdf

- Cat M1 terminals: Support for Class 3 (23dBm) and class 5 (20dBm).

- Half duplex mode: The device alternates between transmitting and receiving (vs. simultaneous transmitting and receiving) in order to simplify the device and reduce costs.

- Connected mode mobility (CMM): The network decides when to transfer the device to a new cell while it is connected to the network.

- SMS: LTE-M supports SMS.

- Power Class 6 (14dBm) was added in the Release 15 spec.

- Release 15 adds Wake-Up Signals (WUS) which are signals that are received by a second radio that will wake up the main radio to monitor the control channels.

LTE-M: Key Ecosystem Partners and Deployments

The GSMA LTE-M Task Force is the industry forum that is accelerating adoption of LTE-M.[48]

GSMA lists 70 deployed NB-IoT networks.[49] The deployment map for LTE-M shows that LTE-M coverage is smaller compared to NB-IoT with availability in North America, parts of South America, Europe, and Australia, and Japan and Thailand in Asia.

---

[48] www.gsma.com/iot/mobile-iot-technology-lte-m/
[49] www.gsma.com/iot/mobile-iot-commercial-launches/

LTE-M: Assessment

LTE-M enjoys extensive support through GSMA. Because it leverages the existing LTE infrastructure and ecosystem, it should be considered as a viable LPWAN technology.

WHAT ARE THE LTE FREQUENCY BANDS?

We noted that LTE-M and NB-IoT are globally supported on a number of LTE frequency bands. These bands are listed in Table 5-3..

Table 5-3. *List of LTE frequency bands supporting LTE-M and NB-IoT*

Channel	Uplink Band[50] (MHz)	Downlink Band (MHz)	Systems Supported
1	1920–1980	2110–2170	LTE-M, NB-IoT
2	1850–1910	1930–1990	LTE-M, NB-IoT
3	1710–1785	1805–1880	LTE-M, NB-IoT
4	1710–1755	2110–2155	LTE-M, NB-IoT
5	824–849	869–894	LTE-M, NB-IoT
8	880–915	925–960	NB-IoT
12	698–716	728–746	LTE-M, NB-IoT
13	777–787	746–756	LTE-M
20	832–862	791–821	LTE-M, NB-IoT
25	1850–1915	1930–1995	LTE-M
26	814–849	859–894	LTE-M, NB-IoT
28	703–748	758–803	LTE-M, NB-IoT

---

[50]www.everythingrf.com/community/lte-frequency-bands

WHAT IS THE DIFFERENCE BETWEEN NB-IOT AND LTE-M?

GSMA's website includes collaterals for both NB-IoT and LTE-M, and many service providers support both MIoT standards so it may be confusing for the casual reader to differentiate the two standards.

- Data rates: LTE-M supports 1400bps in the downlink and 250bps in the uplink; NB-IoT supports 250kbps on both the downlink and uplink→ LTE-M supports higher data rates.

- Available channels: Both LTE-M and NB-IoT support mostly the same set of LTE channels as shown in Table 5-3.

- Mobility: LTE-M supports cell reselection while the wireless sensor is moving while NB-IoT does not and must reconnect to the new cellular base station.[51] → LTE-M is better for use cases where the wireless sensor is moving and continuously connected.

- Both systems are half duplex.

- Security: 3GPP end-to-end security via embedded SIM (eSIM).

- Coverage: NB-IoT has a Maximum Coupling Loss of 164dB vs. LTE-M has a Maximum Coupling Loss of 156dB→NB-IoT supports devices either further from base station or within a building.

- Target battery life for both LTE-M and NB-IoT is 10 years.

[51] www.iotforall.com/nb-iot-vs-lte-m-a-comparison

LPWAN Selection Process

Ultimately, as the IoT system developer, you are tasked with solving the customer's problem and maximizing their return on investment. The design process for a Wireless Sensor Network and the LPWAN selection is especially complicated because of the number of competing technical standards that are available in comparison to Wi-Fi and Bluetooth.

The design process might proceed as follows:

- Document the use case requirements: How much data needs to be sent? How often is the data sent? What is the tolerable latency? Is the data uplink only or both uplink and downlink?

- Power requirements: Is the device powered by batteries or off of the wall? Battery size, cost, and recharging mechanism need to be considered in the design.

- What is the physical size of the device? What are the environmental requirements (such as temperature, humidity, etc.)?

- How long will the device be deployed in the field? The components need to be selected and tested to meet this requirement.

- Will the device be accessible for servicing and upgrades? If yes, how often will the device be serviced and how much does each truck roll cost? If no, then over-the-air updates should be considered.

- In which countries will the device be located? This affects the number of frequency bands and number of RF SKUs that need to be supported.

- Will the network be a public network run by a service provider or as a private network operated by the customer themselves? The tradeoff is the cost of paying the service provider for connectivity vs. having the technical expertise to build and operate the network.

- What are the targets for overall product costs, maintenance costs, revenue streams, and return on investment?

After completing your thorough technical analysis of the best candidate LPWAN systems, it might be helpful to prototype the target application with the candidate LPWAN technology using a developer kit that includes the wireless module, software drivers, and an API for software development. Certainly, developing a prototype to verify performance and reduce risk can be justified before embarking on a large investment on a large wireless sensor application.

HOW ABOUT SATELLITES FOR IOT WIRELESS SENSORS?

Why not use satellites for IoT connectivity for really wide area networks? Certainly, satellites can be considered for distant areas far from terrestrial networks such as ships at sea or wilderness locations.[52] Under consideration would be constellations of relatively inexpensive satellites in low earth orbit. Some examples include

- *Sateliot* uses NB-IoT from space.[53]

---

[52] https://spectrum.ieee.org/satellites-great-option-iot
[53] https://sateliot.space/en/

- *Swarm*, part of SpaceX, provides the satellite network and satellite modems.[54]

- *Iridium* is a global satellite system and satellite terminal products.[55]

We hope to provide more details on satellite-based IoT in a future edition of this book.

5G MASSIVE MACHINE TYPE COMMUNICATIONS (MMTC)

5G will be adding the capability to support wireless sensors via **mMTC**. 5G mMTC is part of the 3GPP Release 13 and 14 specifications[56] and will support 1 million devices per $(km)^2$.[57]

To date, 5G mMTC systems have not been deployed. We will incorporate more information on 5G MMTC in a future edition of this book.

Summary

In this chapter, we have reviewed the key LPWAN systems that are available in 2022 that support wireless sensor network use cases. Selecting which LPWAN system to use is a complex process that must take into account the customer's use case and pain points: number of sensors, data

---

[54] https://swarm.space/
[55] www.iridium.com/
[56] www.mediatek.com/blog/5g-what-are-embb-urllc-and-mmtc
[57] www.gigabyte.com/Solutions/mmtc

rate, types of data, message size, message frequency, latency requirements, range from the sensor to the gateway, power and battery requirements for the sensors, product lifetime, mobility, countries where the sensors are deployed, security and business viability of the LPWAN ecosystem, and the customer's targets for total cost of ownership and return on investment.

Please consult some of the references that we have provided in this chapter to get more information.

Problem Set

You are tasked by your local government with deploying a temperature measurement system across your city. The goal of the project is to identify parts of the city where the health of the citizens may be jeopardized by extreme temperatures and warn them via an app on their phones.

- Assume that the city is in Europe and that you do not need to worry about global coverage.

- The city is 10km x 10km square.

- Your budget includes 1000 wireless sensors and an Edge Gateway to collect the data that are then sent to the cloud for analysis.

- The sensors are uniformly distributed across the city on street lamps that are 10m above the street. The sensors are only situated outdoors.

- The city consists of a series of concrete buildings and trees with a maximum height of 20m located on flat terrain.

- Every hour, each sensor transmits a temperature reading consisting of one byte on the uplink.

- Messages from each sensor are encrypted with a private key for that sensor.

- The target reliability is 99% of the 1000 sensor readings are received correctly every hour.

- The measurements are collected at City Hall which is conveniently located at the center of the 10km x 10km square city.

- The receive antenna on the gateway at the top of City Hall at a height of 100m.

- The measurements are fed into a cloud analytics package that will process the temperature data and will send an alert to the citizens of the town if extreme temperatures are detected.

- The gateway sends a downlink message consisting of one byte once a day to each sensor to trigger a health check from the sensor.

- The sensor responds with its health status in a 2-byte message.

- If the sensor indicates faults, then a maintenance crew will need to be sent to repair it.

- The sensors are built to withstand extreme weather.

- The sensors will be deployed for 10 years, and each sensor is powered by batteries that are charged via a solar panel.

The scenario is illustrated in Figure 5-7. **Which LPWAN would you select and why? Explain your reasoning.**

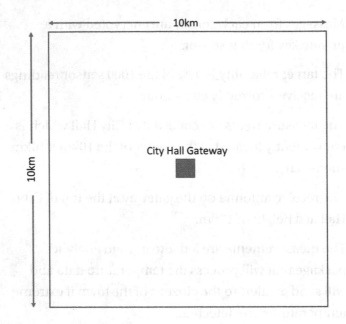

Figure 5-7. *Smart city scenario*

CHAPTER 6

Building Your IoT Solution

Chapter Overview

In the preceding chapters, we discussed the principles of wireless connectivity and wireless standards that can be used to connect an IoT solution.

In this chapter, we will walk you through the process of integrating the key components into your wireless-enabled IoT product: wireless hardware, platform hardware, wireless drivers, and application software.

After reviewing the components that go into the solution, we will address product validation, qualification, certification, and then scaling of the solution for high volume manufacturing. Product support is also a key consideration, especially for IoT products that require a long lifetime. Finally, we will present a couple of case studies to provide concrete examples.

© Anil Kumar, Jafer Hussain, Anthony Chun 2023
A. Kumar et al., *Connecting the Internet of Things*,
https://doi.org/10.1007/978-1-4842-8897-9_6

Product Requirements

We recommend that you follow good engineering practice and thoroughly document your product requirements before starting your product design. At a very minimum, the requirements should be listed in a spreadsheet or a specifically defined database that is accessible to all of the product team members.

Items that we typically include in our product requirements documents are shown in Table 6-1. The Key Parameter Indicator (KPI) is a defined quantity that can be accurately measured by the product validation team to indicate that the final product quality has been met.

Table 6-1. *Example of IoT product requirements for wireless*

Requirement	Comments
Use case	*Describe the use case with enough detail so that the key requirements can be derived*
User persona	*Clearly define who will be using the product and what they will be using it for*
Product size (dimensions, mass)	*Dimensions of the device determine how tightly the components are integrated into the product; size and mass are important if the device is portable or handheld*

(continued)

Table 6-1. (*continued*)

Requirement	Comments
CPU type	*The type of CPU is determined by the computational requirements of the workload; for example, is machine learning and artificial intelligence required on the platform? This in turn influences the wireless bandwidth requirements. For example, if image recognition is done within the IoT device and then the resulting description of the scene or metadata (e.g., "a person is detected") is sent, the CPU computational requirement and power consumption will be higher but the wireless bandwidth is lower. On the other hand, if the jpeg image captures are sent with minimal image processing on the CPU, then a CPU with lower computational performance and power consumption could be used but the wireless bandwidth could be higher*
Network topology	*The network topology determines the distance between nodes, the transmit power requirements, and the power consumption and battery requirements of the IoT device. For example, how many IoT devices are required? Are the IoT devices connected to a central server via a star or mesh network? A star network may simplify the design, but each node must have sufficient transmit power to close the link to the central access point. A mesh network may shorten the distance between nodes and reduce the amount of transmit power and increase network robustness but increase the latency*
Wireless throughput	*Peak and average data rate determine which wireless technology to use*

(*continued*)

Table 6-1. (*continued*)

Requirement	Comments
Latency	*How soon must the message from the IOT device be received? Is this a mission critical application? Is time sensitive networking required?*
Message period	*How often messages are sent by the IoT device will affect the battery capacity, the recharging time, the size of the solar panel that might be used, or energy harvesting mechanism. Can the device be asleep and then wake up at a pre-determined time to make its measurements and send data?*
Available wireless spectrum	*Which countries will the device operate in? Will the device move between countries (such as a transportation or shipping use case) and does the device need to dynamically adopt to the spectrum? Will it use the licensed or unlicensed bands?*
Wireless coverage area	*How large is the operating venue? Is it an outdoors or indoors environment?*
Wireless environment	*Are there materials in the venue that could attenuate the wireless signal such as metal shelves or walls?*
Wireless module	*Using a wireless module that includes all of the radio components instead of a custom design using radio silicon and components that implemented on the board is a tradeoff: a wireless module may be pre-certified but may have a higher unit cost than a custom design. A custom design requires wireless and RF expertise and requires the effort to be certified, but in high volume these costs could be amortized*
Operating system	*Does the device support Microsoft Windows, Linux, Android, Chrome, or a real-time OS such as VxWorks? Does the device support containers in a virtualized environment?*

(*continued*)

Table 6-1. (*continued*)

Requirement	Comments
Environmental conditions	Ambient temperature e.g., is the device intended for outdoor use in harsh weather conditions? Are shock and vibration considerations?
Activity factor	How long will the device be operating per day? For example, would it be on and transmitting/receiving during store business hours or continuously 24/7?
Mobility	Will the device be moving and if so how fast will it be moving?
Bill of materials cost	The product cost, the target average selling price and the gross margin, the target market, and target volumes are all considerations in the product design
Target average selling price	The target selling price may affect the choice of the wireless standard that is used
Capital expenses	How much will it cost to install the network including access points, hubs, cabling, compute hardware, etc.
Operating costs	How much will it cost to operate the network? This includes any monthly network charges and cloud infrastructure costs
Product lifetime	How long will the product be deployed after it is sold? You should also consider the difficulty and expense of changing out equipment including halting a production line
Power consumption	Does the device need to operate on batteries? Will there be an opportunity to recharge the batteries and if so how long is the device required to operate before recharging?
Existing infrastructure	Does the facility where the device will be deployed include existing wireless infrastructure such as Wi-Fi Access Points or a Private Cellular network?

Designing Your Solution

The design of the IoT product incorporates all of the product requirements and is an iterative process involving hardware design, software development, RF engineering, power engineering, and mechanical design.

Wireless Selection

We have previously discussed Wi-Fi, Bluetooth, and cellular standards for IoT applications. Using the Product Requirements that you have collected and documented, you can select the wireless standard for your product.

Coexistence

Some use cases may require supporting multiple wireless standards concurrently such as

- Customer Premise Equipment (CPE): Provides a wireless Internet connection via cellular standard that is shared among users via a hot spot

- Wireless IoT Gateway: Uses one wireless standard to receive and transmit data from/to IoT devices and converts data that is sent or received via a second wireless standard

In these examples, transmitting from one radio may create interference on another radio in the device.

Coexistence can be achieved via

- Hardware-based RF filters: Prevent interference from radio signals in adjacent frequency bands

- Coordinating when each radio is allowed to transmit

Hardware Design

Hardware design for the wireless component begins with comprehending the interfaces from the wireless module and providing the appropriate connections on the circuit board. This step requires accessing the documentation provided by the wireless manufacturer.

An important consideration for IoT products is that the product could be built over 10 years or more. This means that all of the components, including the wireless modules, need to be manufactured by the vendor in sufficient volume for this amount of time. The OEM and ODM need to work with each part vendor to ensure that the parts will be available for 10 years or more or else have replacement parts that can be used without impacting the board design or overall performance.

Another important consideration is that the parts on the board need to meet the environmental and usage requirements of the final product. Of particular importance is meeting the temperature requirements. For example, if the product needs to support an ambient temperature of -40 to 85C within the product enclosure, then each component needs to meet this. An appropriate thermal design could be used to ensure that the components on the board will meet the temperature requirements.

Antenna Selection and Placement

Once the wireless standard and frequency bands are selected, the type of antenna can be selected. Placement of the antennas is critical and can affect wireless throughput. Other design considerations can impact the antenna selection and placement; for example, if the device needs to be hermetically sealed to mitigate moisture and dust, then keeping the antennas within the case may increase signal attenuation and reduce the received and transmitted data rates.

The country where the device will operate limits the allowable transmit power levels, and the device certification will need to account for the antenna gain.

Operating System

Though this is not in scope for this book, the operating system that is used on the IoT product has ramifications for the wireless components. In particular, the wireless driver and wireless features that are supported are dependent upon the selection of the OS. The OS selection depends upon the target market, end-user preferences, applications, and product costs.

Wireless Drivers

Depending upon the operating system, the software drivers for off-the-shelf wireless modules are available from the manufacturer or from the open source community such as kernel.org or from third party operating system vendors. These drivers support the interfaces that are available on the wireless module.

For example, consider the Intel AX210 Wi-Fi 6E module. The AX210 has a PCIe interface for Wi-Fi and a USB interface for Bluetooth.

The available software drivers can be found:

- Windows10 and Windows11 Wi-Fi and Bluetooth drivers can be found on the intel.com website.[1]

- Linux Wi-Fi and Bluetooth drivers can be found on the kernel.org website.[2]

---

[1] www.intel.com/content/www/us/en/download/19351/windows-10-and-windows-11-wi-fi-drivers-for-intel-wireless-adapters.html

[2] https://wireless.wiki.kernel.org/en/users/drivers/iwlwifi

Compatibility issues occur when there are differences between the operating system on the platform and the operating system that the wireless module was integrated with by the software engineering team. These differences could be kernel that is used or the operating system release.

For a custom wireless solution that is developed by the ODM on the IoT board, the driver would need to be developed by the software engineering team. The custom driver would utilize the specific commands provided by the manufacturer to configure the wireless device, connect to another device, and then send and receive data.

RF Tools

In addition to the wireless driver, most wireless vendors provide software tools that enable the device manufacturer to configure the device transmit power levels, modulation, and other features for RF testing. These tools are especially useful for debugging the integration of the wireless module on the board, measuring the wireless capabilities of the device after integration of the board, antenna into the enclosure, as well as for certification testing.

Application Software

The OEM and end customer may have specific software applications that rely upon wireless connectivity.

Connecting to the Cloud

In many IoT use cases, the goal is to analyze the data from the on-premise Edge to derive insights and actions that benefit the customer. For example, in a retail use case, the data on each transaction would be uploaded from the Edge Point-of-Sale terminals and analyzed to determine shopper buying patterns, the effectiveness of targeted advertising, store location, store layout, impact of influencers, etc. This process of data collection and analysis has to be easily scalable to thousands or millions of edge devices that are uploading their data to the cloud for analysis.

The customer may implement their custom cloud analysis services or may build upon an available platform such as Microsoft Azure, AWS, etc. These services include device manageability capabilities...

Prototyping

To reduce the development period, it might be beneficial to develop the hardware and software in parallel. To facilitate the software development, it might be useful to start with an off-the-shelf developer kit that incorporates a CPU with the wireless solution. The developer kit would enable the engineering team to develop a mockup of the software solution, test the RF and wireless capabilities, and remove some of the risks of integrating the host application with the rest of the network.

Validation

The validation team will derive the test plan and test procedure based on the product requirements. On the wireless portion of the test plan, the validation team will validate the wireless features of the product, from the testing of the wireless drivers with the operating system to measuring wireless performance include compliance to a particular Wi-Fi or Bluetooth, etc. standard, connecting to access points or other devices, transmit power levels, transmit data rates, receiver sensitivity, received data rates to robustness with adjacent and co-channel interference.

Quality and Reliability

Qualification is the process of testing the IoT product to ensure that it meets the target environmental and lifetime requirements. For example, the product might have been designed to meet a specific extended temperature range by selecting components that meet the temperature conditions and then designing a thermal solution consisting of forced air cooling or heat sinks. The final product is then tested in an environmental chamber to verify that it meets the required operating temperature range without failing.

Validation of long-life IoT products may require accelerated life cycle testing.[3]

Certification

The completed IoT product is an electronic device and must receive certification in each country where it is intended to operate. This certification is required to ensure that the device's radio emissions are within the legal limits in frequency bands and power levels.

The device certification is simpler if the radio component of the IoT product such as the wireless module is already pre-certified in the destination country. In some countries, the complete device certification of the IoT product and the wireless module may require additional

---

[3] https://en.wikipedia.org/wiki/Accelerated_life_testing

paperwork. In other cases, additional RF testing of the complete product may be required. These tests can be conducted by the vendor if they have the necessary radio expertise and facilities or by a third-party certification house.

The product may also need industry certifications. For example, being certified as a Wi-Fi Alliance product means that the product has been tested to meet a Wi-Fi standard and can be listed on the WFA website.[4] Similarly, the Bluetooth SIG has its process to qualify that a device with Bluetooth can be labelled as compliant and carry the Bluetooth label.[5]

For devices using Android, validation against the Compatibility Test Suite (CTS) may be required.[6]

IoT products for cars may need to pass the Automotive Electronics Council (AEC) Quality certification tests such as AEC-Q100.[7]

Scaling Your Solution

Once the early production units have been validated, qualified, and certified, the device can be approved for production, and high-volume manufacturing can begin. This manufacturing process may be performed by a contract manufacturer or ODM.

Deployment of the Product

Installing the IoT product in the operating venue is performed by a System Integrator (SI) working with the customer. From the wireless perspective, the SI needs to ensure that wireless performance is optimized

---

[4] www.wi-fi.org/certification

[5] www.bluetooth.com/develop-with-bluetooth/qualification-listing/

[6] https://source.android.com/compatibility/cts

[7] www.aecouncil.com/Documents/AEC_Q100_Rev_H_Base_Document.pdf

with the physical positioning of the device. For example, in a warehouse with numerous metal shelves, the performance of the wireless device is impacted by the number of shelves between the device and an access point. In this case, the access points should be positioned so that the path between the devices ideally has the least number of shelves.

For example, for Wi-Fi there are Wi-Fi Analyzer tools that are available for performing a site survey and then optimizing installation of the network. These tools monitor signal strength, channels that are being used, coverage, throughput, and detect rogue networks.

Device provisioning to set up each device, authenticate, and access the network will also be performed by the SI.

Customer Support

Once the IoT product is deployed to the operating venue, it is expected to operate for the required number of years without servicing by the customer or installer. In reality, issues are bound to happen, and the product will need maintenance, including the following:

- Operating system upgrades and patches.

- Security patches to address security advisories.

- Unit fails in the field.

- Unit needs rebooting.

- New equipment such as Access Points are installed.

- Changes to the operating venue: Realignment of store layout such as moving of store shelves changes radio environment and degrades performance.

Total cost of ownership increases if technicians are required to go to the operating venue for maintenance of the product. This becomes a scaling issue if there are hundreds or thousands of the products deployed over a wide geographical area.

Remote Manageability is a feature on some IoT products that allows technicians at a central location to access the device through an out-of-band mechanism. A commercial example of this is Intel vPro.[8] This capability requires a separate, low power Microcontroller Unit (MCU) that is accessible via a secure wireless link. This MCU is kept awake while the main CPU is turned off and can be used to reboot and access the main CPU remotely. This capability can eliminate a "truck roll" of having a technician visit the facility to make the repair and reduce maintenance costs and the total cost of ownership.

Case Studies

In this section, we discuss two IoT case studies to make the concepts of this chapter more concrete.

Case Study 1: Digital Signage at a Retail Store

Digital Signage is a large display that is used in retail, corporate, transportation, or medical venues that conveys timely information to consumers, employees, or visitors. In the retail environment, digital signage may be used to indicate sales, display ads, present food menus, display upcoming events, news, etc.

---

[8]www.intel.com/content/www/us/en/architecture-and-technology/vpro/what-is-vpro.html

Digital signage products operating unattended during business hours of the venue. Content may be updated on a regular basis in real-time, such as financial news and stock prices or news headlines in a corporate environment. An example of Digital Signage is shown in Figure 6-1.

Because there may be numerous devices in a store or shopping mall, maintenance can be a big expense, and the devices should be as robust as possible. Remote servicing would facilitate applying software patches or reconfiguring units with reduced repair costs.

Security is important to ensure that the content that is displayed is accurate.

The requirements are summarized in Table 6-2.

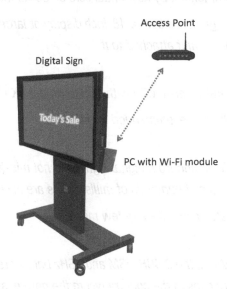

Figure 6-1. Depiction of digital signage product

Table 6-2. Example of IoT product requirements for wireless

Requirement	Examples of Typical Values
Use case	Digital signage at convenience retail store that displays items on sale; the content, which may include 4K graphics or videos from key influencers, is updated in real-time; the sign operates during store hours (12 hours per day, 7 days per week). There is no Ethernet wiring in this store
User persona	Retailer would like the consumers who are shopping at the store to be aware of items on sale this week that are also recommended by key influencers on social media
Product size (dimensions, mass)	The sign consists of a 48-inch display or larger with a 6-inch compute unit attached to it
CPU type	General purpose CPU with GPU to render 4K video and graphics
Wireless throughput	56Mbits/s recommended for 4K video[9]
Latency	Traffic to and from digital signage is not mission critical and latencies of hundreds of milliseconds are acceptable
Message period	Updated content every few minutes
Available wireless spectrum	For Wi-Fi, the 2.4GHz ISM and 5GHz bands are used, subject to restrictions in the country where the device is deployed
Wireless coverage area	Digital signage units need to be able to connect to Wi-Fi access points that may be within 10–20 meters

(continued)

---

[9]www.adobe.com/creativecloud/video/discover/bit-rate.html

Table 6-2. (*continued*)

Requirement	Examples of Typical Values
Wireless environment	*In a retail environment, there could be store shelves and product. In an office environment, there could be walls, offices, and cubicles. In a transportation city environment, there could be buildings and vehicles*
Wireless module	*Off-the-shelf Wi-Fi modules*
Operating system	*Microsoft Windows, Linux, Chrome, or Android*
Application software	*Digital signage unit runs a media player application that is connected to a central cloud server that provides updated content*
Environmental conditions	*Digital signage units are deployed in indoor retail stores and malls where people are and room temperature conditions are sufficient; in transportation use cases such as train or bus stations, the units may be deployed outdoors and may be subject to strenuous temperature and moisture conditions*
Activity factor	*The digital signage unit operates during retail operating hours (12 hours per day, 7 days per week); in transportation environments, the digital signage may be operating 24 hours per day, 7 days per week*
Mobility	*Digital signage unit may be fixed in a permanent location, or it could be repositioned as the store is reconfigured for holiday sales – this is the value of wireless connectivity*

(*continued*)

Table 6-2. (*continued*)

Requirement	Examples of Typical Values
Average selling price	$100 for a media player[10] and $3000 for a display[11]
Product lifetime	*Digital signage devices may be deployed for 5 or more years in order to recoup the investment of purchasing and installing the devices*
Power consumption	*The digital signage unit is connected to AC power*
Existing infrastructure	*Digital signage devices may connect over the existing Wi-Fi network unless an upgrade to the latest Wi-Fi standard is being performed*

Case Study 2: Forest Monitoring System for One Trillion Trees

Planting a trillion trees to mitigate climate change was presented in a *New York Times* article.[12] The challenge is ensuring that seedlings grow to mature trees as they are vulnerable to being disturbed by adverse weather, soil, lack of water, and destruction by disease, insects, humans, and animals. It would be good to observe the growth of the trees, measure temperature, moisture, barometric pressure, detect smoke, fire, and adverse weather conditions, and the presence of humans or animals who may be disturbing the trees.

---

[10] www.xogo.io/

[11] www.amazon.com/DMC-Taiwan-Display-Digital-Signage/dp/B07TZQN555/ref=sr_1_4?keywords=digital+signage+monitor&qid=1658865535&s=pc&sr=1-4

[12] www.nytimes.com/2022/07/13/magazine/planting-trees-climate-change.html

It may be problematic to have humans visit remote locations on a regular basis to check on the newly planted trees. Is there a way to remotely monitor the growth of a huge number of trees over a number of years in remote locations around the world?

One example from the literature is SeaForest which is a Raspberry Pi based device that measures data and transmits via 3G/4G.[13]

The scenario is depicted in Figure 6-2. Some of the difficult technical challenges with this example include developing an IoT sensor solution that can scale to millions or billions, capability of withstanding extreme environmental conditions for 20 or 30 years without servicing, and the need to transmit wireless data reliably over long distances.

The tree monitors need to be ruggedized devices capable of being deployed for 20 years without servicing and capable of withstanding extreme temperature, moisture, shock, and vibration conditions.

Suppose that each tree monitor unit is responsible for observing 100 trees. If there are a total of 1 trillion trees, then there needs to be 10 billion tree monitor units. Among the many challenges is enabling billions of tree monitor units to transmit their data reliably to the cloud data center.

We can envision that there would be numerous tree monitoring systems developed in different countries by different manufacturers using different wireless standards ranging from 5G, ZigBee, Wi-Fi, BLE, LoraWAN, satellite services, etc. While a device capable of connecting over multiple wireless technologies is possible, this would increase the cost of the tree monitoring device, and when scaled to a billion tree monitors the overall cost may become prohibitive.

---

[13] A. Marcu, G. Suciu, E. Olteanu, D. Miu, A. Drosu and I. Marcu, "IoT System for Forest Monitoring," 2019 42nd International Conference on Telecommunications and Signal Processing (TSP), 2019, pp. 629-632, doi: 10.1109/TSP.2019.8768835.

For the purposes of this example for this book, we will focus on a tree monitor device using LoRaWAN for wireless connectivity.[14] LoRa offers 5km range and the LoRa edge server can support 1000 devices. The corresponding product requirements are listed in Table 6-3.

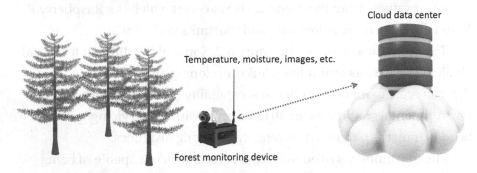

Temperature, moisture, images, etc.

Cloud data center

Forest monitoring device

Figure 6-2. *Depiction of remote tree monitor device*

---

[14] Dushyant Kumar Singh, et al., "Wireless Communication Technologies for Internet of Things and Precision Agriculture: A Review," 2021 6th International Conference on Signal Processing, Computing and Control (ISPCC), pp.765-769.

Table 6-3. *Example of IoT product requirements for wireless*

Requirement	Examples of Typical Values
Use case	*Remote forest monitoring system that can record temperature, humidity, smoke, images, and audio in a remote location under outdoor environmental conditions for 20 years or more*
User persona	*Climate and forest scientists who would like to validate the growth of the trees over a number of years*
Network topology	*Tree Monitor Units are connected in a star network to gateway that is connected via 5G or satellite to Edge Server*
Product size (dimensions, mass)	*Small, hermetically sealed and tamper proof enclosure attached to existing tree*
CPU type	*Very low power, general purpose CPU that can be run on battery charged by solar or energy harvesting*
Wireless throughput	*Message types include* • *Image of tree showing growth and potential diseases and insect infestation* • *Audio captures (that might indicate presence of humans cutting trees down)* • *Temperature* • *Amount of sunlight* • *Humidity* • *Air pressure* • *Soil moisture* • *Air quality/smoke* • *Location of trees (GNSS)* *Each message may consist of kbytes*
Latency	*Message latency can be minutes or hours*

(continued)

Table 6-3. (*continued*)

Requirement	Examples of Typical Values
Message period	Data can be sent on a monthly basis unless there is an emergency such as a fire or other natural disaster
Available wireless spectrum	Ideally, same spectrum used worldwide to simplify regulatory and to enable worldwide distribution
Wireless coverage area	Tens of kilometers between tree monitor devices and edge node that is connected to the cloud
Wireless environment	Potential obstructions due to trees, hills, and terrain
Wireless modules	Pre-certified LoraWAN module. GNSS unit to provide location information. Potentially include Bluetooth to support additional sensors
Operating system	Linux with minimal memory and compute footprint
Software applications	Automated upload of data to cloud services such as Microsoft Azure, Google Cloud, or Amazon AWS
Environmental conditions	Within sealed enclosure: ambient temperature -40 to 85C; unit must be resistant to rain, snow, ice, dust
Activity factor	Low duty factor with each device transmitting data once per month
Mobility	None-tree monitors will be in permanent locations
Average selling price	Target $5 for complete tree monitor unit in high volume
Product lifetime	20 years
Power consumption	Battery powered with solar panels; battery needs to continuously charge and discharge over 20 years
Existing infrastructure	None

Summary

In this chapter, we assembled the discussions from the preceding chapters into the steps required to design and manufacture a wireless IoT product. The next steps for the reader are to define their IoT product in the following exercise.

Problem Set

The reader is invited to fill in their product requirements in the following table.

Requirement	Values
Use case	
User persona	
Product size (dimensions, mass)	
CPU type	
Wireless throughput	
Latency	
Message period	
Available wireless spectrum	
Network topology (sketch out design)	
Wireless coverage area	
Wireless environment	
Wireless module	

Requirement	Values
Operating system	
Environmental conditions	
Activity factor	
Mobility	
Bill of materials cost	
Average selling price	
Product lifetime	
Power consumption	
Existing infrastructure	

CHAPTER 7

Conclusion

Chapter Overview

We wrap up our discussion of wireless connectivity for the Internet of Things and provide suggestions for next steps.

Recap

In the preceding chapters, we have presented key foundational concepts in applying wireless connectivity to the Internet of Things. We have discussed some of the relevant wireless standards, how they work, and the use cases where they can be applied.

Our hope is that you will be able to utilize what you have learned as you develop your IoT applications and product designs. We have purposely not provided a cookbook of IoT recipes with prescriptive suggestions on what you, the designer, should do; instead, we hope that you are able to make appropriate design decisions based on the constraints of the IoT product that you are developing.

The IoT ecosystem is dynamic and in constant flux. Even during the time that we started writing this book in 2020 to now (spring of 2022), there has been an upheaval in the daily life of most people and the corresponding set of IoT use cases and technologies:

© Anil Kumar, Jafer Hussain, Anthony Chun 2023
A. Kumar et al., *Connecting the Internet of Things*,
https://doi.org/10.1007/978-1-4842-8897-9_7

- The Covid-19 pandemic has changed the way we work, learn, shop, and interact with others.

- The rise of remote work, teaching, socializing, and shopping has increased the use of wireless connectivity by most of the population.

- The pandemic has impacted manufacturing, health, and retail operations, with increased need for robots, telehealth, and an increased use of wireless connectivity in these industries.

- Even as the Covid-19 pandemic becomes endemic, many of these changes to the way of working, learning, shopping, and manufacturing will remain.

Future of IoT Connectivity

Wireless connectivity continues to evolve with new wireless standards and implementations of these standards.

Here are some examples to consider:

- Swarm is a satellite-based service for connecting the IoT devices.[1] Swarm provides a data rate of 1 kbps and operates 137–138 MHz (downlink) and 148–150 MHz (uplink).

---

[1] https://swarm.space/

- Wi-Fi 7 will be officially standardized in March 2024.[2] As of the spring of 2022, there have been announcements of Wi-Fi 7 products from MediaTek[3] and Qualcomm.[4]

- Wi-Fi 8 is on the heels of Wi-Fi 7, and the IEEE is developing this standard with a timeline of standardization in 2027.[5]

- 6G is under development by 3GPP with a timeline of launching in 2030.[6] 6G will offer terabit data rates, location and context aware services, and support XR. 6G satellite coverage and low power capabilities will extend the application of 6G to IoT devices in remote locations.

Future editions of this book will incorporate new wireless technologies as they are introduced.

Next Steps

The best way to solidify your internalizing of the concepts from this book is to design your next IoT product with wireless connectivity capabilities. In particular

---

[2] https://ieee802.org/11/Reports/802.11_Timelines.htm

[3] www.mediatek.com/technology/wi-fi-7

[4] www.qualcomm.com/news/releases/2022/05/04/qualcomm-debuts-wi-fi-7-networking-pro-series-worlds-most-scalable

[5] E. Reshef and C. Cordeiro, "Future Directions for Wi-Fi 8 and Beyond," in IEEE Communications Magazine, vol. 60, no. 10, pp. 50-55, October 2022, doi: 10.1109/MCOM.003.2200037.

[6] www.techradar.com/news/6g

- Review the connectivity requirements for your application, including range, throughput, latency, security, etc.

- Experiment with different connectivity technologies and the hardware and software implementations using available developer kits.

- Understand the tradeoffs between the different technologies and standards and pick the right wireless solution for your application.

Good luck on your product development, and drop us a line on how we can improve future editions of this book.

Index

© Anil Kumar, Jafer Hussain, Anthony Chun 2023
A. Kumar et al., *Connecting the Internet of Things*,
https://doi.org/10.1007/978-1-4842-8897-9

Printed in the United States
by Baker & Taylor Publisher Services